The Leaders Welcome *Print Matters*

Print Matters provides a comprehensive, easy read for both the beginning advertising student and the seasoned professional. The book offers a wealth of information presented in a practical fashion. It's an outstanding addition to anyone's advertising library.

Joseph Basso, Esq.
Rowan University

This is a very interesting book, with excellent examples, clear explanations, and easy-to-apply theories if you're looking to develop effective advertising campaigns.

Margo Berman
Professor of Advertising, Florida International University
Author, *Street-Smart Advertising: How to Win the Battle of the Buzz*

This text offers a practical, thorough, applied approach to print advertising and is a must for any course on print advertising. The text provides step-by-step instructions on how to create effective print advertisements, but also provides sufficient theory for students to understand why print ads are designed in a particular manner. This text is excellent for instructors who want their students to learn how to create print ads, not just learn about print advertising.

Kenneth E. Clow
Biedenharn Endowed Chair in Business
College of Business Administration
University of Louisiana at Monroe

Print advertising ain't dead. Quite the contrary. In this ever-changing world of fast, hip, digital communications, we may forget that one thing never changes—the life and death impact of great writing. Advertising scholars Hines and Lauterborn offer great advice on the power of words—advice for clients, planners, strategists—all students of advertising.

Richard Cole
Professor and Chair
Department of Advertising, Public Relations, and Retailing
Michigan State University

Hines and Lauterborn are right on with this book. The importance of drawing in and holding the reader in print advertising can't be overstated, since it is far and away the most important medium for solid delivery of the advertising message.

The authors show that this works both ways: studies demonstrate that print is the best medium, and they show those in the advertising business how to make sure they use it to best advantage.

No shallowness in this book—Hines and Lauterborn cover all bases. What a boon this book will be for those wanting to learn all about advertising. Love their textual and visual illustrations.

Elenora E. Edwards
Managing Editor
The Tennessee Press Association

Great champions master fundamentals first. This book is a master foundation for championship print advertising. I hired and fired a lot of would-be talent. I wish I had this book earlier in my career. I could have said, *"Come back and see me when you have memorized this."*

This book is a master foundation for great print advertising. If you want a job in persuasive communications, memorize this book before you go on any interviews.

Sean Kevin Fitzpatrick
Former Chief Creative Officer
McCann-Erickson World Group

Randy Hines's monthly column offers practical and common-sense advice to newspapers across the country. So, it comes as no surprise that this book follows the same successful formula: Textbook advice written in non-textbook language with contemporary examples illustrating his points. He introduces you to what you should know and reintroduces you to what you already know—signs of the good teacher he is. You'll take much away from this classroom of Professor Hines.

George Geers
Editor
New England Press Association

The book provides an excellent summary of essential consumer behavior and research concepts that every copywriter needs to know.

Jonna Holland
Associate Professor
Department of Marketing
University of Nebraska–Omaha

In this highly readable, usable volume, the authors show thatplain, simple, effective language still matters—maybe more than ever in today's over-marketed, over-communicated marketplace. And regardless of the media you are using, the principles they explain so clearly will help you craft more effective advertising messages.

Rick Kean
President
Business Marketing Institute
Former Executive Director
Business Marketing Association

Companies that advertise do better than companies that don't advertise. It's expensive and consumers say they hate it, yet it continues to be the defining quality in a brand's success or failure. In *Print Matters,* Randall Hines & Robert Lauterborn explain how advertising has changed, what works, what doesn't, and why. It's a good, useful and very readable book from which I expect to be quoting fairly regularly.

Joe Marconi
College of Communications
DePaul University
Author, *Creating the Marketing Experience*

As we are now fully engaged in the era of interactive advertising media, it is critically important to reinforce the basic principles of effective advertising . . . this book captures the essence of persuasive print techniques, compelling ad copy, and useful hands-on lessons that apply now more than ever. I have used it for online IMC Multi-Channel Media courses to the delight of the graduate students who appreciate such well-honed print wisdom and insight.

Sheila L. Sasser
Department of Marketing & IMC
College of Business
Eastern Michigan University

. . . a great conversational style with focused descriptions, explanations, definitions, and illustrations that will give great guidance to anyone trying to master the essentials of creating more powerful print advertising.

Alice Tait
Professor, College of Communication and Fine Arts
Central Michigan University

Print

Matters

How to Write

Great Advertising

Randall Hines

Susquehanna University

Robert Lauterborn

University of North Carolina, Chapel Hill

Racom Books/Racom Communications

Chicago, IL

Published by Racom Communications, Inc.
150 N. Michigan Ave.
#2800
Chicago, IL 60601
www.racombooks.com
(ph) 312-494-0100
(fax) 312-494-1600

Editor: Richard Hagle
Design: Sans Serif, Inc., Saline, Michigan 48176

Printed in the United States of America

ISBN: 978-1-933199-10-8

Contents

✦ Appendix A

✦ Appendix B

Chapter 1

The Importance of Print

This is the shortest but possibly the most important chapter in this book. Why? Because it lays out the overall framework and reasoning for everything that follows. And that is: Print matters still. In fact, it matters more than ever, even—maybe especially—in a world of continuous rapid-fire media innovations because it provides the standard—the acid test—for relevance and communication power.

Why print? Because it's the purest form of advertising—an idea given power visually and crafted to move people with words. If you don't have an idea, it shows. If you can't write, people know. You can't hide emptiness behind a mesmerizing glare of glitzy TV production or trade on the familiar voice of a spokesperson to make a connection for you. It's just you and the reader. So print is the acid test for advertising as well as advertising people.

The Primacy of Print

An instructive interactive game we play with students is to get them talking about current television commercials they love. Often they are able to describe their favorites virtually scene-by-scene, fairly accurately repeat the dialogue, and

1

even hum the music. The catch comes when they are asked to identify the advertiser. Horrifyingly (if you paid for this commercial), they sometimes can't even name the category. More often, they ascribe the work to the wrong company or brand, usually the category leader.

We're not talking about rare exceptions here. Year after year, class after class, this is the rule. The ploy never fails. Occasionally, a commercial breaks through and bonds the brand to the work (Volkswagen's distinctive "curve" commercials, for example, or anything Apple does, including its iPhone), but the average television commercial is not only considered by some a waste of money, it produces a negative return on investment for brands that are not the leaders in their categories. Doubt it? Try this test yourself with any random group of people who aren't in marketing or advertising.

What fascinates us is that this is *not* true for most print advertising. People almost always recall the advertised brand accurately when they describe print ads they like. Why is this so? One reason is that people experience print differently from how they experience television.

People "watch" television while multi-tasking. Although much has been written lately about multi-tasking media activities, the topic is not a new one. Decades ago, researchers like Herb Krugman demonstrated that the number-one activity of people allegedly watching television is reading. Number two is talking to someone, either in person or increasingly on their ubiquitous cell phones. Today's researchers found that the Internet plays a big role while the TV is on. Television does not require us to pay attention. So we don't. In a desperate attempt to alter this unalterable truth, advertisers seek to entertain. Is it any wonder that it is the entertainment, not the sponsor, that is remembered?

Another growing problem about television advertising is how digital video recorders allow viewers to skip right past commercials in previously recorded programs. TiVo and other technology toys, according to Nielsen Media Research, were in 17 percent of U.S. homes by mid-2007. In fact, Nielsen now wants to gauge viewership of commercials, instead of the programs, to create more realistic ratings for advertisers. The new issue of commercial ratings even delayed the upfront buying season for the fall 2007 network programs.

In contrast, print requires our attention. If you lose your concentration when you're reading and your mind wanders, what do you do? Why, you read the sentence or paragraph or page over again—too often more than once. A woman named Evelyn Wood built a speed-reading franchise on this simple truth. Her instructors don't teach you to read faster; they teach you to *concentrate* better so you don't have to reread. That's why Evelyn Wood graduates not only seem to read faster, they also remember better.

People process print differently, too. An Israeli researcher demonstrated this with an often-cited experiment. He exposed a group of young people to a simple story, half of them in a video mode, the other half in print. Tested at similar intervals—two days, two weeks, two months or whatever—the subjects revealed fascinating differences not so much in their ability to recall the basic story, but in the connections they had made with the material. Their relative ability to repeat the plot line differed only slightly, but when asked questions such as, "What do you suppose Rachel's life was like before this story began?" and "What do you think is going to happen next?" the TV kids went "Huh?" The print kids, however, had developed entire scenarios that combined material already in their heads with the story they had read. "I think Rachel grew up in the city, in a house near the harbor," said one. "Rachel and Ben are going to get married and have three children, two boys and a girl," said another.

What does this tell us? That what we read goes into a different part of the brain from what we merely watch. Readers are active participants in the communication process, while TV viewers are passive.

"Reading is Fundamental," says a venerable literacy program. And so it is. Therefore, the fundamentals of writing advertising to be read are also critical. That's what this book is about. How to not only attract a reader, but how to involve him or her in the world of the brand. How to not only know what to say, based on what the reader needs to hear, but how to say it with such professional craftsmanship that your print advertising message penetrates the reader's mind, creates action and builds lasting bonds.

Parting Shot

The tombstone (in Exhibit 1.1) from Auckland, New Zealand, is not officially a print advertisement, but notice the stonemason's chagrin when he finished the long text, only to discover a misspelling by omitting a letter near the end of the very last line. He did the only thing possible on his 1853 medium. He used a caret mark and carefully chiseled in the missing "K."

Today we have easier methods of correcting our mistakes, but we do have to find them before they are in print for a permanent record of our accomplish-

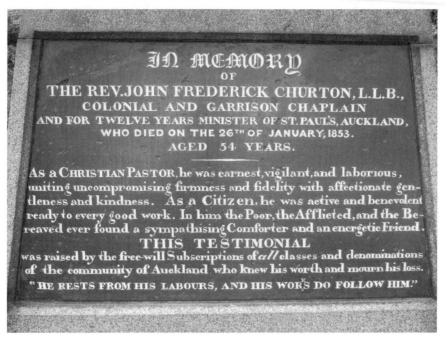

Exhibit 1.1 Old-Style "Proof Correcting"

ments. Advertising students, business owners, and ad professionals must always proof their work carefully before turning it in, whether to a professor, the media, or a client. Perhaps this visual reminder will haunt us to be excellent proofreaders of our own advertising assignments, whether for class or for a client. And it should make us diligent consumers of all ads we read.

This book should be valuable for a variety of audiences. We conceived the idea initially to help advertising, mass communication, and design students to learn how to think about and create advertising that works. But its message applies equally well to the men and women working in advertising for a company (whether on the agency or client side), or for any print medium. And then, of course, there is the small business owner or entrepreneur who doesn't have an ad department and can't afford to hire an ad agency. Yet that individual has the task of creating exciting print ads to move merchandise or create demand for services.

To all of you and any others we might have missed in our listing, please read on. The proof is in the print. Print matters!

Chapter 2

Are You Talking to Me?

> *"Know thy customer—all wisdom centers there."*
>
> (with apologies to Montaigne)

In Focus

- How do consumers encounter the three levels of the brand experience?
- What are attributes, benefits, determinants, USP, and UBP?
- How are qualitative and quantitative research related?
- Which research techniques are most commonly used in advertising?

This chapter talks about understanding a product or service by understanding its customers, spending time with them, and becoming expert on how they use it and what they use it for—what it helps them to do, to feel, to become. It's about research.

Apple's Macintosh computers arrived in 1984 on the wings of a vision of people who resented the attempts of IBM to mold them to fit technology and put them into identical boxes. Apple's leaders and the creative people in its then-agency Chiat/Day perceived that there were people out there who "think different." The fact that Apple and its agency still used those very words in advertising more than twenty years later demonstrates the validity of the research that brought them that insight. Its head-to-head comparison ads with PCs starting in 2007 carry over that "think different" mentality.

One of the fastest-growing job functions in advertising today is called **Account Planning**. No, it's not about planning in the sense of scheduling, nor does it have anything to do with accounting. Account Planning (or **Brand Planning**, as some agencies refer to it) is about developing insight into the person whose behavior you're about to try to change before you sit down to create an ad. Who is that person? Not just a demographic statistic, like "women aged 25-44" or some other nearly useless number. Who is that person in terms of how she sees herself? What's in her world, and how does she relate to it? And how do you make that product or service you're commissioned to advertise *relevant* to her?

Branding guru and University of California, Berkeley, professor emeritus of marketing David Aaker says that the consumer experiences a brand on three levels. The first is **functional**: What the product or service does, how it works, what it's made of. (We'll get to the other two levels, **emotional** and **self-expressive**, later.) Not surprisingly, numerous studies have demonstrated that some functional attribute or benefit is the primary focus of most advertising. In the words of an old saying, "Sell the hole, not the drill." Check for yourself: Next time you're near a newsstand, pick up an issue of, say, *Business Week* and see how many ads talk primarily about the product and what it does. Do the same quick research exercise in any magazine you like and read regularly.

Differences and Distinctions

In an article in *Business Week Small Biz* (April/May 2007) Doug Hall, author of the book series *Jump Start Your Business Brain*, said your ad must be clear about what's in it for the consumer:

> Customers are greedy. They want to know what's in it for them—that is, what they will receive, enjoy, or experience in exchange for their investment in your company, product, or service.

We should spend a minute here talking about the difference between an attribute and a benefit. An **attribute** is something that may be said about a product. For example, an ad might say that GE's newest portable electric drill has a one-piece casing made of Lexan®. If you happen to know that Lexan® is a shatter-resistant composite material, then you might infer the **benefit**, which is that if you drop it onto your driveway while you're twenty feet up on a ladder fixing the rain gutter, it won't crack in half. But why count on the reader making that connection for himself? Doesn't it make more sense to lead with the benefit, and use the attribute as a reason why?

Another way of simplifying this has been done by Jerry Vass in *Soft Selling in a Hard World*. He calls attributes "features." To make it less confusing for the consumer, he writes: "Features are our stuff and benefits are the customer's stuff."

Imagine an ad showing a guy up that ladder dropping the drill, but not looking particularly worried. "Why is this man smiling?" the headline might say. "Because that new GE drill he dropped isn't going to break when it hits the ground," the subhead might explain. The copy would then go on to give the reader what a pioneer American advertising agency named Compton used to call "permission to believe," explaining that the drill body is virtually shatter-proof because it's made of Lexan®, GE's nearly indestructible engineered plastic.

See how it works? Make it easy for the reader. Don't make him guess. Tell him what the benefit is first—that's "what's in it for him," after all—then prove it, by citing the attribute (or feature) that makes the benefit possible.

If you do just that much, you're already going to be one-up on most of your competitors or your client's competitors who haven't figured this out yet. And a lot of them haven't. Just check out their advertising.

Even a Unique Attribute Isn't Enough

Part of the problem is that most current advertising practitioners were brought up to believe in something called a **Unique Selling Proposition**. The phrase was coined forty years ago by Rosser Reeves, a famous ad man with the then-prominent Ted Bates agency. It's our contention that the USP is responsible for more misguided advertising than any other idea ever hatched. What it encouraged people to do was to find something they could claim was unique about the client's product or service. Deep down, Reeves himself probably meant, "Go find a benefit that matters to the potential buyer," such as the classic "Fast, fast, fast relief" claim he made for the headache medicine Anacin, an early Bates client. (Its advertising used repetition, but was much less annoying than the contemporary "Head On" commercials.)

Unfortunately, what the USP has too often been interpreted to mean since is, "Go find something unique about the product." Period. The question of whether the allegedly unique attribute has any value to the consumer is too often never asked, particularly in the case of technical products. For example, the post-2000 demise of all those dot.com companies built on unique technology that had no perceived relevance to consumers was a grotesque consequence of this same sort of shortsighted thinking or, rather, nonthinking.

Because the USP applied unthinkingly can and often does lead to such errors, we propose a substitute phrase: the **Unique Buying Proposition**. The USP has often turned out to mean "what the client wants to say." But the UBP minimizes that risk because it can be best characterized as "what the consumer needs to hear that the client can say." What the consumer needs to hear is the *benefit*—that "What's in it for me?" question the advertising really needs to answer "fast, fast, fast."

"Two scoops of raisins" in a box of Kellogg's Raisin Bran was coined by the copywriter who was thinking of a UBP for the product. He determined that fact at home after he poured a box onto his kitchen table. It's still the leading brand in its category.

The iPhone has plenty of technical features that could consume an entire full-page ad. However, to appeal to the buying public, the ads in late 2007 pushed its benefits for the consumer. What it does for the individual is more important than what geeky Apple engineers did to the new product.

There are several advantages to our UBP approach, not the least of which is that it forces the agency (or the in-house creator of the ad) and the client to find out exactly what it is the consumer needs to hear—that is, what the consumer needs to hear before he or she will be moved to buy.

But There's More

Let us draw the distinction here between an attribute or a benefit and a **determinant**. An attribute, as you read a few paragraphs ago, is something that can be said about a product. If it's something that can only be said about some particular product, it may be a USP. A benefit is an expression of the "so what" of an attribute—what that characteristic or quality or component or capability does for the consumer. This may be a UBP. However, the critical words here are "may be." Many features and benefits that are unique (or are claimed first and, therefore, may be perceived by the consumer to be unique) are nonetheless irrelevant.

This is not mere parsing. Unique or not, some features and benefits have nothing to do with why the consumer would actually buy one specific brand rather than a competitive brand. They are not determinants of consumer or customer behavior.

This can be an especially contentious issue in engineering-driven companies. A company's research scientists and engineers may have worked for many years to produce a product with some breakthrough technical feature, so naturally they want to trumpet their achievement in the advertising for that product.

The problem arises when that new feature, no matter how challenging it was to develop, is not among the factors that consumers will consider important when they are evaluating similar products. Money spent to advertise it may turn out to be wasted. (Of course, if product development were always driven by perceived customer needs, copywriters wouldn't have to fight that battle, but that's another story.)

Engineers Aren't Always to Blame

The arguments aren't even necessarily about technical features, however. In a famous case involving a campaign for paperboard milk cartons versus plastic milk jugs (see Exhibit 2.1), one of the company's sales executives insisted strongly that the advertising should stress that paperboard cartons fit into refrigerator doors because that was a unique advantage compared to gallon-sized plastic jugs. Sure enough, that was a USP. But the fact was, it had always been true, and consumers had still switched overwhelmingly to buying milk in plastic jugs. It was an *attribute*—with an obvious space-saving benefit—but it clearly wasn't a determinant. It didn't change a mother's behavior and, therefore, unique or not, it didn't matter.

How do you know what does matter? Aha, now it's time to talk about research—research with a small "r" first because sometimes very simple research can yield just as much valuable insight as big "R" research studies costing tens of thousands of dollars.

"You can observe a lot by just watching." (Yogi Berra)

The first and most indispensable form of research is **observation**. To remind himself of what was really important, one sales manager hung a big sign on the wall opposite his desk that said, "What are you doing in here, dummy? The customers are out there." An aspiring copywriter would do well to commit that line to memory. Nothing brings reality home like a field trip to the supermarket to watch people shop. Observe the people whose behavior you're going to try to affect. What do they do now? Do they roll up and down the aisles snatching up items purposefully, or do they amble along, picking up things at random and reading the labels? Do they shop with a list? What's on the list—categories or specific brands? (Think about your own shopping list.) Do they use coupons? You can't ever know enough about what people do, much less why they do it. (A very good book on this subject is *Why People Buy*, by Paco Underhill.)

Don't ever forget that in the end the only purpose of advertising is to *affect someone's behavior*. Perhaps you want a consumer to try something she's never tried before, or perhaps you want her to switch from a brand she's been buying for years to a new brand, or perhaps you want her to keep on buying your client's brand despite all the advertising she sees that's trying to tempt her away. Whatever the desired behavior is, make sure you know exactly what it is you're supposed to be trying to make happen. All advertising must have *specific, measurable objectives* stating exactly whose behavior you're supposed to affect, exactly what your client wants those people to do, how much or how often and by when. Without such criteria, you'll never know if you're successful.

That's just as true for so-called "corporate advertising"—advertising that talks about a company—as it is for product or service advertising. One outspo-

UNIVERSITY STUDIES SHOW PAPER MILK CARTONS GIVE YOU MORE VITAMINS TO THE GALLON

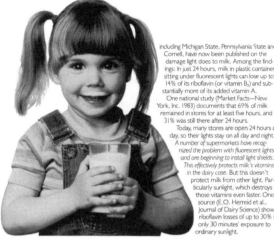

From the moment children are born they need the nourishment you find in milk. Milk is one of a child's best sources of riboflavin, or vitamin B₂. And a good source of vitamin A.

These are vitamins that help a child grow and stay healthy, have soft skin and bright eyes. In fact, scientists include both vitamins in a list of leader nutrients that play a key role in human nutrition.

Important vitamins lost in plastic containers

But did you know that milk can lose some of these important vitamins when you buy it in transparent plastic containers? Over 50 independent studies conducted by scientists at major universities

---

Important Facts About Milk

• Milk can provide nutrients it would take a variety of other foods to provide.

• Milk is rich in protein, calcium, riboflavin (vitamin B₂) and a good source of vitamin A.

• Recent research by scientists and nutritionists is building up evidence that adults, especially women, need milk's key nutrients as well as children do. Cornell University studies show that young women who exercise need extra riboflavin. Other studies show that women can lessen the risk of osteoporosis, or brittle bones, in later life if they drink milk regularly.

---

including Michigan State, Pennsylvania State and Cornell, have now been published on the damage light does to milk. Among the findings: In just 24 hours, milk in plastic containers sitting under fluorescent lights can lose up to 14% of its riboflavin (or vitamin B₂) and substantially more of its added vitamin A.

One national study (Market Facts—New York, Inc. 1983) documents that 69% of milk remained in stores for at least five hours, and 31% was still there after 24 hours.

Today, many stores are open 24 hours a day, so their lights stay on all day and night. *A number of supermarkets have recognized the problem with fluorescent lights and are beginning to install light shields. This effectively protects milk's vitamins in the dairy case.* But this doesn't protect milk from other light. Particularly sunlight, which destroys those vitamins even faster. One source (E.O. Herreid et al., Journal of Dairy Science) shows riboflavin losses of up to 30% in only 30 minutes' exposure to ordinary sunlight.

Bigger loss in low-fat milk

Vitamin A loss can even be worse in low-fat or skim milk. When fat is skimmed from milk, much of the natural vitamin A is skimmed off with it. So Fed-

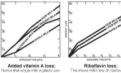

Added vitamin A loss:
Notice that whole milk in plastic containers loses 18% under fluorescent light in only two hours. Low-fat milk loses up to 28%.

Riboflavin loss:
This shows milk's loss of riboflavin in plastic containers under fluorescent light. Again, low-fat milk loses even more.

Source: "Protecting Your Milk from Nutrient Loss," by Dr. G.F. Senyk and Dr. W.F. Shipe, Department of Food Science, Cornell University.

eral law requires dairies to add vitamin A back to low-fat and skim milk. They "fortify" it. Here's the catch. Low-fat milk is even more susceptible to light—which actually destroys the vitamin A that has been replaced. In fact, in only 24 hours light can destroy up to 90% of vitamin A in low-fat and skim milk that comes in plastic containers. Because Amer-

icans are becoming conscious of fat and cholesterol, low-fat and skim milk now account for over 50% of milk consumption in many areas of the country.

So more and more people are getting shortchanged on their vitamins in the milk they drink.

Paper cartons block out 98% of harmful light

But there is a way to make sure that your children's milk is better protected: buy it in paper cartons. Paper cartons block almost all harmful light. Paper cartons are printed with inks, and that helps

Fluorescent lights penetrate plastic milk containers, and destroy important vitamins. But paper cartons keep most harmful light out and more vitamins in.

block more light. Scientific tests show that light penetration of transparent plastic milk containers can be up to 35 times greater than with paper cartons.

How light hurts milk's flavor

A recent Pennsylvania State University study reports that it "has been realized for some time that milk undergoes flavor deterioration when exposed to light..." And as every parent knows, if children don't like that "off" taste, they'll be less likely to drink milk.

Now—a better way to buy a gallon

Now there's a better way to buy milk by the gallon: the paper Gallon 2-Pak—two half gallons connected by a sturdy detachable handle. While one half gallon is on the table, the other stays cold and fresh in the refrigerator. It's easier to pour, too, than a bulky plastic jug, which weighs 9 lbs. when full.

Buy your children milk in a protective paper Gallon 2-Pak. And give them more to the gallon.

For more detailed facts and statistics about light penetration of plastic milk containers and the destruction of important vitamins—including a detailed listing of the more than 50 studies plus a summary of their findings—write for the free booklet, "Light, Milk and Vitamins." Send your name and address to: Milk Information, Paperboard Packaging Council, 1101 Vermont Ave., N.W., Suite 411 N, Washington, D.C. 20005.

© 1984 Paperboard Packaging Council

Pick up the paper Gallon 2-Pak now wherever Meadowgold, Viva and Page milk is sold

Ad No. PB-234-84 (2-Pak)
Paperboard Packaging Council
This Advertisement Prepared By:
Ogilvy & Mather Advertising
To Appear In:
Tulsa World Tribune
August 30, 1984
September 6, 1984
September 20, 1984
108 Col. Inches
6 Cols. x 18" (13" x 18")
Job No. H-81741
Copy—K. Krimstein   Art—T. Wong   Traffic—M. Kaplan

Exhibit 2.1 Ad for Milk

ken corporate advertising director called most corporate advertising "a euphemism for advertising without objectives." What he meant was that too much of that kind of institutional advertising is fuzzy about what the company wanted readers to do. Buy shares in the company? Write to someone in Congress about a law? Pay a premium for products made by the company? Fuzzy objectives lead to fuzzy, ineffective work. How can you write to accomplish an objective if you don't know what that objective is?

Which brings us back to research. What research is all about, in a nutshell, is finding out what matters to people, relative to the kind of product or service you're selling. One way is to watch them buying and using similar products. OK, we can go into a store to watch people buy, but how do we get to see them using the products? We can't just go into their homes, after all, can we? Well . . . um . . . yes, we can. Or at least a certain kind of researcher can. Most people have heard of Margaret Mead, the cultural anthropologist who lived among South Pacific island people and thus was able to give the rest of the world insight into how these people lived and worked, how their societies were organized, and what was important in their culture. Similar research is now commissioned by marketers to increase their understanding of different groups of consumers.

Notepad

Look at the British Petroleum corporate ad in Exhibit 2.2. BP used to stand for British Petroleum. Now the company signs the ads "Beyond Petroleum." What do you think the company's objective is? Who do you think they are trying to influence? Why? If you were a shareowner, would you consider this campaign a worthwhile investment of $150 million (the estimated budget for 2006)? Why or why not?

Levi's, for example, sent cultural anthropologists to study teenage boys' bedrooms, on the theory that their bedrooms were the only part of the house that was completely theirs, the place where they could express themselves and display their stuff. Levi's was particularly interested in the role various kinds of clothing played in the boys' lives, of course, but they also wanted to know what music they listened to, what sports or entertainment stars they admired, how they spent their time, and their language. Understanding all of that was critical, Levi's reasoned, if they hoped to connect with this age group in advertising. That kind of research—*ethnography*—is another form of observation, more com-

Maybe it's time to get more energy from the Midwest.

Biofuels today BP has been selling ethanol blended fuels in the U.S. for over 25 years. In 2005, BP fuels contained more than 575 million gallons of biofuels. Today, they're available in more than 20 states across the country.

Biofuels investment BP is investing $500 million over the next ten years to create the world's first integrated research center dedicated to applying biotechnology to the energy industry. It's a start.

bp

beyond petroleum*

bp.com

Exhibit 2.2 Corporate Ad for BP

plex than hanging around a supermarket and certainly more expensive, but still about watching people's behavior.

Another way to find out what people think and want is to ask them, which is what Account Planners do. The concept of account planning was developed by British advertising agencies in the 1970s and imported into the U.S. in the early 1980s by the late Jay Chiat, co-founder of the Chiat/Day agency. Now virtually all major agencies use "planning," as it's called. Planners do research, but there is a fundamental difference between what they do and what the people in agencies who called themselves "researchers" did before the concept of planning came to be. Old-style researchers mostly just collected data. They could tell you who, what, where, when, how much, and how often:

> Mothers aged 25-44 with children at home between the ages of 6 and 18 buy 81 percent of all milk sold, their research might say. These mothers overwhelmingly buy milk in super-markets, in gallon jugs, shopping twice a week (Thursdays and Sundays in most communities). So-called "heavy users" buy three gallons at a time, and may send their husbands to a convenience store before supper to buy an additional half-gallon if they run out.

This is all useful information, but it's not sufficient. Did you spot what's missing? What's missing is why they buy milk, and for a copywriter, that's the most useful information of all. And that is what Account Planners find out for you. Planners produce insight into how consumers think, not just data about what they do.

Two Types of Research

Planners use two basic kinds of research: *quantitative* and *qualitative.*

Quantitative research involves lots of numbers, as you might expect from its name. **Surveys**, for example, are a form of quantitative research. Assuming that:

- The *sample* (the people among whom the research is conducted) . . .
- is *representative* of the people whose behavior you want to change (you wouldn't conduct a survey among single, college-aged women on their milk-buying habits, for example, if your target were the above-mentioned mothers)…
- and large enough to be *projectable* (you surveyed enough people in the target population to be confident that your results are truly representative of what the whole group thinks and does),

then a survey can give you great confidence.

Qualitative research is less concerned with numbers but, instead, with quality responses. These are often obtained via open-ended questions, allowing participants to voice their opinions.

Observation—watching actual consumer behavior—is a form of qualitative research; so are **focus groups**.

What a planner will do for focus group research is contact, say, 8 to 12 people who are in the target group (mothers with the characteristics we talked about above) and bring them together to ask them questions and get them talking about what they do and why, relative to the product or service to be advertised. In the case of milk, for example, mothers might say they buy milk for their kids "because it's good for them." Probing deeper, a skilled focus group moderator might get them to explain that the reason they believe milk is good for kids is "because it has lots of vitamins and minerals." More probing might produce the insight that making kids drink milk is all tied up with mothers' images of themselves as "good moms."

Good planners will use both forms of research. They might observe people's behavior and form some initial impressions. Then they might conduct various focus groups

to find out what's driving that behavior. Following that, they might take what they think they learned in the focus groups and do a survey in order to make sure that what the people in the focus groups said holds true for everybody (or at least a sizable proportion) in the designated group.

What Do You Do with All That Stuff?

A planner will now take all that data and insight and more—where people in the target group get their information about products; for example, what they read and whom they trust—and distill it into a Creative Brief for the copywriters and art directors who will develop the advertising itself. See the following Notepad for a typical creative brief template example. The responses help guide the ad planning from start to its finished execution.

Imagine. Twenty years ago, all most copywriters received was a description of the product and some cold facts about the target audience—demographics, mostly. Now you get a much richer picture of the person—at its best, so good that you can see her face as you write to her. You know what she does now, and why she does it. You know what you want her to do, and you know how to connect with her. You know what it is that matters to her about the product or service and how to relate to her as a person.

Earlier we were talking about the three levels David Aaker said were how a consumer experiences a brand. Now you know one reason why advertising focuses so much on the basic functional level—what the product does and how the consumer uses it. That's all the information copywriters used to get. Unfortunately, since most products in a category are pretty much alike and do pretty much the same thing, advertising on that level tends to say pretty much the same thing and look pretty much alike. USPs are rare and quickly copied. Crest was briefly the only toothpaste with fluoride, but Procter & Gamble's worldwide competitors caught up in a matter of months. If you don't have a functional advantage, what do you end up competing on? Price. And that's not very profitable, except for leading brands whose volume allows them to survive on smaller margins.

How do you escape that trap? How do you compete if there's little or no difference between your product and anyone else's? Your advertising can create a difference in how your product is perceived by the consumer, if you understand how she thinks and feels, and if you talk to her about what she cares about, instead of talking at her about the product itself. And thanks in large part to the advent of Account Planning, the insight you need to do that is now available to you.

Taking It to the Next Level

Aaker's second two levels are the *emotional* and the **self-expressive**. Emotional refers to how using the product makes her feel, and self-expressive is about what your product can help her to become. For example, if you wanted to get Mom to buy more milk for her kids instead of soft drinks or Kool-Aid® or whatever, you would know that giving her kids milk makes

Notepad

Varieties of Advertising Research

Advertising has a wealth of research options to help in understanding consumers, analyzing competitors, selecting creative options and evaluating executions. A few are:

Concept testing—a method to evaluate alternative creative ideas.
Focus groups—ideal for getting feedback to open-ended questions, this qualitative technique can assess consumer opinions on many topics.
Copy testing—this helps assure the message is prepared for an audience's readability and comprehension level.

her feel good, because she's doing what she believes is the right thing for them and that this, in turn, supports her image of herself as a good mother. And you can reinforce her belief by reminding her about the vitamins and minerals, which you already know are determinants of her milk-buying behavior.

But remember, it's not about the vitamins and minerals; they're just there to give her "permission to believe." It's about her being a Good Mom.* Thanks to the insight the Account Planner gave you in the Creative Brief, now you can

---

* Crest had the same insight. It maintained its leading market share by positioning getting kids to brush their teeth with Crest as another part of being a Good Mom. Getting fewer cavities was the benefit, and fluoride was the attribute that gave her permission to believe, along with the first endorsement by the American Dental Association. That other toothpastes can say, "Me, too" to all of that doesn't matter. Crest claimed the role of Mom's helper in the kids' teeth category and owns the position to this day.

talk to her about what matters to her—taking care of her kids—in a warm, supportive tone of voice, as though you were friends having a cup of coffee together. That's the great copywriter's talent—making that intimate connection quickly and powerfully, catching and sustaining her attention and interest, and getting her to translate that interest into behavior that rewards your client with her business.

But if it were that easy, this would be a pretty short book.

Recap

Branding guru David Aaker has consumers experiencing a brand on three levels: functional, emotional and self-expressive.

Consumers could care less about a product's features (or attributes); they want to know what will help them (benefits) or make a major difference from the competition (determinant). The unique selling proposition (USP) is what the client wants the consumer to know. The unique buying proposition (UBP) is what the consumer needs to hear.

Much research in advertising is the informal method: qualitative, where the key is to uncover quality answers through focus groups and open-ended questions. Quantitative research is formal and can be generalized for the larger population being targeted.

For Further Reading

Lisa Fortini-Campbell, *Hitting the Sweet Spot.* Chicago: The Copy Workshop, 2001.

Pamela N. Danziger, *Why People Buy Things They Don't Need.* Ithaca, NY: Paramount Market Publishing, 2002.

Mary Lou Quinlan, *Just Ask a Woman.* Hoboken, NJ: John Wiley & Sons, 2003.

Paco Underhill, *Why We Buy: The Science of Shopping.* New York: Simon & Schuster, 1999.

Jerry Vass, *Soft Selling in a Hard World: Plain Talk on the Art of Persuasion.* Philadelphia, PA: Running Press Book Publishers, 1998.

Gerald Zaltman, *How Customers Think.* Boston: Harvard Business School Press, 2003.

Chapter 3

First, Get My Attention

> *"Give me the freedom of a tightly defined strategy."*
>
> Norman Berry
> Former Global Creative Director
> Ogilvy & Mather

In Focus

- How are consumers going to feel and what will they want to become as a result of your product or service?
- What are the five aspects of segmentation and how do they work?
- Contrast the Hierarchy of Needs with the Hierarchy of Customers.
- What are positioning and perceptual mapping and how do they influence behavior?

Potentially promising writers may be ruined for life in elementary school by one misguided question: "What are you going to write about?" Devastating. Warping. And rarely overcome, as witness the plethora of ineffective advertising plaguing the business today. If only early composition teachers assigning students their first papers could be persuaded instead to ask, "Who are you going to write to?" (OK. OK. They'll probably feel constrained to phrase it more correctly, if somewhat stiltedly: "To whom are you going to write?") But think about it. That one simple change implemented this week in second grades throughout the land might create a glorious new era in advertising fifteen or twenty years from now.

Alas, that not having happened a generation ago now requires copywriting professors and copy chiefs and creative directors to retrain the cadre of would-be Kelly Award winners they've inherited, virtually from scratch.

Clients are no help either. They look out at the world from their shipping docks, which only makes it worse. Few understand that the only *sustainable* source of competitive advantage is *superior understanding of the customer*. No, it's not the output of the technological gnomes. Maybe forty years ago, you could have harvested a few years' worth of profitability out of a new product before your competitors caught up. No more in today's tech-savvy world. If a product appears in a test market on Monday morning, before nightfall it'll have been run through the mass spectrometers and gas chromatographs in competitors' labs, and by Tuesday morning, they'll have a knockoff prototype ready for costing. Being first to the marketplace is no guarantee of success anymore, if indeed it ever was.

It's Not Who's First; It's Who Lasts

Apple's iPhone, for example, had knock-off competitors announcing their new gizmos *before* iPhone's July 2007 launch. Other examples abound. What is a guarantee of success? Being first in people's minds and, more important, in their hearts and guts and psyches. The iPod wasn't the first MP3 player on the market. It wasn't even the third or fourth. It was the first MP3 player that talked to people on something other than a functional level, however. Apple and its agency, TBWA/Chiat/Day, understood *why* people wanted an MP3 player and positioned the iPod as the only such product that fulfilled that desire completely and helped the user express himself or herself.

Recall David Aaker's claim that people experience your product or service on three levels: functional, emotional, and self-expressive. Functional is about the product itself—what it does. Sadly, very little advertising gets beyond step one. Prove it to yourself. Pick up any magazine or newspaper and analyze the ads. What percentage of them basically just describe something—how it works, what it does, what it's for?

The real tragedy of this approach is that on the functional level all products are commodities. Oh, sure, there may be some little difference here or there, but it's almost always inconsequential. Basically, all products in a category function more or less exactly the same. So, therefore, how does the customer discriminate among them? On price? Wonderful. In other words, most advertising works in the area where there is the least leverage. (So you really can blame that second-grade teacher: "What are you going to write about?" The kids are still doing it.)

The leverage lies in the next two levels. The emotional level is about how the product (or service or brand) makes you feel. Happy, safe, powerful, hip? The self-expressive level is about what it helps you to become. A better Mom, a masterful lover, the coolest kid on the block. Understand what your prospect wants on that level and you'll be the next John Caples.

Have you ever seen that masterpiece of an ad he created to sell a piano lesson book in the middle of the Great Depression? Did Caples write about how this book used some revolutionary new teaching method devised by a Viennese concert pianist or something like that? No way. He tapped into a visceral emotional/self-expressive need powerful enough to motivate a person to part with his or

Notepad

That successful John Caples' line of "They laughed when I . . ." has been reissued by hundreds of copywriters. One that has aired on both radio and television starts: "They laughed when I told them I was studying French, but when I said to the waiter. . . ." You might recall that commercial was for Rosetta Stone foreign language software. Caples himself used that line decades ago for a correspondence school for French lessons.

In fact, if you conduct an Internet search of the phrase, you'll find literally thousands of uses. (Google listed over thirty-four thousand.) Try to see how many of them were for direct mail pitches. How many are for other types of ads?

her hard-earned money for what might seem in the context of the times a frivolous product. "They laughed when I sat down at the piano," his headline sang. "But when I began to play…." Genius. He transported his readers into an imaginary world where they would be the stars they'd always dreamed of being, surrounded by transfixed admirers, the center of attention for the first time in their lives. Irresistible. And successful.

A contemporary example of an ad that gets results by reaching the consumer on the visceral level is the long-running "A Diamond Is Forever" campaign, developed by the De Beers Company. Used in at least twenty-nine languages, the message has been branded into today's culture that a diamond is the best example to convey an ongoing love for someone. Print, outdoor, and broadcast advertisements point out the many benefits and joys of giving and receiving diamonds. *Advertising Age* awarded it the best ad slogan of the 20th century.

What do you need to know to think like that?

What's My Motivation?

Let's start with **Maslow's Hierarchy of Needs**, the cornerstone concept of psychographic segmentation. Later we'll talk about other ways to **segment**— that is, to cluster people who have something in common into groups so you can talk to a lot of them at once. But let's begin with **psychographic segmentation** because it's the first step toward understanding why people might want to do something you want them to do. According to the late Abraham Maslow (former chair of the Psychology Department at Brandeis University), people everywhere are driven by the same set of basic needs. The most basic needs are physiological—related to survival, really. Starving people need to eat. Freezing people need to get to a warm place. People in pain need it to stop.

Next comes a need to feel **safe** personally and to keep your family and possessions secure. Then people need to feel a sense of **belongingness**, perhaps to a community or a church or even to a sports team. Think of how college alumni still gather and root for the Tarheels or whatever. A level above that comes the need to be **esteemed**—to be valued and to be respected by your peers. And, finally, all that achieved, people have time to do something for themselves at a level called **self-actualization**.

You could apply this model to any social group, even cave people. Think about it. A caveman's first concerns are to find a cave, then build a fire and sharpen some sticks so he can secure and defend his home and food supply. Next, at the belongingness level, he joins a hunting party. Then he wants to be esteemed as the best hunter, perhaps. Finally, with all his elemental needs taken care of, he has the leisure to draw pictures on the cave family room wall!

You can also apply the model to virtually any product or service. A Japanese dental supply company used it to segment people according to their motivations for taking care of their teeth. At the lowest level were people who would only go to the dentist if a tooth started hurting. They built a series of messages around a theme of pain avoidance to reach these people. At the safety and security level, they targeted people with a campaign called "80/80"—the idea that you didn't have to lose your teeth when you got older. If you took care of your teeth properly, you could still have 80 percent of your teeth when you got to be 80 years old. Next came people who were a little insecure socially. The company

Notepad

Try This

Now you try it. Develop messages for Campbell's Chicken Noodle Soup for people you'd imagine to be at each level.

If only all assignments were this easy. You probably told people at the basic level that they couldn't buy a better meal for a buck. Maybe you talked to people at the security level about how soup would keep them and their children healthy. Many Moms used to think chicken soup was the best thing for a sick child. At the belongingness level, people would appreciate the universal family appeal of Campbell's soup. Did you find it a little harder to think of how to talk to consumers who crave others' esteem? Campbell's can be not only a time-saving recipe ingredient, but a building block for someone who wants to impress her guests with a Rachael Ray-style, gourmet-seeming meal.

And what did you say to the self-actualizer? "You eat Campbell's because you like it. You don't need to impress anybody by buying some soup with an expensive label." Same product in each case, but it's positioned differently because the people are motivated differently. One thing that will be the same for each appeal is that it matches the facts. But note that nothing said is untrue or deceptive. It's like when you're out with your friends versus when you're talking to your parents. You are yourself in both cases, but you emphasize different factets of your personality.

reminded them that snagly teeth and rotten breath were turnoffs when you're trying to make friends. People at the esteem level wanted to be more than just socially acceptable; they wanted movie star teeth. So they were potential customers for whitening products, orthodontic treatment, even caps.

And, finally, the company identified a segment of people whose motivations were inner-directed: people who jogged, worked out, and ate a healthy diet for their own personal pride and sense of well-being. The company related to this group by encouraging them to make dental health part of that daily regimen too. See how it works? Different strokes for different folks.

Notice how none of these appeals at any Maslow stage is about how the dentrifice products actually work (Aaker's functional level). They are about how good dental health practices make you feel (safe from pain, socially desirable, etc.), and what you become (a responsible person with a strong sense of self-worth).

Research: Hitting the Sweet Spot

Here's an important word: **positioning**. It's about finding the "sweet spot" in somebody's mind, that place where he or she puts the products and services that deliver best what he or she wants. We'll talk some more about that later.

Of course, in real life you don't guess at people's motivations; you do research to find out for sure. As we described in Chapter 1, the two basic types of research are quantitative and qualitative.

Quantitative research—surveys and polls, for example—gives you statistically valid data, projectible to the population as a whole. As long as your sample is representative—that is, the people you survey all belong to the particular group you want to find out about and you survey enough of them so that you feel confident that what you find out does represent the group as a whole—you can find out how many people do what, how often, for how much. Factual stuff.

Qualitative research—focus groups and one-on-one interviews, for example—gives you meaning to what you've found out and makes the research actionable: it tells you why people do what they do.

It's Not an Either/Or Decision

In some academic circles, there may be proponents of one or the other type, but in advertising we use both. For example, if you were introducing a new type of electric shaver for women, you might do some quantitive research to find out how many women use electric shavers versus blades, and whether preferences are related to demographic characteristics such as age, occupation, income, ethnic group, and so on. You might want to find out how often women shave which areas of their bodies, how long they keep a shaver before replacing it, and how much they paid for the electric shavers they own now.

Then you might do some qualitative research to get an idea of why they use electric shavers versus blades, how they choose one brand over another, their opinions about the wet/dry rechargeable varieties, and what words they use when they talk about the whole process of shaving. (Sometimes we find that engineers and product development people use technical language to describe products and their uses that differ from the language lay people use in everyday conversation about the same subjects.)

The Madison Avenue advertising agency BBDO developed a useful technique called **Problem Definition Research**. When they asked men to say what they'd like to see in, to stay in the category, a new electric shaver, they only got generalities. "I dunno. I guess I want it to shave as close as a blade" was a typical response. Not very insightful or useful. Then someone got the bright idea to switch the question around.

They asked men instead what they hated about shaving with an electric razor. Bingo! The quality of the responses went way up:

Notepad

Using Problem Definition Research

College students are often used in research, so think of an area where you could capture their responses in a negative context, similar to our shaving example.

"What do you dislike about food served on campus?" Their responses may be more insightful than simply asking what do you think about school food.

Now take a few minutes to think of other topics you could research in this manner. Perhaps such findings could become good articles for the campus newspaper.

Likewise, imagine being with a daily newspaper. You might ask subscribers specific questions that would be easy to answer:

"What don't you like about the organization of everyday items in the newspaper?"

"What comic strip(s) would you like to see eliminated from the daily paper?"

This line of questioning is quite common and valuable before a paper undertakes a design makeover.

"I hate the way it doesn't get around that bone in the back of my jaw."

"I hate that it doesn't get the long hairs on my neck."

"I hate that it pulls sometimes."

And so on.

See how much more actionable those responses are? Just pick the shaving problems men identify that your company's or your client's razor can do well at solving and now you know what to talk about. You know what your target audience will relate to. Why did that simple change in how the question was asked make such a difference? Because in the first instance, you're really asking the person to be a product designer, to be creative, to imagine something he's never seen. Most people don't do that very well. But when you ask the question backward, you're asking people about their very own experiences. They're experts on that subject and they'll tell you in no uncertain terms what they think.

In a perfect world, we would have a different conversation with each person whose behavior we're trying to affect. Consultants Don Peppers and Martha Rogers coined the phrase "One-to-One Marketing" and wrote several books about it. Maybe sometimes we can come pretty close to that using the Internet or various mobile marketing and social networking techniques, but most of the time it's necessary to clump people into groups, for efficiency's sake. That process is called *segmentation.*

Among the several criteria we use to segment people are these: demographics, psychographics, geography, buyer behavior, and attitude.

Demographics is pretty much all about numbers. What is the most likely age range of the people we want to reach? Are they men or women or doesn't it matter? Married or single? What do they do for a living? How much do they make? This kind of data is useful, to a point, but it's crude. "Women 18-34" is a typical demographic classification, but it really doesn't tell you much. Not only are 18-year-olds likely to have only the most basic things in common with 34-year-olds, they're likely to be greatly different from one another, depending on upbringing, education, and a thousand other variables.

Psychographics gets at some of those variables. Maslow's Hierarchy of Needs was an early model and is the foundation for most modern psychographic schemes. Perhaps the best known of these is VALS (values and lifestyles), developed by a company called SRI (Stanford Research Institute). VALS segments people into eight distinct profiles based on a combination of the resources they have available and their "primary motivation": How do they view the world? Are they idealistic? Driven to achieve? Or do they like most to express themselves? VALS can tell you in some detail what people in each group like to do, what they value, and even what words to use when you talk to them. It's quite useful for research, wouldn't you agree?

Another criteria for segmentation is **geographics**. Of course, you're certainly more likely to be successful if you try to sell snow tires in the North than in the Florida Keys, but it goes much deeper than that. Where people live can have a great influence on how they think. Think of the images that come to mind when you think of a New Yorker or a Westerner or someone who comes from the Deep South. It's more than a stereotype: People who come from different parts of the country often do have different customs, come from different cultures, and use different words and phrases to mean the same thing.

Notepad

VALS for You

Want to see what type you are? For a simple exercise, log on to www.sric-bi.com and take the VALS Survey. Then jot down a few ideas about how you would persuade someone like yourself to buy a particular product.

After you've done that exercise, go back and read the VALS description of some completely different category from your own. Now think about how you would have to change that appeal to relate to someone in that group.

Where's Waldo?

So how do you know where you should be selling, if it's not an obvious seasonal product? There are two useful tools called CDI and BDI: **Category Development Index** and **Brand Development Index**. CDI tells you how much a product is used in one part of the country compared to another. An "index" means that a score of 100 is based on the national average.

For example, if we look at the salsa category (through one of the data reporting systems such as Simmons or IRI), we may discover that the index for salsa sales in the Southwest is 112, which means that people who live there are 12 percent more likely to buy salsa than the national average. Meanwhile, the index for salsa sales in the Northeast might only be 97, which means that people there are 3 percent less likely than the national average to consume salsa. So you'd think you'd do better in the Southwest, wouldn't you? Maybe so. But what if the brand you're representing is Pace, and you discover that your BDI in the Northeast is 114? That means that although there are fewer salsa eaters in that part of the country, the people who do use the product are 14 percent more likely than average to prefer your specific brand. You have a larger share of the market. See how geographics can matter?

This data won't make your decisions for you, but it does provide more grist for your thinking mill. Should you try to increase the number of people in Boston who consume salsa, on the theory that you will benefit disproportionately? Or should you "fish where the fish are" and go head-to-head with the competition in El Paso to wrest away market share? That decision is a key part of marketing strategy. So it's helpful for copywriters to understand how the decisions they're charged to implement were arrived at by marketing strategists.

Why, Daddy?

Many companies use **buyer behavior** as a segmentation strategy. What they are usually referring to is whether people are heavy, medium, or light users of a product, service, or brand. Some of you are heavy users without realizing it. Do you eat fast food often? Drink a lot of bottled water? Eat pizza frequently? At first glance this might seem to be all you need to know to decide which people you should concentrate on reaching. However, Campbell Soup Company discovered that many of the people who were heavy users of their brand actually only bought the product when they had a coupon. If you think about that, you'll realize that these individuals were a lot less profitable than customers who were brand loyal. Brand loyal users were a lot more valuable no matter what their usage level was because when they needed soup, they would always buy Campbell's, whether or not they had a coupon.

So it's not enough to understand buyer behavior, what people do. You also need to know why they do it: **attitude**, the fifth segmentation factor on our list. We're using attitude here as a synonym for brand loyalty. You wouldn't talk to people who buy your product or your client's product only because they have a coupon or it's half price the same way you'd talk to people who always buy the brand because they think it's the best, would you? Of course not. So that's why you need to know not only what people do, how much, how often, and so on—behavior—you have to know why they do what they do—attitude.

Hierarchy of Customers

Another way to think about how you need to talk to different customers differently is to look at the **Hierarchy of Customers** (yes, based on Maslow) in Exhibit 3.1.

Exhibit 3.1 Hierarchy of Customers

At the base level, there are **Prospects**: people who look like they ought to be good customers.

How do you know that? Kraft did an analysis of people who bought macaroni and cheese and discovered that 20 percent of those people spent about $600 a year on the product, while the other 80 percent averaged $200 a year. Have you ever heard of the **Pareto Principle**? More commonly called the 80/20 rule, it posits that roughly 80 percent of your sales or 80 percent of your profits come from 20 percent of your customers. (A research leader from Ogilvy, Garth Hallberg, wrote a book around this principle that he titled *All Customers Are Not Created Equal*.) Once you know who those big-volume customers are, next you want to find out everything you can about them, starting with all the segmentation criteria we just discussed. When you've built a profile of those top 20 percent customers—how old they are, how much they make, where they live, how big their families are, etc.—you do what's called **data mining**. You root through your database of the other 80 percent to see if you can find people who match that profile. It stands to reason that they're the top prospects to join the ranks of our best customers since they are similar, doesn't it?

The next level is **Users**—people who are buying the product now. Why don't we call them "Customers"? Here's the difference: Users are people who buy our product or our client's product but aren't brand loyal. They buy because they have a coupon or because their boss says they have to or because they've always bought this and it would be a pain to change or whatever. **Customers**, in contrast, are people who can articulate a specific positive reason why they do business with us.

Here are two **Value Propositions** that may help you illuminate this point:

> "Certain specific customers buy our product rather than a competitor's product because they value _____."

Or better yet:

> "Certain specific customers will pay a premium for our product because they value _____."

Once you know the answers to such questions (and you'd *better* know those answers), you know exactly what to emphasize in your "conversations" with those people, don't you?

But if you look back at the diagram, you'll see that Customers isn't the top level. It's great that people buy from us, but what we really want is people who will *sell* for us: **Advocates**. We're all "compulsive sharers," aren't we? When we find that product or service we really like, we can't wait to tell our friends about it. We need to share the good news. Those are our best customers.

One recent term for such advocates is consumer evangelists. Word-of-mouth advertising continues to be a reliable and credible medium. In November 2007, several media outlets reported a finding that there are about 3.5 billion brand-related conversations daily in the United States. Various articles put a price tag on the value of word of mouth for 2007: $1 billion.

The point is, we need to have different strategy for people at each level of the heirarchy, don't we? We want Prospects to become Users, people who at least try our product. We want Users to become Customers, people who buy from us for a real reason. And we want to turn our Customers into Advocates, people who will recommend us to others.

We've come a long way from just writing about the product, haven't we? Now we're beginning to understand how to talk to someone.

It's All in Your Head

We said we'd come back to the subject of positioning. Your "position" is the place your product holds in a customer's mind relative to other products or other ways he or she can satisfy the need your product satisfies. For a thorough understanding of the concept, read the cornerstone book on the subject: *Positioning: The Battle for Your Mind,* by Al Ries and Jack Trout.

Another concept you should understand is the common graphics technique called **Perceptual Mapping**. This is how researchers visually determine where people position your product or service versus others on pairs of key attributes.

Exhibit 3.2 shows a simple perceptual map indicating where consumers place certain foreign automobiles on the scale of quality and price. Maps indicating more than two dimensions are usually more difficult to display and comprehend.

The typical perceptual map compares products or services based on price and perceived quality. But the options are unlimited. For example, you could compare automobiles using such descriptors as "styling," with "sporty" and "safe" as the two extremes. The Volvo is always seen as safe, despite recent efforts by the automaker to blend into the sporty category. The closer cars are to one another, the more they are seen as parity products by the consumers who did the rating.

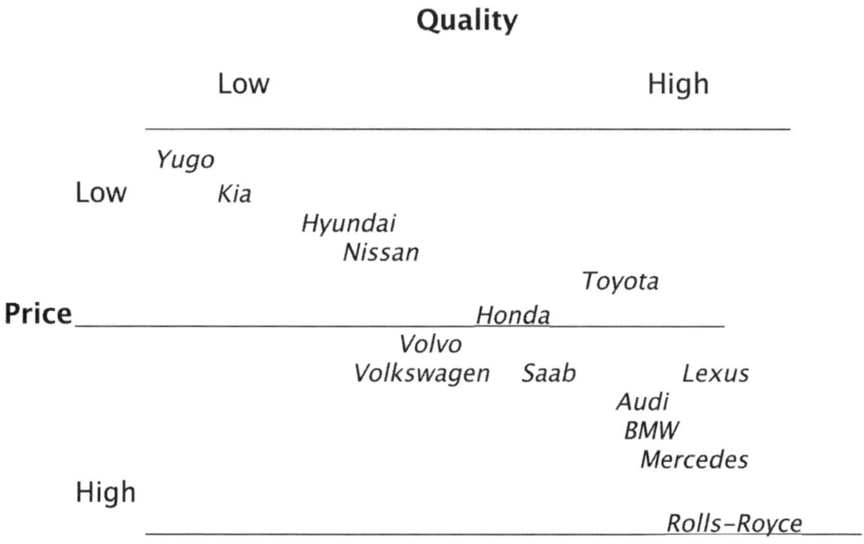

Quality

Low   High

Yugo
Low   Kia
                Hyundai
                    Nissan
                                        Toyota
Price _____ Honda _____
                        Volvo
                Volkswagen   Saab   Lexus
                                    Audi
                                    BMW
                                        Mercedes
High
                                    Rolls-Royce

Exhibit 3.2 Perceptual Map for Select Foreign Automobiles

Notice the absence of automakers in the high-quality, low-price quadrant. Toyota is the closest, which is probably the reason it passed Ford as the world's number-two automobile manufacturer during 2007 and traded places with General Motors as the number-one manufacturer.

Well, by now it's pretty obvious that research is critical to your success as a writer for print. James Webb Young, one of the founders of the famous J. Walter Thompson advertising agency, said the creative process has four steps: Preparation, Incubation, Inspiration, and Perspiration. Preparation is what all that research is about, and there's no substitute for it.

Bottom line: Good writers learn everything they possibly can about the person they're addressing before they write a word.

Recap

Being the first to introduce a product is no guarantee for success. A company has to be first in the hearts and minds of consumers. Maslow's classic Hierarchy of Needs provides psychographic segmentation of customers.

Segmenting people into groups is commonly done through demographics, psychographics, geographics, buyer behavior, and attitude.

The text's Hierarchy of Customers segments consumers into prospects, users, customers and advocates. In the latter group are ones who will be word-of-mouth evangelists for our products and services.

Positioning is where the customer places the client's product or service in her mind (the leader, second best, etc.) compared to other companies. A common way to chart this is with perceptual mapping.

For Further Reading

Garth Hallberg, *All Consumers Are Not Created Equal: The Differential Marketing Strategy for Brand Loyalty and Profits.* New York: John Wiley & Sons, 1995.

Al Ries and Jack Trout, *Positioning: The Battle for Your Mind.* New York: McGraw-Hill, 2nd ed., 2001.

Chapter 4

Visuals Reach Customers

> *"People look at the picture first, then read the headline."*
>
> Herb Krugman
> Former Chairman
> Advertising Research Foundation

In Focus

★ How do photos and other visuals attract attention?

★ What are the best uses of captions?

★ Why is it important to be aware of the legal and cultural aspects of photographs?

★ What are the dangers of clip art and stock photos?

Despite what we have said in the first three chapters, we live in a world of visuals. Photographs and visuals have proven qualities to arrest the attention of both **page scanners** and **engrossed readers**. Compelling image design can create instantaneous connections with a brand. This chapter discusses the headlines that often work together with the illustrations as a synergistic team to make an exclamatory statement. One helps the other without being redundant. Consider the arresting photo of a baby sitting inside of a tire. The photo alone may not sell many tires. For an effective ad, you couple that picture with the headline: "Michelin. Because so much is riding on your tires." Even people without kids may start thinking about having better treads after seeing this ad when heading off for a long weekend or a summer vacation.

In general, literal visuals are used to communicate factual information, so their main task is to identify and illustrate enticing product specifics. Consumers often want to see what an item actually looks like, how it works, and how to spot it (and its colorful packaging) on the retail store shelves. Visuals can show demonstrable product benefits for potential customers. Photos can usually do that better than a long copy block, which may not attract as much attention. Fashion, food and automotive ads almost always use full-color photography to allure consumers. That's another advantage print has over radio. Color pictures do attract much higher readership scores compared to black-and-white or no illustrations. They reflect unedited reality to the consumer.

Graphic Arts

Sometimes, however, graphic artists will grab readers' visual perceptions with an illustration or a photograph that twists reality. Often exaggeration or a cartoon effect is desirable for the ad. Or perhaps your ad rep with the latest digital camera forgot to get a model release signed for the photo that was supposed to run. Time and money are other reasons to go with a sketch versus an actual photo. It costs a lot to hire a professional photographer and model, plus you may have expenses associated with travel, props, other talent, food, and accommodations. And waiting for the perfect weather conditions can delay a shoot for days. So you can visually tell your audience how time is money with a simple clip art illustration, as in Exhibit 4.1.

Even lines (or rules, as they are called) in an ad can convey a deeper message

Sample Clip Art Illustration

Exhibit 4.1 Time Is Money

to consumers. Horizontal lines suggest peacefulness; vertical lines suggest dignity; and diagonal lines suggest action.

Because you only have a brief second or two to capture viewers' attention, the use of artwork is a common method to get readers to stop at your ad. There's no better attention magnet. You need to transmit a creative message quickly, at a glance. Pictures and illustrations are especially important when one considers a society that has become accustomed to less text. Consider signs today. The "No Smoking" warnings have been replaced with a red diagonal slash over a cigarette inside a red circle. Signs declaring "Men" and "Women" on public restroom doors have been supplanted with illustrations that supposedly resemble one of the two sexes.

Advertising agencies and copywriters have found that fewer and fewer residents of the United States are using English as a first language. Many other Americans have poor reading skills. Therefore, an arresting visual may be the primary means to acquire attention. Most individuals scan before they start reading. Even those with great reading skills identify with other folks in a photo. It's just human nature that we look at other people. And it's even better if the people are wearing, using, or consuming your client's product or service.

David Ogilvy said, "Sometimes, the best idea of all is to show the product—with utter simplicity. This takes courage, because you will be accused of not being 'creative.' "[1]

That advice should still be used today. A 2005 Roper Starch survey for the Newspaper Association of America found that the larger the illustration,

Notepad

Try This

Even crosswalk warnings of "Walk" and "Don't Walk" have been exchanged for green and red graphic arts symbols. Get out a piece of paper or use your computer to list how many other similar symbols are being used instead of words. Take five minutes to create your list. Compare your compilation with others. Here's a hint: Think airport.

the higher readership and recall of an ad. Using a base index score of 100, ads without a visual element (line art or photo) scored an 87. Those with illustrations covering 25 percent of the ad space scored a 90. Visuals consuming half the ad scored 109, and those comprising 75 percent of the ad had a recall score of 127. Another study by Cahners found that 98 percent of top-ranked ads used a picture or an illustration.

If your client's service or product lends itself to before-and-after photographs, it's wise to use them. Or the improved lifestyle of a user versus a deadbeat nonuser can be exhibited with photos. Showing readers an illustrative contrast or improvement is much better than trying to explain it. However, new or complicated products and services still need plenty of copy to sell themselves. Nike, on the other hand, can get by with just its classic swoosh.

Use Captions

Captions–the descriptions of what is in the accompanying illustrations or photographs–are always used with news photos because research shows they get 250 percent higher readership than the stories that accompany them. Many times the caption (also called a cutline) is the entry point for getting into the text. Yet many advertising professionals neglect to use captions when they could effectively supplement their photographs.

With such high readership numbers, a cutline can effectively serve as an ad by itself. A large majority of consumers who look at a photo also look for a caption. They want to know why this photograph is crucial to the advertisement. Satisfy that common curiosity by supplying key facts for such eager readers. It could serve as the similar entry point for readers to peruse the copy. But don't simply repeat the obvious. Persuasively sell within that caption. Hook the readers into shifting their eyes to the start of the copy block.

Using Photographs

A key tip when using photographs in ads is to make them bigger rather than smaller. And keep the focus as sharp as possible (unless you are consciously going for a blurred effect). People want to see details, rather than straining to make out images in a small picture. We've seen ads with three or four small photos when one large one would have been more effective, and taken less overall space. Cropping extraneous details and background from a picture allows you to make the crucial visualization bigger for the audience to see. If you decide to flip a photo so the face or movement is directed toward the ad rather than off the page, be careful that lettering does not appear in the picture since it would also be backward. Photos that bleed to the edge of the page do attract more attention, but they do typically cost a bit more.

Notepad

Pick up the closest magazine and flip it open to a full-page ad. Does it have a photo? (If not, go to the next ad with a photograph.) Why do you think this photo was used? Is it relevant to the product or service being featured in the ad? Will it help draw readers' attention to the page? Does it show the product or service being featured in the ad itself? Or does it merely set the mood or finish off the message of the headline? Or is the photo mere decoration for the ad?

Of course, the photos should be relevant to the product or service being advertised. Critics rightly contend that too many ads use attractive models who have no relationship to the sponsoring company's offerings.

There's no problem using an attractive size 2 model in your ad, but many advertisers have realized it's more realistic to portray the average U.S. female, who is six inches shorter and 40 pounds heavier than the runway varieties. Unilever's Dove since 2004, for example, has run a popular multimedia campaign featuring a variety of body shapes. So it's fine to run photos of average individuals in your ads. It makes your presentation more realistic. And profitable, Dove would add.

UNCF helps thousands of deserving students. But we have to turn away thousands more. So please give to the United Negro College Fund. Your donation will make a difference. Visit uncf.org or call 1-800-332-8623.

Exhibit 4.2 Sample Public Service Ad

Here's an example of a large, effective photograph for the United Negro College Fund. Of course, it's up to the publication to determine what size the public service ad will run in each case, since the space is being donated by the medium.

Exhibit 4.3 Ad for Santa Fe Cattle Company

Santa Fe Cattle Company developed a series of ads for its chain of steak houses, using print and outdoor. The close-up photo of the woman in Exhibit 4.3 is not what you would expect to sell steaks. But it does draw the readers to the ad. And the unexpected humor in the headline helps entertain the audience at the same time.

Legal, Cultural Cautions

Many organizations are rather protective of their logos and facility photographs that appear without approval in advertisements. For nonprofits, check with that organization's publications office to examine its policy. Many for-profit companies are similarly hesitant about their logo or product being used in unauthorized endorsements for another entity.

Consumers interpret visual messages differently, based on their cultural and personal backgrounds. In the U.S. the word *football* refers to a sport with two teams of 11 players each and a goal at each end of the field. That game of football is vastly different from the game of that name played around the rest of the world. Only in the U.S. that sport is called soccer and has a relatively limited audience. (Even veteran import David Beckham is having a hard time getting more Americans interested in soccer.)

A photo of war may evoke emotional ties to World War II, Vietnam, or Iraq, depending on the age of the viewer. European young people would apply their own conflicts to such a visual message. Just as many university students are making lifelong brand choices now, Baby Boomers did the same thing when they were in their late teens. So nostalgic photos are quite meaningful and effective for this growing older group. You can trigger emotional memories in consumers with the right photograph.

Even though photos convey significant messages, you can't assume one that's appropriate for a U.S. audience would render the same effect in a global campaign. (We discuss color's impact and interpretation in later chapters.) Many acceptable symbols—such as the OK sign made with the thumb and forefinger—have profane interpretations for other cultures. Popular celebrities in South America or Europe are relatively unknown in the United States and would attract minimal response. Comparative advertising makes for a good visual, but it's illegal in many countries worldwide. Germany, for example, just in this decade approved the practice of comparative ads.

Stock Photos Can Backfire

Stock photos and clip art samples are always available for a quick visual downloadable solution. These numerous top-quality photos are free, just waiting for your decision to use them in your ad. A quick search will turn up several sites offering thousands of royalty-free photographs. We found these, for example:

www.usda.gov/oc/photo/opclibra.htm
www.ars.usda.gov/is/graphics/photos
www.pbase.com
www.dpchallenge.com
www.freefoto.com
www.morguefile.com
www.nwyhstockimages.com
www.sxc.hu
www.comstock.com/web

Exhibit 4.4 "Dueling" Stock Photos

With so many options, chances are slim that the same visual would appear in your ad or Web site and another's, even the competition. But it does happen, as evidenced in Exhibit 4.4. These two ads use the same model's identical photograph for two entirely different purposes.

Stock photographs have even caused legal problems when the individuals are portrayed as endorsing a product or service. The UK's Advertising Standards Authority took offense with several posters featuring photos of people who were endorsing a housing development. They were not residents, of course, and Clapham Homes had to remove the ads.

Recap

Visuals attract attention, which is why a huge majority of ads contain them. One large photo is better than several small ones.

Captions (or cutlines) that explain what's in the picture are another magnet for readers' eyes. Use them to help draw consumers into the text of the ad.

Be wary of using photos in ads without permission. Another ad caution concerns gestures and customs that may have different connotations for an international audience.

Stock photos and clip art are easily available, but the same ones could be used by a competitor or in another ad that reflects poorly on your company.

Notes

1. David Ogilvy, *Ogilvy on Advertising.* New York: Random House, 1985, p. 16.

For Further Reading

Patricia Johnson, *Real Fantasies: Edward Steichen's Advertising Photography.* Berkeley, CA: University of California Press, 2000).

Paul Messaris, *Visual Persuasion: The Role of Images in Advertising.* Thousand Oaks, CA, Sage Publications, 1997.

Chapter 5

Headlines and Subheads

"Now that you have my attention, is there something you wanted to say to me?"

Mae West
American Actress

In Focus

How do headlines attract readers to the ad?

How can heads be used to target appeals to certain audiences?

How do headlines and visuals work as a unit?

Compare the three main types of headlines.

What are the rules for headline writing?

What kinds of subheads are used in ads?

A good headline accomplishes a major task. It breaks through all the advertising clutter of competing ads to get a reader to notice its message, pause to read it, and then—when successful—convince the viewer to read about the product or service being featured in the body copy. Selling is done through various aspects of the ad, but the headline is definitely essential in grabbing shoppers by their eyeballs so they can consider the claims of a particular manufacturer, retail store, or service provider.

At the same time, U.S. households have had it up to here with the onslaught of more and more marketing communications attacking their senses. That's why about 145 million telephone subscribers have signed up with the Federal Trade Commission's Do Not Call Registry. In *Coming to Concurrence: Addressable Attitudes and the New Model for Marketing Productivity,* based on a study out of the Yankelovich opinion research group, J. Walker Smith and his co-authors point out that one of the fastest-growing product categories is the type that blocks advertising messages. Millions of consumers use spam blockers on their computers and buy the latest electronic gadgets to thwart television commercials. So there's even more pressure for the copywriter to design tempting messages that break through that unwanted, detested clutter.

There's no magic formula for writing headlines. Some ads don't even use them, but most copywriters swear by them. Other ads merely drop in the company name. A few ads just inflate the size of the opening line or two of copy to draw the reader into the rest of the message. Some print ads—for example, billboards—will often use nothing but the headline as the only design element. And headlines don't always have to be at the top of the layout, as we'll discuss in Chapter 8.

"In a print ad, 75 percent of the buying decisions are made at the headline alone," said the veteran copywriting expert John Caples, whom you've met earlier. However, despite Caples' assertion about the sales decisions, today's consumers are discerning and doubtful about product claims. The headline is joined by other ad elements to accomplish the difficult feat of closing the deal. Many feel that the headline gets the customer, and the copy asks for the order. Headlines do get more exposure than the smaller copy block. Readership of headlines is usually five times or more than the body copy itself. Since the bulk of the closing of the convincing sales job is primarily relegated to the ad's copy, the headline has to quietly or loudly grab the shopper's attention. So you can easily see how three out of four buyers attribute the headline as the convincing element of the ad.

The classic introductory advertising textbook, *Kleppner's Advertising Procedures*, in its 17th edition (2008), echoes this crucial job of the headline:

> The headline is the most important part of a print advertisement. It is the first thing read, and it should arouse interest so the consumer wants to keep on reading and get to know more about the product being sold. If the headline does not excite the interest of the particular group of prime prospects the advertiser wants to reach, the rest of the advertisement will probably go unread.[1]

One important thing to keep in mind when writing ad headlines is the audience. Various studies have shown that women control anywhere from 65 to 85 percent of household-buying decisions. (The Kleppner text above says women "purchase or influence 85 percent of all products.")

Consultant Martha Barletta, in *Marketing to Women: How to Understand, Reach, and Increase Your share of the Largest Market Segment,* says women account for 70 percent of new businesses startups and control 92 percent of vacation decisions. Therefore, keep that in mind when designing these interest-generating headlines for such products and services:

In order to stop readers, headlines must catch their awareness.

> In all forms of advertising, the "first impression"—the first thing the readers sees, reads, or hears—can mean the difference between success and failure. If the first impression is boring or irrelevant, the ad will not attract your prospect. If it offers news or helpful information or promises a reward for reading the ad, the first impression will win the reader's attention. And this is the first step in persuading the reader to buy your product.[2]

The headline is often more time-consuming and difficult to craft than the copy that follows. In fact, once the head is written, it may dictate the form and style for the rest of your commercial message. With the slant already determined by the title, some ads can almost write themselves.

But it's no simple task getting that headline to project the right attitude with words that say to the casual reader, "Stop! Look at this! This is something you need!" Headlines need to grab sets of appropriate eyes, but at the same time they may be ruling out nonprospects. That's not always a bad thing. You want prospects so be specific with product benefits. "How to Cover Your Gray Hair" probably appeals to the many readers who have that condition. But the title would eliminate (naturally) bald people and those who still have a whole mop of youthful hair in its original or re-engineered color.

On a similar note, many suggest that copywriters should avoid using the word "if" in heads. It either qualifies the buyer or the product. Such a conditional statement might somehow weaken your message. "If You Need a Plumber, Call Bubba's Plumbing" won't even earn a glance if residents don't have a current plumbing need. However, other veteran copywriters have expressed valid reasons for eliminating nonusers of products or services. Readers want to read— or at least will take the time to read—ads that interest them. Not every subscriber of the publication is going to become a customer. Prospects are the ones who will buy the product or service. So it's OK to use headlines that zero in on busy readers who need what your company or your client is selling.

Heads and Visuals: Working as a Team

Elements of a print ad work as a unit. It's always wise to have that specific photo or graphic element in front of you as you struggle to compose the headline. It often gives you the impetus to provide the headline joke, the punch line for what appears in the picture. Or vice versa.

The Radio Advertising Bureau started a full-page print ad campaign by De-Vito/Verdi in 2006. Appearing in media trade publications, the ads feature a photo at the top, followed by a generic product with the identical small headline "If it works, don't ignore it."

One ad featured a crumpled soccer player in obvious agony. Below that was a protective athletic cup with the campaign headline, "If it works, don't ignore it." Another featured a blue jeans-clad home handyman on his knees. The back of his jeans is revealing the infamous "plumber's crack." Beneath the photo is a belt, with the similar "If it works, don't ignore it" headline. (See Exhibits 5.1 to 5.4 for these and other examples.)

Along the bottom of each ad is the identical logo and claim that radio advertising works, reaching 228 million people every week. (For a more thorough discussion of ad campaigns, please see Chapter 11.)

As we described in previous chapters, the copywriter and the art director use the creative brief to work as a team, whose foremost duty is to garner awareness with the headline and the visual. One could stand alone in a few ads. But in an overwhelming number of cases, the two are indivisible. The finished ad is greater than the sum of its parts. One element may play off the other. Or one could even be worthless without the other. Just look at the bottom half of the RAB ads in Exhibits 5.1 to 5.4 to see how senseless they would be as complete ads without the photo.

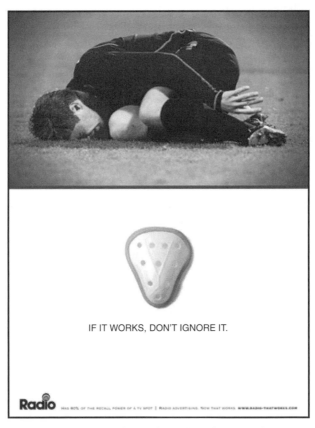

IF IT WORKS, DON'T IGNORE IT.

Exhibit 5.1 Headline and Visual Working Together

Exhibit 5.2 Headline and Visual: Together Again

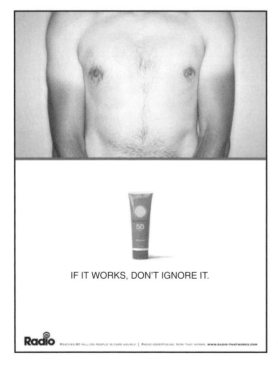

Exhibit 5.3 Headline and Visual: Yet Again

IF IT WORKS, DON'T IGNORE IT.

Radio

Exhibit 5.4 Headline and Visual: One More Time

Saab's "Born From Jets" print and TV ad campaign needed both that head-line and a view of the sleek car to see the connection. (The Swedish automaker produced jet engines before it entered the automotive industry.) You'll note in these headlines as well as many others in publications how the illustration and the photo are inseparable. Some of its other headlines, usually accompanied by a photo of the car in an airplane hangar or on a runway, are:

- Air-crafted.
- Stow your gear for takeoff.
- Any similarity to a jet is purely genetic.
- Now departing.
- The Saab 9-5 Sedan. Never fly coach again.
- Have a safe flight.

- You're closer to owning a jet than you think.
- Fly non-stop.
- Prepare for takeoff.

Types of Headlines

Headlines, pre-planned or not, typically fall into one of three categories. Some authorities will actually produce a list of up to about a dozen separate alignments. One of the classic texts, Philip Ward Burton's *Advertising Copywriting*, listed eight headline varieties, for example. These various categories are far from ironclad, of course. Sometimes a head will fit into more than one type or fall into a miscellaneous class.

1. One broad category is headlines that provide *news*. Readers are used to scanning newspaper and news magazine headlines that summarize the content of the articles. If you mimic the practice of providing your readers with news—a new product, a new service, new features, new prices—it may entice them to read the rest of the advertisement. The word *new*, in fact, is always among the top buzzwords of persuasive advertising.

   News is up to the consumer to interpret. A bigger, tougher SUV model may not attract much attention from green-minded individuals wanting more than a dozen miles to the gallon. The headline "Pay on time. Get paid back." provides Discover customers with a new money-saving feature of their credit card.

2. Many heads will promise a *benefit* to the consumer. After all, you want to attract the readers' attention, so why not offer something that your product or service can provide? Headlines that work best are those that promise a benefit to readers, a feature they will value. Don't forget the Hierarchy of Needs discussed earlier with such motivators as greed, fear, power, prestige, etc. Make sure you appeal to the reader's self-interest, not the client's. Don't be shy and hide a benefit in the copy. A busy reader may not get that far if not enticed.

   The benefit of a different camera is evident in this headline: "Their point-and-shoots would miss and miss. Then the Nikon D40 came to town."

3. A third major category is the *curiosity* headline. As the name implies, this headline is meant to hook the reader's interest so the rest of the ad will be consumed. This is a catch-all category, of course, since most ads want to grab readers' eyes. But this particular headline will arouse curiosity about the product or service.

In a recent *Glamour* issue, for example, we saw inquisitive heads such as "Some Discoveries Are worth Sharing," "Bad News for People Who Can't Walk and Chew Gum," and "If It Doesn't Fit, It's Ugly Anyway."

Rules to Follow—Usually

Advertising books will often suggest the top 10 or so rules for writing award-winning headlines. (We found four such lists on the Web in less than half an hour.) If only it were that simple. Newsroom copy desks craft headlines that summarize the essence of the story that follows. They will select key words—usually short—that lure readers into wanting more information. Just as newspaper story headlines vary, depending on the elements of that article, advertising heads will also differ for several reasons. There's no clear-cut, simple solution for crafting the most appropriate grabbers of attention. And every rule can be broken for the right reason. Here are a few, in no particular order, that you should adhere to most of the time:

- **Use Active Voice**

One admonition that appears on most lists is to create active voice headlines in the present tense for a stronger presentation to readers. That rule is a valid carryover from news headlines as well. Active voice just sounds stronger and more direct. Compare: "The Size You Need Is Stocked By Our Store" vs. "Your Size Is Here." Notice also the fewer words needed in most cases for active voice phrases. That gives your ad some extra benefits. One is that the type size can increase because you're using half the words of the passive voice example. Another is that you can also add white space around your shorter title to give viewers' eyes a refreshing pause.

Likewise, present tense verbs carry more immediacy than future tense or past tense. "Lightyear Tires Will Increase Your Mileage" may sound conditional or a little iffy to some readers. It's more direct to say definitively, "Lightyear Tires Increase Your Mileage." It's more factual.

- **Name the Benefit**

Knowing the importance of the headline's role in capturing awareness, you should try to sell the product's advantages to the consumer. How will this item or service make the customer's life better? Will they get better gas mileage from this new additive or whiter clothes from this improved detergent? You can't assume the reader will wait around until the body copy to get to the benefit.

Headlines should clearly inform readers what the benefit is, then tell them how the item being promoted is capable of delivering on the promise. What's the special formula in the additive that cleans your carburetor or fuel lines that mileage definitely increases? Provide the reason your product can make the benefit possible.

- **Keep It Positive**

Phrasing things in the positive is better than using negative words. Veteran newspaper editors used to admonish their rookie reporters to write that the defendant was found innocent, even though the official court jury's finding was "not guilty." The reason? To protect the paper from a libel suit if the word "not" was dropped from the story through a composing or editing error.

Also, negative headlines can leave a negative impression in customers' minds. If the giant print in the ad says, "Buddy's Glue Will Not Leave an Ugly Mess," some readers will recall only the key words: *Buddy's Glue* and *Ugly Mess*.

And undoubtedly that's the opposite combination you were hoping for when crafting that head. Your parents or grandparents can remember the infamous Richard Nixon speech when he proclaimed, "I am not a crook." A majority of Americans who read about his Nov. 17, 1973, proclamation recall only the key utterance in that phrase: *crook.*

- **Make Your Words Count**

Among other things, this means to count your words. However, short headlines aren't always better than longer heads, except for billboards. You need to placate those harried readers, so don't bog them down with excessive wording in your grabber titles. If you can say it in fewer words, that's fine. Never waste words in a headline. As stated above, shorter heads can use larger font sizes and still have white space around them to garner more attention. Still, use what you need and not one extra word.

Even though some pundits suggest a maximum of 10 headline words, say what you have to say—even if that means using more than 10 words. Just say it succinctly. Use as many words as you must to drive your message home. Ogilvy disputed the mantra that no one reads long headlines. He always maintained that if the readers were engaged—meaning they were interested because the writer had done a good job—they would read longer headlines. One of his many classic headlines (Exhibit 5.5) used 18 words: "At 60 miles an hour the loudest noise in this new Rolls-Royce comes from the electric clock."

Meanwhile, two of the most successful 20th-century ads contained the Volkswagen heads "Lemon" and "Think Small." (See Exhibit 5.6.) Naturally the copy was devoured in both ads so readers could understand what the short labels were talking about. "Think Small," in fact, ranks as *Advertising Age*'s top ad campaign of the 20th century.

- **Work With the Visual**

You've seen the ads for Michelin tires with the headline: "Because so much is riding on your tires." That headline works so well because the photograph in the ad shows a young infant sitting on top of a Michelin tire. That image reinforces the impact of the words. Unfortunately, its newer ad campaign claims "A Better Way Forward," which says very little.

Look at many ads and you'll see the obvious. The headline and the visual form a team. Many surveys give the edge to the photo's impact on drawing

The Rolls-Royce Silver Cloud—$13,995

"At 60 miles an hour the loudest noise in this new Rolls-Royce comes from the electric clock"

What makes Rolls-Royce the best car in the world? "There is really no magic about it— it is merely patient attention to detail," says an eminent Rolls-Royce engineer.

1. "At 60 miles an hour the loudest noise comes from the electric clock," reports the Technical Editor of THE MOTOR. Three mufflers tune out sound frequencies—acoustically.

2. Every Rolls-Royce engine is run for seven hours at full throttle before installation, and each car is test-driven for hundreds of miles over varying road surfaces.

3. The Rolls-Royce is designed as an *owner-driven* car. It is eighteen inches shorter than the largest domestic cars.

4. The car has power steering, power brakes and automatic gear-shift. It is very easy to drive and to park. No chauffeur required.

5. The finished car spends a week in the final test-shop, being fine-tuned. Here it is subjected to 98 separate ordeals. For example, the engineers use a stethoscope to listen for axle-whine.

6. The Rolls-Royce is guaranteed for three years. With a new network of dealers and parts-depots from Coast to Coast, service is no problem.

7. The Rolls-Royce radiator has never changed, except that when Sir Henry Royce died in 1933 the monogram RR was changed from red to black.

8. The coachwork is given five coats of primer paint, and hand rubbed between each coat, before *nine* coats of finishing paint go on.

9. By moving a switch on the steering column, you can adjust the shock-absorbers to suit road conditions.

10. A picnic table, veneered in French walnut, slides out from under the dash. Two more swing out behind the front seats.

11. You can get such optional extras as an Espresso coffee-making machine, a dictating machine, a bed, hot and cold water for washing, an electric razor or a telephone.

12. There are three separate systems of power brakes, two hydraulic and one mechanical. Damage to one will not affect the others. The Rolls-Royce is a very *safe* car—and also a very *lively* car. It cruises serenely at eighty-five. Top speed is in excess of 100 m.p.h.

13. The Bentley is made by Rolls-Royce. Except for the radiators, they are identical motor cars, manufactured by the same engineers in the same works. People who feel diffident about driving a Rolls-Royce can buy a Bentley.

PRICE. The Rolls-Royce illustrated in this advertisement—f.o.b. principal ports of entry—costs $13,995.

If you would like the rewarding experience of driving a Rolls-Royce or Bentley, write or telephone to one of the dealers listed on opposite page.

Rolls-Royce Inc., 10 Rockefeller Plaza, New York 20, N. Y. Circle 5-1144.

Exhibit 5.5 The Classic Ogilvy Ad for Rolls-Royce

Think small.

Our little car isn't so much of a novelty any more.
A couple of dozen college kids don't try to squeeze inside it.
The guy at the gas station doesn't ask where the gas goes.
Nobody even stares at our shape.
In fact, some people who drive our little

flivver don't even think 32 miles to the gallon is going any great guns.
Or using five pints of oil instead of five quarts.
Or never needing anti-freeze.
Or racking up 40,000 miles on a set of tires.
That's because once you get used to

some of our economies, you don't even think about them any more.
Except when you squeeze into a small parking spot. Or renew your small insurance. Or pay a small repair bill. Or trade in your old VW for a new one.
Think it over.

Exhibit 5.6 The Classic VW "Think Small" Ad

viewers into the ad. However, both certainly impress the viewer. One often leads into the other, forming the punch line that completes the message. And it's not always the photo that finishes off the interest-getting point. It can be the head following the visual. In the words of the old saying, "The whole is greater than the sum of its parts."

Don't merely echo one with the other. The two need to complement and supplement each other. The photo should not merely illustrate the head. It might show the product in use, but with an unusual, humorous, or otherwise distinctive application. (Exhibit 5.6 illustrates this point.)

• Know Your Audience

As mentioned above, it's impossible to design an ad or its headline if you don't know your target audience. Think of a specific prospect and use selective words. Give her a name and think of her age, occupation, and marital status as you design your creative. Visualize your customer using the product or service in your ad. How does it help that person? You have to know the people your ad is addressing or you won't know the language and attitude to use. What's on their minds? What's their "hot button"? What do they need that your client can provide? Your ad headline should immediately answer their question of "What's in it for me?"

• Shun All-Cap Headlines

Studies have proven that all capital letters are both harder and slower to read than caps and lowercase letters. Used sparingly in short headlines, all caps may be OK to capture reader attention. However, avoid using them in longer heads because they are more difficult to read and lead to a loss in readership. Furthermore, the capitalized headline will take much more space than one written in caps and lowercase. This concept is discussed in more detail in Chapter 7.

• Avoid Most Punctuation Marks

While a few practitioners think a period is needed at the end of every headline, most heads are far from being full sentences, so they don't need that treatment. Additionally, the period, besides taking room, signifies the end. You want readers to continue with the headline thought into other elements of the ad—visuals, subheads and copy. What marks should be used then? Certainly a question mark is needed if the title asks a question. Never use an exclamation point (or, perish the thought, multiple ones). Its overuse merely enhances the image that you're shoveling puffery at the audience.

And quotation marks? Some copywriters, including Ogilvy, say they increase recall. Perhaps the implication is that the quote seems personal. You may notice that most newspaper news stories use a single quote, rather than the double ones, for actual quotes. That's simply a device to save space. Feel free to imitate the practice. But if the headline isn't a testimonial statement by a source, skip the quote marks and leave a little white space instead. Again, their absence may let you pop up the head size a little more for added impact. Ellipses, when necessary, can be used, of course.

- **Take Chances**

Some headline advisers may caution you against humor, puns, or other abnormalities of good copywriting. Puns, often called the lowest form of humor, are criticized for having no selling power. But if *good,* puns can get readers to think of the client's product or service; then they can serve a purpose. People do like to be entertained. But the admonition to shun a pun is because so many of them are bad.

Humor, of course, needs to be nonsexist and nonracist. And remember: The purpose is to sell something, not to merely entertain for its own sake. The biggest problem with using humor is that the laughs often overwhelm the subject of the ad. People will remember the gag or the one-liner but can't tell you what the product, much less the brand, was.

Subheads

Known by various names, the smaller headlines in an ad help guide readers, attract attention of skimmers, and create contrast on the page to improve an ad's visual image. The word **subheads** typically refers to those small, bold-faced headlines that appear within the text of a long copy block, either ad or news-editorial material. Often called **crossheads**, they help break up the text and serve as entry points for busy readers. Writers drop them into copy after three or so paragraphs to outline the main points and break up long copy blocks. Used to that end, they are common in direct mail pieces. *Subhead* is also a generic term applied to the sundry other types of additional headlines used in an ad layout.

Shorter headlines that appear above the main headline are called *kickers,* just as they are on the news side of the publication, although their use has declined with news stories these past few years. They often are set in a different style (italics, for example) or weight. Copy desks traditionally made kickers half the size of the main head. They usually consist of a phrase that gets your audience's attention, perhaps by introducing your client's product or service. A kicker typically is not enough to drive customers to their computers or retail outlets. It's just a starter in the sales process.

One variety of a kicker is called a **read-in**, because it's the beginning of the headline. Take a look at Exhibit 5.7. It starts the wording in the headline in its smaller position above the main head. For the Mercedes-Benz and Swatch's

Save Gas By

Thinking Smart

Exhibit 5.7 Sample Read-In Head

Smart® minicar's 2008 U.S. introduction, a read-in might say: "Save Gas By," followed by the larger, main head: "Thinking Smart."

Opposite of a regular kicker, a **reverse kicker**, sometimes called a *hammer*, uses the upper line as the brief, but larger-sized headline. The hammerhead might be only one or two words as shown in Exhibit 5.8. The extra white space created is one of the reasons a **hammer head** is used. Using this subhead example, a reverse kicker might simply say: "Smart." The longer and smaller headline underneath that one word could be: "How to Buy Your Car in 2008."

Smart

How to Buy Your Car in 2008

Exhibit 5.8 Sample Hammer Head

Another version of a secondary headline is called a **deck** or **drop head**. Rather than above, this smaller head appears under the main headline. It often elaborates on the main headline. The value of decks cannot be overlooked since they provide additional details that could catch the eye of readers who weren't grabbed by the major headline phrase. The deck below in Exhibit 5.9 shows

Driving Smart

**Easily park in spots
other cars pass by**

Exhibit 5.9 Sample Deck

how the Smart car has an advantage when it comes to parking in tight spots. Major news stories in the 19th century and early 20th century typically contained multiple one-column decks, each providing more details about the story that eventually followed. Most decks in ads today are no more than two or three lines long.

An offshoot of the deck is one that continues the thought of the ad's major headline. Called a **readout**, it finishes the sentence or thinking started in the above headline. Exhibit 5.10 shows an example where the readout continues the concept of the main head: "Senior citizens can attend college" followed below by "For free next semester." The readout itself can be placed at various spots on the line: flush left, indented, centered or even flush right.

Senior citizens can attend college

For free next semester

Exhibit 5.10 Sample Readout

Headlines and various subheads have tremendous responsibilities for an advertisement. The main head can grab the attention of all readers as well as specific readers needing the service or product being promoted. Both, when used, should entice readers into the body copy. Another common function of the head is to coordinate with the visual—either photo, artwork or graphic—to balance and enhance the ad message.

Recap

By their size alone, headlines attract attention on the printed page—enough, it's hoped, to catch the reader's eyes to look at the accompanying ad.

In most ads, the head and the visual work as a team to present a unified message to viewers. The RAB and Saab campaign examples are described accomplishing that goal in this chapter.

Headlines typically fall into one of three categories: news, benefit and curiosity. Rules for writing heads are subjective, but they include: use active voice, name the benefit, keep it positive, make words count, work with the visual, know your audience, avoid all-capital headlines, avoid most punctuation marks, and take chances.

Subheads help direct readers into and through your ad.

Notes

1. W. Ronald Lane, Karen Whitehill King and J. Thomas Russell, *Kleppner's Advertising Procedure.* Upper Saddle River, NJ: 2008, pp. 508-509.
2. Robert W. Bly, *The Copywriter's Handbook: A Step-by-Step Guide to Writing That Sells.* New York: Henry Holt and Company, 1990, p. 11.

For Further Reading

Martha Barletta, *Marketing to Women: How to Understand, Reach, and Increase Your share of the Largest Market Segment.* Chicago: Dearborn Trade Publishing, 2006.

Robert W. Bly, *The Copywriter's Handbook: A Step-by-Step Guide to Writing That Sells.* New York: Henry Holt and Company, 1990.

Philip Ward Burton, *Advertising Copywriting.* Lincolnwood, IL: NTC Business Books, 1999.

Herschell Gordon Lewis, *On the Art of Writing Copy.* Chicago: Racom Books/Racom Communications, 2004.

J. Walker Smith, Ann Clurman, and Craig Wood, *Coming to Concurrence: Addressable Attitudes and the New Model for Marketing Productivity.* Chicago: Racom Books/Racom Communications, 2005.

Chapter 6

Copy That Makes the Sale

> *"One difference between a writer and a talent is the number of wastebaskets the writer has filled."*
>
> John Ciardi
> American poet and critic

In Focus

✳ How does copy cause consumer action?

✳ What makes the copy in the VW Lemon ad work?

✳ What are inherent dangers of international ad translations?

✳ Why is the copy from the Power of the Printed Word campaign effective?

A legendary New York ad agency copywriter named Ed McCabe (Scali, McCabe & Sloves was his agency) once admitted he'd rewritten the copy for an award-winning Volvo ad 256 times.

"How do you know it was 256," a skeptic sneered, "not 255 or 257?"

"Because I counted the pieces of paper I'd wadded up and thrown away," McCabe replied.

The art of writing is rewriting, as another sage said. But first you have to know what you're trying to accomplish in that struggle for perfection, which is what we're going to talk about first in this chapter: the role of copy.

Even before that, though, let's define what we mean by "copy" to make sure we're all on the same page. Copy is that block of words in a print ad that people read (we hope) right after they've been stopped by the illustration and read the headline (which functions like a caption, you'll remember from Chapter 2). The writer half of a typical writer/art director team is called a copywriter.

So to review: We know that people experience ads by looking at the picture or illustration first. If they're intrigued or, better yet, compelled by the image—if what you've shown them is relevant to something they care about—they'll read the headline. About 90 percent of the time, most people don't go any farther, research says. But if you've done a good job of connecting with them, if you've made your UBP (Unique Buying Proposition) clear and they're interested, they'll read more.

OK, copywriter—you're on. It's up to you to make the sale. "Sale" sometimes is quite literal (in direct marketing, for example, where it's often also termed the call-to-action; the action, of course being the sale). At other times, it's a surrogate for whatever action you want the reader to take, such as punch up a Web site, clip a coupon, go to a store, etc. It's extremely important you know exactly what action you want consumers to take. Advertising is not about delivering a message. (One veteran of the business used to say that's what we have Western Union for.) It's about causing some specific, measurable, and, ultimately, mutually profitable behavior to take place. Don't write a single word until there's agreement among the client, the account people, the creative director and you as to exactly what that single-minded behavioral objective is.

Now that you know what you've got to accomplish, how do you go about it? What's the function of the copy? How do you construct it to hold and deepen the reader's interest and cause that person to do what you need him or her to do?

That Golden Lemon

The first sentence of copy picks up where the headline left off. "Lemon," said the headline on a classic Doyle Dane Bernbach ad for the original Volkswagen Beetle. "What's that all about?" the reader wondered. "They can't really be saying this car's no good." Intrigued, he (the ad was primarily aimed at educated, literal-minded males, such as engineers) reads on. So the first duty of the copy is to expand upon the point the illustration and headline introduced. Imagine the question(s) you may have raised in the reader's mind and respond—quickly—all the while moving the proposition forward.

"This Volkswagen missed the boat," says the first line of the copy.

"Oh, really?" ponders the reader. "Looks OK to me." And, of course, he reads another sentence. He has to, to find out why the car wasn't shipped. See how the story line is being advanced and the reader drawn in?

So why did the "Lemon" miss the boat? Because "The chrome strip on the glove compartment is blemished and must be replaced," the copy tells us, adding, "Chances are you probably wouldn't have noticed it; Inspector Kurt Kroner did."

"Wow! Are they that meticulous?" the reader wonders. Of course, they are. Germans know how to make quality products and are very disciplined and serious, aren't they? And besides, the copy actually named the inspector. Isn't that a delicious touch? How much more credible is it to add the specific detail of the inspector's name as opposed to just saying, "One of our inspectors noticed it"? Details make the difference.

Here's the next line: "There are 3,389 men at our Wolfsburg factory with only one job: to inspect Volkswagens at each stage of production." Notice, the copy doesn't say "more than 3,000"—it says exactly 3,389. See how much more credible that is? If they said "more than 3,000," you'd say they're guessing. It's approximate. It's weak. But when they say "3,389," you're sure it's true. They counted them! So there's a tip: Never use a round number. Never say "10 percent." Use "10.2 percent." Never say "about a hundred." Say "99" or "101." It's much more believable to your readers. And you have an offensive maneuver against those competitors. In the words of Herschell Gordon Lewis, the great direct response copywriter, "Specifics outpull generalities."

Remember again to whom Koenig was writing this ad: men with engineering-type minds, people who appreciate, nay even demand, precision.

"Every shock absorber is tested (spot checking won't do), every windshield is scanned," the copy goes on to say. "VWs have been rejected for surface scratches barely visible to the eye."

"Final inspection is really something!" Koenig tells us, really warming up to his task now. "VW inspectors run each car off the line onto the Funktionsprufstand (car test stand), tote up 189 check points, gun ahead to the automatic brake stands, and say 'no' to one VW of fifty." Notice how the copy really rolls here, just like the car? It doesn't say "drive," it says "run" and "gun." You can see it all happening in your mind's eye, almost hear it happening.

What's the benefit of all this? You can guess, but Koenig is going to make it easy for you. "This preoccupation with detail means the VW lasts longer and requires less maintenance, by and large, than other cars." Note that "by and large." You can be sure that the lawyers made him put that in, lest he be seen as giving an implied warranty. It's great to be enthusiastic, but you have to be careful that you don't make promises you might not able to keep. (We'll talk more about the legal issues in Chapter 13.)

Let's do a little something for the dealers while we're at it, he must've thought about here, so he dropped in this parenthetical aside. (It also means a used VW depreciates less than any other car.) Gee, no qualifier this time. They must have actual numbers to back that statement up.

Finally comes the payoff, a play to the wry sense of humor Doyle Dane

Bernbach's research said characterized the people most likely to buy Volkswagens: "We pluck the lemons; you get the plums."

What an elegant piece of professional copywriting! The headline and illustration work perfectly together (as discussed in Chapter 5) to intrigue you and make you want to read more. The lead continues the setup; each sentence carries you to the next.

Now it's time to submit evidence supporting the claim. A wise old creative director from Compton—the once-famous agency that became Saatchi & Saatchi—called that step "giving people permission to believe." Once you've brought them into the ad, and engaged them, people want to believe you. They're hooked emotionally, but that other half of their brain—the rational, spoilsport hemisphere—is saying, "Wait a minute. How do we know that's true?" So you put in a few supporting facts, what the old textbooks used to call the "reason why" what you're saying is so. With that done, you bring it all to a nice, neat conclusion, tying the story back to the headline.

By the way, did you notice that the sentence lengths are varied? It's the difference between rhythm and monotony. And that the tone is conversational? The ad copy isn't selling you a car. It's talking to you, telling you a story.

I'm sure you won't be surprised to learn that this campaign is in the Advertising Hall of Fame. And so is the copywriter. That brilliance has been copied, of course. There's the old saying that imitation is the sincerest form of flattery. In the 1980s Hanes underwear had a similar hard-nosed inspector (this one was number 12) who made sure only flawless underwear shipped out of the Hanes plant. She would snarl, near the end of the print ad and commercial, "They don't say Hanes until I say they say Hanes." Can you recall any other former or current advertisements that make a big issue out of quality control?

A few more lessons you can learn about body copy come from another Hall

Notepad

Be Cautious of International Translations

One of the dangers of using ads in other countries is to literally translate or mistranslate the copy from one language into the host tongue. Great embarrassment—not to mention expense—results from such word blunders.

Parker Pen's ballpoint in Mexico was supposed to carry the tagline: "It won't leak in your pocket and embarrass you." Unfortunately, the wrong word was used to actually state: "It won't leak in your pocket and make you pregnant."

The Dairy Association had no idea that its simple "Got Milk?" slogan would have any problems going south of the border. But the Mexican ads translated the phrase, "Are you lactating?"

After printing thousands of signs, Coke found out that the Chinese translation for its brand was "bite the wax tadpole."

Clairol's Mist Stick, a curling iron, was exported to Germany before the company discovered that the word Mist means manure, which would hardly attract German women.

It goes both ways. Electrolux, translating its Swedish slogan, assured English-speaking readers that "Nothing sucks like an Electrolux."

It's wise to consult an established ad agency of the country where a product is being introduced. Its employees are aware of culture, idioms and other setbacks that can wreak havoc with your advertisements.

of Fame campaign, this one from International Paper, called The Power of the Printed Word. (Please see the Appendix B for a dozen examples.) It was a series of 16 two-page spread magazine ads designed to help young people read, write, and communicate better. Here are a few of the authors and titles: "How to write with style," by novelist Kurt Vonnegut; "How to write a personal letter," by the humorist Garrison Keeler; and "How to write a business letter," by publisher Malcolm Forbes. In its ten-year run, the campaign won just about every advertising award there is. More importantly, readers asked for more than 39 million reprints of the ads! How's that for a tribute to the copywriter who shaped the contributions of each ostensible "author?" His name is Billings Fuess, who worked most of his career for Ogilvy & Mather, an agency famed then and now for intelligent print advertising.

Each Power of the Printed Word ad was a carefully crafted 1,500-word masterpiece. Turn to the Appendix and notice, for example, that the subheads—the usually bold-faced short sentences or sentence fragments between the paragraphs—serve two purposes. Not only do they visually break up the copy block and make the ad more inviting to read, they actually carry the story. If they're done well, a reader in a hurry ought to be able to scan just the subheads and get the main message of an ad.

Remember the milk carton campaign in Chapter 2? Scan the subheads in that campaign's core newspaper ad. "University Studies Show Paper Milk Cartons Give You More Vitamins To The Gallon," said the headline. (Please note the illustration shows a young girl with a "milk moustache"—at least a dozen years before a milk industry campaign made that its signature visual!) There are 1,500 hundred words of copy, but a person disinclined to read it all could just read the subheads and still get the message: "Important vitamins lost in plastic containers." "Bigger loss in low-fat milk." "Paper cartons block out 98 percent of harmful light."

Another lesson you can learn from that ad: Always caption illustrations and diagrams, as mentioned in Chapter 4. People will approach them the same way they approach the whole ad; they look at the picture and read the caption. And they get mad if the caption isn't there, which is, unfortunately, sometimes the case.

We could go on and on, but let us give you a self-study suggestion. One of the most important awards The Power of the Printed Word campaign received was the Kelly Award, presented annually by the Magazine Publishers of America association to the best print advertising campaign in the country for that year.

Go to www.magazine.org, find the Kelly Awards and study not just the winners but all the ads that have been nominated. Nearly every one is a mini-tutorial on how to do good work. Notice, too, which agencies have won more than once and which agencies' submissions have been contenders year after year. See who the winning copywriters were and are. Those are places where you could learn something about writing and people you could learn from, don't you think? If you aspire to be a serious writer, try to work where print is valued and where serious writing is done. If you are a college student looking for an internship where you can actually learn something, try to obtain one at these winning agencies.

Chapter 7

Select the Proper Font

> *"Type is the most pervasive graphic tool of our society."*
>
> James Stovall
> Author and educator

In Focus

- ✸ How do you identify a font or type family?
- ✸ What are the major categories of fonts?
- ✸ How are the relationships between and among the elements on a page created?
- ✸ What are the proper uses of type varieties?
- ✸ What are other type considerations?

Thanks to twenty-plus years of computer use, we now have countless more fonts to choose from when designing a print advertisement. No longer are ad agencies forced to always send copy to an outside printer and wait for what seemed like an eternity for expensive typesetting services. Nor do they have to use rub-off lettering or borders from rolls of tape for their print creations as they did twenty years ago. In-house creative departments can handle the bulk of that work now, saving time and money for the full-service ad agency. Even small businesses have the capability and software today to design and produce their own ads themselves.

Desktop publishing and hundreds of available fonts have made typeface selection a quicker—if not easier—process. There's not always just one perfect text to select for pitching a product or service. But there may be a few wrong typefaces to avoid among the growing options.

Some national marketers will have a font designed exclusively for their ads. Choosing a font that complements and reinforces your message is vital. The emotional impact of a font on readers cannot be overlooked. Fonts can carry psychological power.

Advertising guru David Ogilvy, who died in 1999 at age 88, appreciated that fact. "You may think that I exaggerate the importance of good typography. You may ask if I have ever heard a housewife say that she bought a new detergent because the advertisement was set in Caslon. No. But do you think an advertisement can sell if nobody can read it?"

Major Font Characteristics

Certain characteristics identify a typeface as a type family, or what we commonly call a font. The font includes the letters as well as numbers and punctuation marks. It's hard to find universal agreement on the categories of type as well as the exact terminology.

Most common is **serif**, often called **roman** or **old style**. It's characterized by thin strokes (or feet) at the end of the letters. All of the letter forms will have a variety of thick-to-thin transitions. Serif is often used for books (such as *Print Matters*) and other longer passages because the strokes help the reader's eyes maneuver through the text. Some authorities say it is more readable because it holds the base of the line better than other kinds of typefaces.

S	T	A	𝒯	𝔈	𝔘
serif	sans serif	slab serif	script	Old English	decorative

Exhibit 7.1 Sample Typefaces

The next most popular type is **sans serif**, also known as **gothic**. The ends of these letters have no extensions or feet. (The French word "sans" means "without.") There's very little, if any, thick/thin transition in the lettering.

A combination face is the **slab** (or square) **serif**. Sometimes called **Clarendon** or **Egyptian**, its letters have little or no contrast in the thickness of the strokes, but they do have thick, horizontal serifs (or slabs).

Above you see examples of these fonts spelling out "STATE U" using a 28-point size for each letter.

Script type is cursive, almost resembling calligraphy in many instances. Some examples have lowercase letters that seem to connect with each other.

Old English text (see Exhibits 7.1 and 7.2) is sometimes included within the script category or simply given its own status. It's by far the oldest letterform, made famous by Germany's Johannes Gutenberg, generally credited as the inventor of movable type, over 560 years ago. The ornate, old-fashioned design, however, limits its use in modern advertising.

A final category is **decorative** (also called novelty or ornamental). It's a broad section, encompassing a range of informal, distinctive typefaces. Some adapt graphic devices embodied into a letter, such as a sun for the letter "O" or a horseshoe for "U." Others use fonts that resemble wooden planks or rope. These lighthearted shapes can be appropriate at times, especially for graphically reflecting the nature of a headline.

Most designers use one type family for headlines, subheads, and feature elements and another for body text in an ad. Some textbooks will call them display type (usually 18 points and above) and text type (often 8 to 14 points), respectively. An inch equals 72 points or 6 picas (12 points to a pica). The same family can appear as regular, italic, bold, all capitals, small capitals, underline, reverse, or even shadow.

Type Personalities

You can then **e x p a n d** or **condense** selected text by various degrees. Be careful of extremes, of course. Usually you'll alter a word's width only for a specific reason. If you're comparing the interior roominess of your client's new SUV model with the competitor's smaller version, you can see how such devices could be appropriate for that particular ad's headline or other display type: O u r S U V vs. Brand A.

Type design, so underappreciated, is rarely noticed unless it clashes with your product or service. If you're trying to establish an atmosphere for the company or its offerings, selecting the proper font goes a long way in creating such a culture.

An informal, casual typeface could be disastrous for a client trying to position itself as a prim and proper organization. A country club in an exclusive resort community, for example, wouldn't even think of using most of the novelty fonts that apply rope and fence posts for letters. But a barbecue restaurant might be quite suitable for such an informal font.

"Type can have character and personality," writes James Stovall in *Infographics: A Journalist's Guide.* "It can speak to us in many ways, not just by what it represents in terms of words but also by its own shape and design."

Back in 2006 Spike TV decided to revise its on-air logo to give it a tougher image to better attract its target audience, young male viewers. Its former lightweight logo with a cursive font was replaced with stronger block letters to accompany its new tagline, "Get More Action." Niels Schuurmans, the network's creative director, explained the modification in a news release: "We are a destination that will inspire and define men through bold, action-packed original entertainment."

Some of your clients may think the classic Old English text lends a sense of sophistication and formality to their products or services. However, you want to balance such an image with the simple requirement of being readable.

Religious organizations sometimes make the mistake of thinking such hard-to-decipher text gives their ads a sense of religiousness. No offense, but King James is no longer commissioning ads in the 21st century. That font may still work occasionally in a house of worship ad, of course. You might wish to contrast a contemporary service with the more formal style attended by our grand-

Exhibit 7.2 The Readability Challenge

parents. Or to compare the latest iPhone with earlier, now antique, cell phones that were as big as a shoe.

You always want to strive for legibility. A few companies still insist their ads will stand out more if they are Old English text in all capitals. Nothing can be further from the truth. The Old English script letters are almost impossible to decipher when used in all caps. (See Exhibit 7.2.)

The Detroit Tigers decided to slightly modify the fancy "D" logo on their baseball caps one season back in the early 1960s. It was a minor change since it was a slightly different style of the Old English font that had been used since the 1890s. According to one rumor, a baseball-loving typesetter at the *Detroit Free Press* pointed out that the flamboyant "D" selected for the American League team had suddenly evolved into a "V" in the ornamental font revision.

Old English "V"   Old English "D"

Exhibit 7.3 Sample Old English Typefaces

It shows you how confusing such lettering can be. Since readability is your goal, don't make the mistake of using too much—if any—Old English text. And avoid all caps at all costs.

A few ads are effective without any type. But those ads are rare. Typically, text does the sales job in an ad after a headline, photo or graphic gets the reader's attention. The smaller words provide details that will interest the potential consumer. Selecting the proper font is a challenge. You want to put words in the ad that will attract readers in the most visually interesting way. Should all the text be the same font or should you use variety?

Element Relationships

Robin Williams—the designer, not the actor—tackles that challenge in her book, *The Non-Designer's Design Book*. (Also see Exhibit 7.4.) She maintains that multiple elements on a page create an association that falls into one of three categories:

> A *concordant* relationship occurs when you use only one type family, without much variety in style, size, weight and so on. It is easy to keep the page harmonious, and the arrangement tends to appear quiet and rather sedate or formal—sometimes downright dull.
>
> A *conflicting* relationship occurs when you combine typefaces that are *similar* in style, size, weight, and so on. The similarities are disturbing because the visual attractions are not the same (concordance), but neither are they different (contrasting), so they conflict.
>
> A *contrasting* relationship occurs when you combine separate typefaces and elements that are clearly distinct from each other. The visually appealing and exciting designs that attract your attention typically have a lot of contrast built in, and the contrasts are emphasized.

You certainly don't want to bore your readers. No one will be enticed to read the ad if the copy creates a gray, lifeless appearance. So make sure you avoid a **concordant** relationship where everything seems to be uniform—unless you occasionally want that formal impression. For certain clients, products, or services, the ceremonial look might be appropriate.

Likewise, giving readers an ad where the font **conflict** is too minimal should be shunned. When the differences are negligible, readers may not even notice the slight differences. But if they do, they may wonder why the change is so slight. Was it a mistake? Or do they think the default setting kicked in and changed the text size? Did the publication not have the right font and substitute a similar one?

So, if you want to show differences in fonts, show grand variations. Don't have 10-point and 11-point type in the same ad. Use 10-point and 16-point.

Mollie's Lollies

Best Candy
Best Selection
Best Prices

Downtown Perth

Concordant Relationship

Mollie's Lollies

Best Candy
Best Selection
Best Prices

Downtown Perth

Conflict Relationship

Mollie's Lollies

Best Candy
Best Selection
Best Prices

Downtown Perth

Contrast Relationship

Exhibit 7.4 Relationships of Type Elements

Change a short text block in one to boldface and italic for even more contrast. It will be one of the best ways to attract the reader's attention to the ad.

Beginning graphic designers, business proprietors, and students, when designing print ads, will frequently blunder with overuse of such options as boldface, italic, all capitals, and reverse type. It is definitely an effective way to create contrast. However, it's necessary to learn the proper methods to employ or ignore these various devices.

Boldface

Thicker, **boldface** type helps a particular word, phrase, or sentence stand out from its surroundings in an advertisement, whether it's on a billboard, print ad, direct mailer or computer screen. An ad that's full of gray text without bold elements may seem boring to the casual reader. Thick and thin contrasts of type will make a page more appealing to the eyes. That's one of the common selling points of the Yellow Pages. Having an optional boldface business name among the gray listings will help it jump off the page for the consumer.

But if the purpose of using boldface is to emphasize key phrases or subheads, what purpose is accomplished when everything is darkened? Remember, when you emphasize everything, you are emphasizing nothing. Readership studies over the years have shown that all-bold type is slower to read and comprehend than normal text. The thickened, darker letters can almost blur together for many readers. This is especially true on newsprint.

Your computer's regular word-processing fonts have a bold option that slightly darkens highlighted text. For an even stronger emphasis, however, you might wish to download or purchase a few typefaces with an extra-bold style. This is especially crucial for headlines or smaller display type.

Boldface can be effective when the darker text highlights a limited amount of copy. Too much emphasis with a bulkier version of the typeface, however, will only slow down readership.

Italics

Just as boldface type is used to attract attention, *italics* within a block of roman type will do the same thing. Italic type, however, doesn't have the advantage of being thicker and darker than its neighbors. In fact, it's leaning to the right and even slightly frail looking to some observers.

The slant of italic type helps it stand out for prominence. But an entire lengthy paragraph of italics is almost always too much, since nothing is being isolated for emphasis. Because roman fonts are straight, an italicized word, phrase or sentence that leans will attract the eye. An entire copy block, however, could be overlooked as too much of an eye strain for readers.

Surveys confirm the obvious—that all-italic copy is slightly more difficult to read and understand and thus takes longer to comprehend. Just to be on the safe side, it's wise not to mix italics with boldface in the same line. That may be too much variety for the eye to take in a single line of copy.

ALL CAPITALS

Many retailers insist to ad sales reps that they want their company name to be in **ALL CAPITAL** letters. Then they think to themselves, "Why not put all of the ad copy in larger all caps too?" Yes, the client is the customer, but in this case the customer is not always right. We'll spend considerable time warning about mis-use of all caps because it's a common problem that's easy to fix.

Remember our earlier illustration about Old English fonts being illegible in all capital lettering? You'll drive your readers insane if you expect them to read lengthy copy blocks that are all uppercase letters, even in a crisp roman type. The eye is not used to such lettering beyond a few words here or there. SMALL CAPITALS, by the way, are almost as bad as all capitals and should be used sparingly for text as well.

Yet another reason to avoid all-caps text is that it takes up more area in the valuable advertisement than normal capital and lowercase lettering. When ads need to convey vital information in a limited amount of space, why waste that real estate with inflated letters? A 12-point all-caps copy block takes more space than comparable copy in 14-point type with regular capital and lowercase letters. It may be necessary to prove this to a retailer who insists on the all-capital advertisement. (See Exhibits 7.5 and 7.6.)

All-caps: THIS IS AN EXAMPLE OF 12-POINT AD COPY.

Normal: This is an example of 14-point ad copy.

Exhibit 7.5 Sample Copy Blocks

The Case Against All Caps

Typography is one of the make-or-break elements in print advertising. Legibility is the key. If an ad is difficult to read, it may not be read at all.

ONE OF THE MOST COMMON TYPOGRAPHICAL MISTAKES IS THE OVERUSE OF UPPER CASE CHARACTERS. SOME ADVERTISERS ARE CONVINCED THAT ALL-CAPS MAKE THEIR WORDS MORE IMPORTANT. BUT IN REALITY, ALL UPPER CASE COPY IS ALMOST IMPOSSIBLE TO READ. ESPECIALLY IN LARGE BLOCKS LIKE THIS.

If you slogged your way through the above paragraph, you're in a rare company. Most people don't want to get involved with such an indecipherable blob of type. All-caps are not reader-friendly at all.

An upper case character is like a golfer's driver, the biggest, most powerful club in the bag. While a driver is vital, it's not supposed to be used on every shot. In an average 18-hole round, a driver will be used 14 or 15 times—usually for tee shots on par four and par five holes.

Setting an entire ad in all-caps is just as unthinkable as using a driver for every shot. All-caps should be used sparingly. In fact, I can think of only three instances in which all-caps are acceptable: (1) in short headlines (and sub-headlines) with short words, (2) in some logos and (3) to emphasize an OCCASIONAL word in the body of an ad.

If you have an advertiser who is stuck in an upper case rut, you might want to prepare a little demonstration for your next presentation. Produce two versions of the same sentence, one in all-caps and one in upper and lower case. Use your computer to print them in large letters on separate, letter-size sheets of paper. For example:

NOW IS THE TIME	Now is the time
FOR ALL ADVERTISERS	for all advertisers
TO SEND CLEAR MESSAGES	to send clear messages
TO THEIR READERS.	to their readers.

Ask your client to participate in a simple readability experiment. Reach into your briefcase and announce that you are going to show two headlines for about the length of time it takes to turn a page of your paper. First, hold up the all-caps version for a (silent) count of three seconds, then lower it and ask what it says. Do the same thing with the other headline. Chances are, your client will find the second one considerably easier to read at a glance.

Explain that the second headline is more legible, because people read word shapes—not individual letters. Since upper case characters are the same height, there is no distinguishing profile. On the other hand, upper and lower case type creates a variety of character sizes and shapes. As a result, it is much more inviting to readers (i.e. potential customers).

Many advertisers don't realize how typography influences readership. Telling them "don't run all-caps" is not likely to change their minds. But showing them—with a graphic comparison—can help you build a strong case against all-caps.

© Copyright 2007 by John Foust. All rights reserved.

John Foust is an advertising consultant. Contact: jfoust@mindspring.com; 919-848-2401; PO Box 97606, Raleigh, NC 27624 USA.

Exhibit 7.6

All-capital words with their rectangular shape are slower to read because the human eye is used to the shapes of letters since prekindergarten days. We know at a quick glance that a descender (the part of a letter that falls below the invisible line on which it sits) falls into a small quantity of letters: g, j, p, q, or y.

Highway safety experts have determined there's an advantage of putting "Pittsburgh" instead of "PITTSBURGH" on highway signs. Perhaps the split-second quicker recognition of lowercase and uppercase words (compared to all capitals) will pay dividends when the reading motorist is driving 65 miles per hour (or higher) and has to change lanes swiftly on Interstate 76.

Putting a company name or title in all caps is not a readability problem. But an advertisement that contains more than that can usually be improved by resorting to uppercase and lowercase lettering. (By the way, back in the linotype era, typesetters kept capital letters in a case or drawer *above* the one with small letters. So the uppercase contained the capital letters, and the lowercase held the small letters. The moniker remains today.)

Small-capital text is a little-used function. As the name implies, you can create letters that are capitalized, but are not much larger than lowercase letters: SMALL CAPITALS. You often see it used for the names of companies or products. Again, going overboard with its use is the major problem with small caps. It's still slower to read than regular lettering.

Reverse Type

This advice may be getting monotonous. Nevertheless, too much of a good thing can spoil an ad. **Reverse type**, in which the letters are white or light colored on a black or dark background, does stand out and get recognition. In fact, the block of black or color on the page helps create contrast and balance for the ad layout. It will attract the reader's eye, much like a photograph will in viewing the page. That's why you see lots of reverse ads in a newspaper or magazine.

Black print on white paper always creates the best contrast, of course. Anytime you change that formula you're going to suffer regarding ease of readability. In some ads the white type appears on top of an illustration. It does help save space. But if light shades are within that photo or artwork, the reverse letters should not be placed there or they can easily disappear from view.

White on a black background, although the best contrast choice for reverse type, can still cause detection difficulties. If the font happens to be a serif variety,

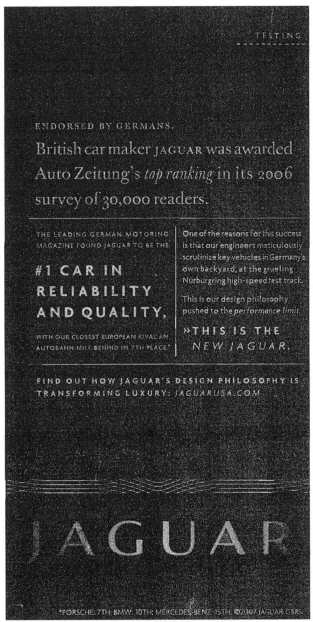

Exhibit 7.7 Jaguar: The Perils of Reverse Type

This Jaguar reverse-type ad from *The Wall Street Journal* became a readability problem because the black background actually reproduced to only about 85 percent black on the original newsprint. Unfortunately, the reverse print was not white, but varied from a medium gray to a light gray. Extra leading was used in the ad, but the smaller, thin text is difficult to read. Many of the letters seemed to disappear into the newsprint. Reverse can still be quite effective for ad layouts, if these precautions are heeded.

Reverse Type Tips

Use slightly larger font size

Use slightly more leading than normal

Use minimal copy blocks

Exhibit 7.8 Sample Reverse Type

some of the thin ends of the white letters could disappear. This is especially true for ads reproduced on newsprint.

If you desire to use reverse type, the suggestions in Exhibit 7.8 will make your effort more effective. A copy block of single-spaced text will blend and blur if it's too small. So it's wise to go to a slightly larger font size than you normally would if the text were black on white. Perhaps your 10-point text could jump to 12, or your 12 could now become 14. These simple tips on size would have helped the Jaguar ad in Exhibit 7.7.

Just because that big dark box creates good contrast for your advertisement, don't make it too big. Avoid the temptation to make the entire ad reverse if there's lots of text. Too much reverse-type copy is too difficult for most people to read.

Another caution concerns running white text across the product or some other graphic in the ad, as mentioned above. You've probably seen ads where the white text was printed on top of a gray or light-colored object. Perhaps the text was set too wide to fit on top of the item, so the left and right margins disappeared in a sea of off-white newsprint. If the reverse text is clearly legible on a dark background or full-page photo, there's little problem. In fact, in many cases, that's the only way to get the ad message across. And large photos are effective, as you can tell by leafing through most magazines.

A related problem is using a color text, let's say pink, on top of a maroon box.

The contrasts have to be sharp—between the paper and the ink—to get maximum readability. This is sometimes a problem with Web pages, where a dark-blue type often floats upon a black background screen.

A light ink color should never be printed on a screened box that's less than 80 percent shaded. Light gray on dark gray, for example, provides little contrast, even for readers with perfect vision. (See Exhibit 7.7 for an example of that.) A similar problem occurs when black ink is placed on top of a dark product or background.

Flip through some magazine advertisements and look for reverse text examples where the contrast is poor. How would you improve such ads?

Other Considerations

Shadow text should rarely be used. It typically gives a fuzzy feel to the type, almost as if the registration was off during the press run. This is especially true of outlined shadow text.

Often increased for reverse type, **leading** is that vertical spacing between lines of text. The term hearkens to the time when typesetters used small strips of lead between lines of type to create white space so a descender would not extend into the line of text below it. But it should not be limited in its use. Quite often you will want to "air out" (add space within lines of) a copy block to help it look more inviting.

Most computer programs automatically add about 20 percent of extra spacing to the lines of text. So 10-point type, for example, will be set on a 12-point line to enhance readability. Feel free to adjust that percentage, but be careful about decreasing the amount of space unless it's done on purpose for a good reason. Headline leading, for example, will almost always need to be set closer together because large type will make the space between lines too excessive at 20 percent.

The word **solid** means you have set 10-point text on a 10-point line. In that situation, some descenders will make contact with the ascenders from the line directly below in many font choices. It can be used, but only for special occasions.

Suppose you were comparing the interior roominess of your client's car with a competitor's version. This can tie in with the psychology of font use mentioned earlier when employing expanded or condensed texts. If your ad wants to stress a roomy interior, you might want to increase the leading in that section.

Kerned War   Normal War

Exhibit 7.9 The Necessity of Kerning

Then when you talk about the cramped quarters in the other vehicle, you could use solid or even tighter for emphasis. Try 12-point condensed text within a 10-point line for a super-stuffed effect, but make sure the words are still legible.

Another term affecting text is **kerning**, defined as the process of moving type elements closer or farther apart than standard. Kerning is commonly applied to eliminate extra spacing within headline and other large display capital letters, especially "T," "V," "W" and "Y."

Larger-sized capital letters have more breathing room devoted to their left and right sides as buffers. Some letters and words within advertisement headlines would look strange if they weren't kerned to close up that extra amount of space. The unusual distance between letters will look awkward.

Please see Exhibit 7.9, for example, where the lowercase "a" slides in slightly under the top right edge of the capital "W" in the kerned example. Without kerning, the excess area between the "W" and the "ar" may appear to be a full space to some readers.

Text Alignment

Speaking of moving things around, one of the other key choices for ad designers is the **text alignment**. All elements of an ad should be placed in particular locations for a reason. Just throwing things within a border will not produce an effective sales message.

"The principle of alignment states that nothing should be placed on the page arbitrarily," writes Robin Williams. "Every item should have a visual connection with something else on the page."

So your carefully crafted text block might be adjusted in width so it aligns with the above photograph's right and left margins. When things line up, you avoid the haphazard look of an unorganized ad (and the image of its unorganized sponsor).

The Western eye is used to starting from the left when reading. Having a

This text block is an example of flush left and
ragged right. As you can see, the right
margin will vary with short and long lines.

This text block is an example of flush
right and ragged left. As you can see,
the left margin will vary with short and
long lines.

This text block is an example of justified
alignment on both the left and right margins.
Making margins even creates uneven spacing
between words.

This text block is an example of centered
alignment. Both the left and right margins
will vary with short and long lines.

Exhibit 7.10 Alignment Options

left-side alignment is also called flush left/ragged right, since the words on the right side will fluctuate at the end of the lines. An informal style with high comprehension, flush left is becoming more common for reading material, such as books, newspaper columns and magazines. Because of uniform spacing between words, readers have little difficulty breezing through copy. The uneven right margin adds visually pleasing white space in the copy and helps eliminate most hyphenations. (You can avoid them altogether with an optional click on your computer.)

However, despite the ease of that reading style, it's perfectly OK to experiment with other alignments for advertisements. Three other options are available, in addition to the growing popularity of text wrapping around a graphic or product.

The opposite of flush left is flush right (or flush right/ragged left). We're not used to moving our eyes to an inexact location on the left to pick up the next line of text. But it can be effective at times. For example, if a model is looking into the ad from the left side, running the copy block aligned along the right border could work. It's no longer a taboo, but flush right is not an alignment that should be overused.

A second variation is to have both margins justified. Your text lines will be flush left and flush right. The only exception will be partial lines that close out a paragraph. Although ragged right is growing in popularity for the media, you'll still find many books and newspapers following a justified style. Some designers may feel it adds formality to the words in this format.

To get such an even margin, space is redistributed between words on the line. This often results in expanding many words awkwardly with extra spaces or squeezing letters or spaces tightly to get them on the same line. Along with a slightly slower comprehension and reading rate, justified text usually has more hyphenations. (Some studies, however, claim that justified margins are just as effective as ragged right. We can't agree because of the distorted spacing problems readers encounter.)

The third option is to center the text within the confines of the copy block. This is also fairly common among beginning ad designers. It helps elements on the page fall into place beneath one another. It often gives the reader a feeling that the document may be formal, such as a graduation announcement. Unless you're going for the classic look, however, centered text can produce a somewhat boring ad.

Another problem with centered text is to make sure the lines have varying lengths. If it were not for having just seven short words on the last line in the centered example in Exhibit 7.10, one may think the space bar simply went a little wacky while typing the last line of text. If you choose centered, make it more obvious with short lines mixed in with longer ones. You may want to purposely create line breaks so key phrases are not broken from one line to the next, such as "Diet Dr Pepper."

The text wrap feature can be a clever way to surround a product, model or graphic device with copy. It can be effective in small doses. Having text on all sides of an irregularly shaped object can be confusing to the reader. Does the text continue across the figure or do you stop and drop to the line below to continue reading?

If it's a large graphic, readers could actually lose their line as they jump across the object. Because flush left is simpler to read than flush right, text wrap that has the ragged right bumping against a product retains high readership scores. Find a print ad that uses text wrap in a way that could easily confuse the reader.

Computer software makes text wrap a popular feature for many designers. You need to be careful that text doesn't bump up too close to the object. Another caution concerns the length of some lines. Be careful about using a mere word for an entire line while wrapping your text around an irregular-shaped item in the ad.

Column Width

Speaking of the width of your copy column, make sure yours don't get too long or too short. Both extremes can harm your ad's impact with readers. Most graphic designers realize that optimal reading occurs when the length of the copy is approximately one and one-half times the font's alphabet. In other words, 39 characters would go through the A to Z and then A to M letters, whatever its size or font. (See Exhibit 7.11 for the suggested ideal length for two different-sized fonts.)

The minimum recommended length for a line of copy would be one alphabet length, or about 26 characters. The suggested maximum length is two alphabet lengths, or about 52 characters of any specific font. So a specific line length in inches or picas for a copy block should not be determined too soon, of course. The text family and the size selected will determine exactly the ideal length for any line. So a four-inch copy block column (24 picas wide) would be too small for most varieties of 24-point text but too wide for 10-point text. Extra leading or spacing could also contribute to a line being longer than the maximum 52 characters without harming legibility ease.

Breaking any one of these somewhat subjective rules is always a choice in

11-point Bookman Old Style (39 characters wide)
abcdefghijklmnopqrstuvwxyzabcdefghijklm

14-point Times New Roman (39 characters wide)
abcdefghijklmnopqrstuvwxyzabcdefghijklm

Exhibit 7.11 Alternate Ideal Column Widths

designing print advertisements. You may want to use all caps for special emphasis, for example, despite our dire warnings, even though you know readability will suffer. But that's your option—and the personal joy—in creating ads.

Recap

A font or type family (letters, numbers and punctuation marks) is identified by particular characteristics.

Major categories of fonts are serif, sans serif, slab serif, script, Old English and decorative (or novelty).

Multiple elements on a page create various relationships: concordant, conflicting or contrasting (ideal).

Type varieties that need to be used with caution include boldface, italics, all capitals and reverse. Other considerations are shadow text, leading, kerning, text alignment and line length (or column width).

For Further Reading

Randy Hines and Joe Basso, *The Writer's Toolbox: A Comprehensive Guide for PR and Business Communication.* Dubuque, IA: Kendall/Hunt, 2005.

David Ogilvy, *Ogilvy on Advertising.* New York: Random House, 1985.

James Glen Stovall, *Infographics: A Journalist's Guide.* Needham Heights, MA: Allyn and Bacon, 1997.

Robin Williams, *The Non-Designer's Design Book: Design and Typographic Principles for the Visual Novice.* Berkeley, CA: Peachpit Press, 1994.

Robin Williams, *The Non-Designer's Type Book: Insights and Techniques for Creating Professional-Level Type.* Berkeley, CA: Peachpit Press, 1998.

Chapter 8

Designing an Ad

> *"Don't create relationships with elements that don't belong together."*
>
> Robin Williams
> Graphic Designer

In Focus

★ What design elements make up most ads?

★ How do the three key design principles of equilibrium, proportion, and contrast work together?

★ What are the proper layout uses of white space and color?

★ What is dangerous about printing text on top of photos?

★ How have SAUs developed and what is their current status?

★ What are the special problems in the competitive environment of B2B advertising?

Which elements make up the typical print advertisement? Although it's far from unanimous, most ads contain the following ingredients: headline, photograph and/or visual, subhead(s), copy block, and logo/trademark. But they're not necessarily in that order. And many ads successfully function using only two or three of those features.

Previous chapters have talked about the crucial visual element, the headlines and subheads that help attract attention and direct the reader, and the sales job performed by the carefully selected text. Now it's time to put everything together. Sounds simple enough, but it wasn't universally applied until about fifty years ago. Another one of the leaders calling for integration of text with artwork was William Bernbach of Doyle Dane Bernbach. Although he came from the copywriting ranks, he knew an ad's success hinged on a perfect blending of copy and visual. Thus, partnerships were formed with art directors and writers collaborating on single ads as well as major campaigns.

Understanding three major design principles of equilibrium, proportion, and contrast will help an ad look organized. More importantly, their use will help make a print advertisement look inviting. If consumers overlook your ad, it fails to convey your message.

Equilibrium

Forget the high-wire act for equilibrium. This one is more like the playground seesaw or teeter-totter. Balance can be manipulated by size, color, weight, and placement of items within the advertisement. A print advertisement with perfect stability—with objects evenly divided on both sides of an invisible, centered vertical line—is symmetrical. Such formal balance can be effective in giving an ad a peaceful, established, or dignified appearance. Many beginning ad designers fall into the easy trap of centering all visuals and text. When that happens, boring is a frequent adjective to describe the look.

The opposite, of course, is asymmetrical, or informal, balance in which more elements (photo, graphic, or text) are on one side of the layout than the other. Arranging items on the page to please readers and entice their interest usually results in an informal arrangement. A frenzied, circus layout can be used if you want to create a chaotic effect. However, it's extremely rare that elements would ever be placed randomly on a layout. Even extreme imbalance probably involves a lot more work for the designer than centering everything. As a result, the ad is usually more interesting.

An ad's equilibrium should always encourage readership and should avoid overpowering the print message. The typical reader notices the look of the ad long before reading any copy. Eye movement in the Western hemisphere typically starts in the top left and gradually flows to the bottom right. This visual flow is often called a Z pattern. Keep that in mind so your model in the top left of the ad isn't glancing off the page to the reader's left. How you design your ad can change this normal flow. Don't feel that you have to insert an entry point in the upper left of your ad, of course. Ads would be boring if they all followed the identical Z pattern. But the flow should direct consumers to the copy you want them to read.

Proportion

Proportion means that the ad designer creates a relationship in size between and among visual elements. Besides size, proportion can be used with colors, darkness, white space, bleeds, and thickness. The interior of the ad needs to have pleasing relationships.

Although a few do appear occasionally, square ads are considered monotonous by most designers—as well as many consumers. Usually it's best for ad designers not to evenly divide ads into equal halves or quarters. (Maybe that's why three-by-five index cards were created, rather than four-by-four ones.) Called different terms throughout the centuries, the ratio of width to depth is epitomized by the Parthenon, considered the most perfectly proportioned structure in the world. Recall the classic "Ogilvy" ads, in which a large photo dominates the page. It is not a 50-50 proportion, but more like 35-65 or 65-35.

Contrast

Having a copy block in 12-point text and the headline in 16 point creates very little difference between the two. Good contrast—with type size, fonts, and thickness as well as white space, visuals, and color—creates dramatic variations within the ad. If items are totally harmonious, you provide no clues for readers as to the relative importance of specific elements. If everything has the same emphasis, nothing is really emphasized. Nothing stands out. Different thicknesses

Designing Ads:
Everybody Wants in on the Act

Ad design has evolved over the past century. David Ogilvy, for example, when advertising high-ticket, luxury items such as quality watches or Rolls Royces, used a large photograph of the product with its requisite caption, followed by an intriguing headline. Then he convinced buyers with intelligent copy and closed with the logo or brand name. His formula was so successful it was soon called simply the "Ogilvy." Variations would sometimes run the headline across the top of the layout if that element seemed stronger than the visual.

Art, music, and fashion made inroads on ad design, as did high-tech innovations near the end of the 20th century. However, the recent onslaught in the volume of advertising messages has created in many consumers an anti-advertising attitude.

North Americans encounter from 3,500 to 5,000 marketing signals a day, compared to only 500 to 2,000 during the 1970s, said J. Walker Smith, president of Yankelovich, a North Carolina-based consumer research firm, in his book, *Coming to Concurrence: Addressable Attitudes and the New Model for Marketing Productivity.*

As a result of that deluge of communications, potential buyers shun many advertisements. They protest the forced exposure of commercials at movie theaters, for example. TiVo allows viewers in the U.S., Canada, U.K., Australia, New Zealand, and the Netherlands to record programs they want to watch later (called time shifting) without commercials. Other competitors, such as ReplayTV, offer the same feature. TiVo immediately heard complaints from customers when it tested pop-up ads back in March 2005.

After only one year, more than 62 million individuals had signed up for the Federal Trade Commission's Do Not Call Registry for both home and cell phone numbers. One year later, 98 million phones were registered. Today it's over 145 million phones.

Magazine readers frequently complain about ad banking, the practice of running consecutive full- and multiple-page ads in the front of many publications, especially fashion and women's magazines. These types of clutter and complaints make it imperative that your ad layout encourages readership.

Indeed, a classic study by The Readership Institute claims that good advertising design can actually sell newspapers. The survey of 37,000 readers of various-sized papers determined that good ad content and layout can positively impact a publication's readership.

"Readers want fun, energetic and creative content," said Ellen Meany, at the time the ad committee chair of the Society for News Design. "The creative process should be about the reader. In fact, it's often about the client."

Unfortunately, the client often wants to clutter a layout with extra store details, additional products, and extraneous bits of information. Eye-pleasing white space is determined to be wasted space by too many advertisers.

Exhibit 8.1

of type, different type weights (bold, italic, etc.), or the judicious use of reverse boxes produce contrasts that are more likely to catch readers' attention.

Contrast should likewise be used with colors. Using a 60 percent blue with a 40 percent blue doesn't create much contrast. Perhaps 80 percent with 20 percent blue would indicate a sharper dissimilarity. Or go with different colors altogether for even more contrast:

> Contrast can be created in many ways. You can contrast large type with small type; a graceful oldstyle font with a bold sans serif font; a thin line with a thick line; . . . a horizontal element (such as a long line of text) with a vertical element (such as a tall, narrow column of text); . . . a small graphic with a large graphic.[1]

Next in this chapter we'll discuss how to create contrast with white space, the pros and cons of using color, spot color, black and white "color," shading basics and dangers, cautions of printing text within photographs, and SAUs. Design tricks such as kerning and text alignment are discussed in Chapter 7.

White Space

Too many clients fight any suggestions about using white space in an ad. "Why should I pay for empty space?" they clamor, while insisting that six more elements should be jammed into a three-column ad that's three inches high. Clients raise these same objections to the use of white space in outdoor ads, transit ads, and even direct mail pieces.

White space is considered the designer's friend because its use actually helps draw readers' eyes to the elements bordering it. It emphasizes the text, photo, or logo that has room to breathe as a result of the white space.

Ketel One Vodka has run several full-page magazine ads that carry a large headline across the top one-fourth of the page. Its unique black text stands out because the remainder of the page is nothing but white space. One such ad's headline on the back cover of *Inc.* magazine during 2007 said:

Dear Ketel One Drinker

On those awful days when you're

feeling your age, just remember,

we're 316.

Exhibit 8.2 shows another example of that white space concept effectively taken to an extreme measure by Crest. Readers may have to squint at first to realize there actually is tiny text in the middle of the page. It's almost lost by the sea of white space surrounding it. Yet its size and placement within the sea of white space will make the consumer want to read it.

Consultant Edward Henninger often discusses the value of negative space—a term he prefers for white space in his workshops and writings. Although his comments here are referring to entire page layouts, one can see the application to ad design as well:

Notepad

Look through some magazines for ads that contain an unusual amount of white space. Did they attract your attention immediately just from that feature? Is the use of white space effective in these ads?

Now try to find some ads that could use some white space. Are these ads packed with too much information? Is all of it necessary? Could white space be found if some graphics were smaller or photos were cropped better?

In a nutshell: empty space is space you haven't filled yet. It's an area of the page in which you should place an element such as a photo or graphic. But negative space is already filled with an element—the space itself. Empty space does nothing for the page—in most cases, actually, it detracts from the page. Negative space, however, creates a positive force by its effect on the other elements on the page.[2]

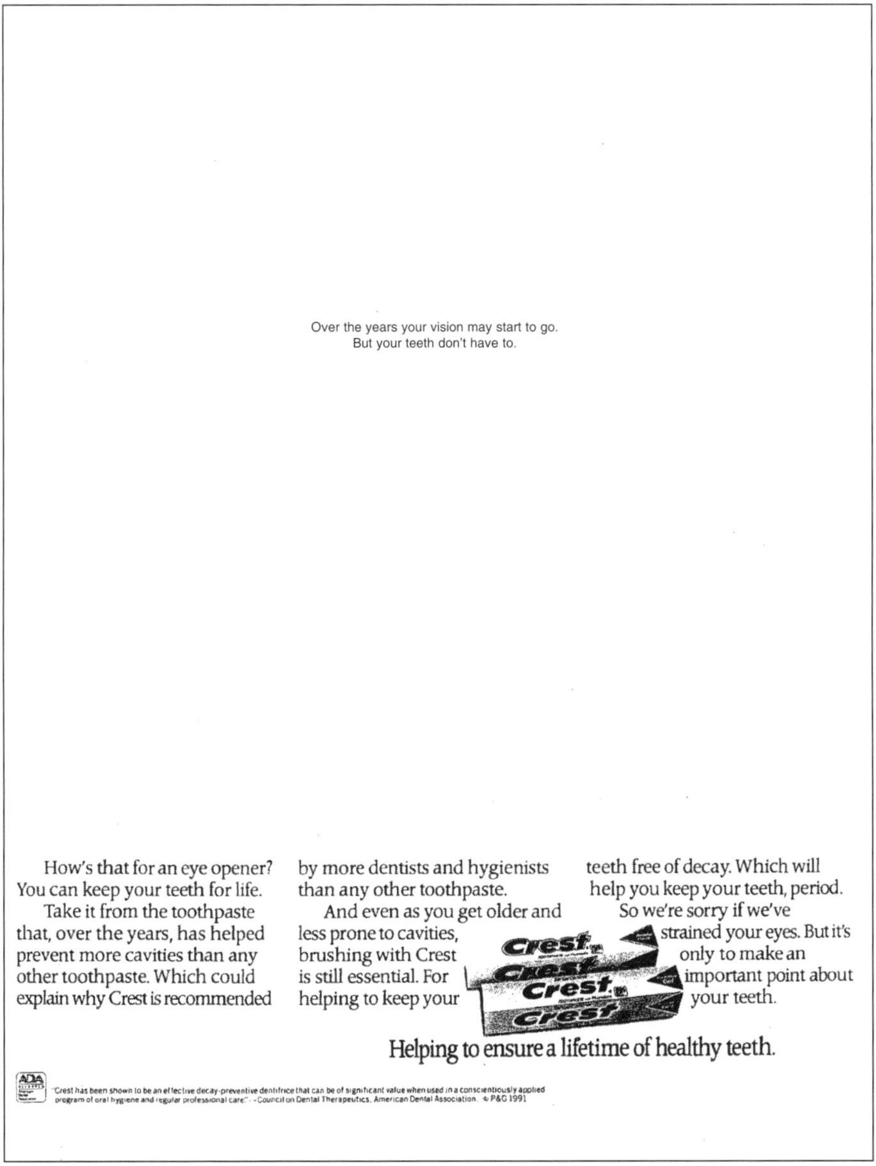

Over the years your vision may start to go.
But your teeth don't have to.

How's that for an eye opener? You can keep your teeth for life. Take it from the toothpaste that, over the years, has helped prevent more cavities than any other toothpaste. Which could explain why Crest is recommended by more dentists and hygienists than any other toothpaste. And even as you get older and less prone to cavities, brushing with Crest is still essential. For helping to keep your teeth free of decay. Which will help you keep your teeth, period. So we're sorry if we've strained your eyes. But it's only to make an important point about your teeth.

Helping to ensure a lifetime of healthy teeth.

"Crest has been shown to be an effective decay-preventive dentifrice that can be of significant value when used in a conscientiously applied program of oral hygiene and regular professional care". - Council on Dental Therapeutics, American Dental Association. © P&G 1991

Exhibit 8.2 Crest Ad's Unusual Use of White Space

Color

Over the years studies have proven that color ads almost always draw more readers than black-and-white ones. Roper Starch research claims that full-color ads pull in 60 percent more newspaper readers than those in black and white. One of the occasional exceptions is when an alarming, stark black-and-white ad literally pops off the page among a sea of full-color magazine advertisements. But that practice in contrasts has been around long enough that the effect is no longer so dramatic.

Full-color (or four-color) advertisements do provide viewers with a truer sense of the product being featured. That's especially true when the color appears in an untouched photograph. Of course, top-quality color has limited application in many newspaper pages with its porous newsprint. (That's why preprinted inserts are popular for department stores, grocery stores, and many other retailers.) But other print applications are ideal landscapes for influencing your message with color. (See Chapter 10 about billboard visibility.)

The American Psychological Association (www.apa.org) and other groups have classified colors into strata of emotions and moods. Of course, culture plays a major role for interpreting colors as well. White, for example, may symbolize purity for Western civilization, but in many Asian countries white is the representation of death. Latin Americans often consider purple the color of death. Pink is considered the most feminine color by North Americans, but yellow is the worldwide leader in that regard. Blue, the most popular corporate color, has the widest appeal. Light hues soothe, while dark blues suggest dignity.

For those using color other than for the ad's photograph, it's wise to consult expert advice regarding which colors harmonize and which ones clash. You could do an Internet search to examine a color wheel, which shows what colors tend to harmonize. However, if they are too close in shade, they will lack contrast and will blend together. Those colors separated by another color on the wheel are considered complementary and are effective in ads, especially when they are not bumping against each other in the layout. Tints opposite one another on the wheel are considered clashing. They can still be used to highlight prominence.

For advertisers with limited budgets, spot color can be practical and almost as effective as full color. The insertion of one additional color (perhaps in shades of dark green and light green, which counts as only one extra color) along with black text creates a look and feel quite different from simple black and white. Even black (or another dark text color) can be used with its own shades of gray to create multiple colors on the same press run. Total black (100 percent) could be contrasted with some elements that are dark gray (70 percent) along with others that are lighter (20 percent). A major caution about shading is not to use reverse text inside a tinted box unless there's extreme contrast. Using white letters in a 50 percent green rectangle will hurt legibility. We suggest at least 80 percent as a rule of thumb for reverse color boxes. The use of spot color is readily available in daily newspapers with an additional charge for the extra press run.

Overprints: Printing Text on Top of Photos

Sometimes a headline or other type element is superimposed onto a photograph or illustration. It might be done to save space, especially if the picture fills the entire ad space. Many magazine ads are full-bleed pages with a photo filling the whole page. Or perhaps the photo doesn't have a feature that pops out and grabs the attention of readers. Putting text over visuals—overprinting—has been deplored by many advertising executives because it dilutes overall impact. For example, some letters of the overprint can get lost in the shading of the graphic if there isn't sufficient contrast. Thus, legibility is often sacrificed.

Similarly, reversed letters (in white) might disappear in the skylight background or on a light-colored item of a model's clothing. Occasionally, the black text will become invisible when printed on top of a car's tire or a model's dark hair. An old (and occasionally still recurring) joke among direct response people is making the order form in black with the type directions reversed in white. That means that the customer/buyer—who wants to respond or buy the product—is faced with trying to write his or her information on a black form (obviously an impossibility).

The rules about reverse type will help guide copywriters who need to use a photo for the canvas of their words. Just make sure that the placement of all words keeps them fully visible for the reader.

SAUs

The standard advertising unit was established back in 1984 by the American Newspaper Publishers Association. SAU is the system of standardized sizes of newspaper columns in order to create a measure of uniformity to the multifaceted manner of purchasing space in a variety of papers in multiple markets. It's still important to know about SAUs if you deal with newspapers, even though the specific sizes have changed.

Column widths had been all over the page, literally, making it practically impossible for national advertisers to buy space without altering their ad sizes from paper to paper, even within the same region or state.

Although a few publications never came around to the new dimensions, most broadsheets eventually adopted the SAU of one column being 2-1/16-inch wide in a six-column format. Two columns are 4-1/4 inches, with the extra space being the blank gutter an ad would consume crossing both columns. It made possible the popular concept of one-insertion, one-billing for major advertisers. State press associations loved it as a marketing tool for national advertisers. But not for too long in all cases.

The advent of the new millennium was not kind to the SAU. About that time a U.S. trend started catching on that saved the newspaper industry millions of dollars each year. Newspapers literally shrank to reduce newsprint consumption. (The slender switch actually started in Canada a few years earlier.)

With more and more papers adopting the narrower newsprint rolls, column widths likewise shrank, curtailing the SAU standardization. Although there are still today a few wider holdouts—*The Wall Street Journal* being one of the major ones finally switching in 2007 with a massive three-inch reduction—a majority of daily newspapers have jumped on the thinner-is-better (and cheaper) bandwagon. For them, the current average roll is 50 inches, used to print four pages printed, folded and sliced. But that is slowly shrinking as well. The *Tulsa World* went down to 48 inches for its press run width back in June 2007. Many others are following with similar reductions.

Even for those papers that have shrunk widths, there's still lack of uniformity. The 50-inch web roll is only an average. The six-column ad, for example, typically ranges from 11-1/2 inches (at *USA Today*, for example) to 12 inches wide. And, as pointed out above, some papers are thinking of going even narrower. We won't open a can of worms and start talking about tabloid columns or sizes.

When the confusion started early in 2000, the Newspaper Association of America issued a statement that the new widths were not replacing the standardized ones. It suggested that some newspapers may want to adopt a preferred ad submission size (or PASS) for their new, narrower columns. In a six-column format, one column width would be 1.833 inches under PASS. "We believe that the PASS will provide another tool to help newspapers and their advertisers do business better," the NAA said in a news release at the time.

The term SAU is still being used, but often by Web designers for their unique sizes of banners, tiles, skyscrapers, buttons and pop-ups or pop-unders. Based on an Internet search, we found that several daily papers have adopted the old SAU phrase for their revised, narrower column measurements, which merely adds to the confusion for advertisers, designers, and sales reps. PASS has not become as popular in the lingo as SAU did.

What Happened to the Fundamentals?
Reflections on judging a B2B ad competition

That's the question my fellow Business Marketing Association ad competition judges and I asked after spending a long day looking at business-to-business work that advertising students would have had their GPAs busted for doing. But once they've graduated, students' learning responsibility transfers to creative directors, agency owners and clients to make sure they don't slip into bad habits.

Let me give you some examples

Observe the type you're reading. Serif, isn't it? Do you know why? Because it's more readable. Why then do so many B2B ads use sans serif type in the body copy? Because it's prettier? Because it pleases the art director's aesthetic sensibility? Because all those award-winning ads in Communication Arts are using it? The business we're in is about communication and persuasion. Doesn't that trump fashion?

David Ogilvy said it best, as he said best so many things about communicating clearly and effectively: "Why would you go out of your way to make it more difficult for your customers to read your message?"

Actually, what he was referring to with that line was Bugbear Number Two: reverse type. Every study done over 60 years has shown that white type on a black page is harder for people to read, especially in body copy. Put type over an illustration and you compound the problem. You know what happens when you make stuff more difficult to read? People quit reading.

We winced at a dozen other offenses in the same vein: weird fonts, excess leading, line lengths across the page, body typeset in all caps. Doesn't anybody teach this stuff anymore?

While we're picking on the art directors, let's throw in layouts that have no focal point, that are difficult for the eye to track, that throw in extraneous elements. What's all that about? Trying to be different? Trying to be "eye-catching?" The result is often more eye-confusing or brain-repelling.

But let's not blame all the mess on the art director. Maybe what he or she

Exhibit 8.3 Business-to-Business Advertising Basics

is trying to cover up is the total lack of an idea. Dazzle 'em with footwork; maybe they won't notice we have nothing to say.

Maybe the art director wasn't even part of the process until the end. Bill Bernbach's greatest contribution to our business was to pair the copywriter and art director as equals. Prior to the so-called "creative revolution," copywriters virtually developed ads on the back of an envelope and tossed them over the partition. "Here, draw me one of these." Really.

Now we understand that way of working was 180 degrees wrong. People don't read the headline and then look at the picture. They look at the picture and then read the headline, which actually functions more like a caption. When we see an ad showing a race car because the product works fast, we can be pretty sure it's been developed backward. We saw a lot of that sort of cliché thinking in the ads we were judging. The shame isn't that the ads get thrown in the reject pile for the competition; it's that 95 percent of the client's money got wasted showing something he doesn't sell. That's not just incompetence; it borders on criminal behavior.

No, you don't have to put a big illustration of the product front and center in every ad, but you do need to do something relevant. One nice piece of work showed a tough-looking worker and said, "Would you like to explain to this guy that he has to dig up the cable he just laid because you didn't use [the client's product]?"

What that ad did is talk TO SOMEONE, not just ABOUT SOMETHING. Too many B2B ads read like catalog pages. For goodness sake, you're talking to a human being out there. Engage the reader. Solve his or her problem, don't just bleat about the product.

In one ad, we counted 27 uses of the words we, us, and our. Zero uses of the word you. What are you thinking, people? Nobody looks in a mirror for a thrilling view of you; they want to see their own faces. They want to read about themselves in your advertising.

Please resolve to do better. Don't tell us the category is boring or the client doesn't have enough money. There are no boring categories, only empty writers and art directors. And a tight budget doesn't mean you get to do your job less well; on the contrary, it means you need to be especially brilliant because the work won't run as often. It also makes it even more important that you pay attention to the details we talked about above that improve, not impede communication. Do work that all B2B people can all be proud of. And nothing less.

Robert F. Lauterborn

Exhibit 8.3 Business-to-Business Advertising Basics (continued)

Recap

Most, but not all, ads contain headline, photo or visual, subhead, copy and logo/trademark. Some ads will only use a couple of these elements.

Ad design utilizes the three major layout principles of equilibrium, proportion, and contrast.

White space helps draw attention to other ad elements and should be used properly. The emotional language of color draws more readers to ads than black-and-white ones, but it does cost more. One can wisely use aspects of color economically, however, such as shading and spot color. Printing text on top of visuals can save space, as long as there is adequate contrast so letters do not disappear.

Standard advertising units began in order to provide newspaper column widths that were the same in almost all newspapers. But the inconsistent narrowing of newspaper widths to save on newsprint costs has eliminated much of that standardization today.

Many business-to-business ads fail to communicate effectively when they attempt to be fashionable instead.

Notes

1. Robin Williams, *The Non-Designer's Design Book*. Berkeley, CA: Peachpit Press, 1994, p. 53.
2. Edward F. Henninger, "Make Negative Space Work For You—Not Against You," *By Design,* 2006.

For Further Reading

George Felton, *Advertising Concept and Copy, second edition*. New York: W.W. Norton, 2006.

Mario Pricken, *Creative Advertising: Ideas and Techniques from the World's Best Campaigns*. New York: Thames & Hudson, 2002.

Alex White, *Advertising Design and Typography*. New York: Allworth Press, 2007.

Chapter 9

Direct Marketing

> *"You must open your sales letters . . . in such a way that you compel your prospect to read on right to the end, and take action."*
>
> Alan Sharpe
> Direct mail copywriter

In Focus

- How and why has direct marketing exploded in recent years?
- How does direct mail effectively reach individuals?
- How important are the right mailing list, proper envelope, kind of postage, letter's appeal, postscript, related documents, and timing in making a successful direct marketing program?
- Why are catalogs so popular?
- What are advantages and pitfalls of e-mails?
- What has contributed to the tremendous growth of online advertising?

irect marketing, so often overlooked when planning an advertising campaign, often boasts numbers that are tangible evidence of its importance. After all, more than half of all advertising dollars are allocated to direct marketing. And money spent on direct mail advertising trails only network television and newspapers. Moreover, it's certainly money not wasted. It's claimed an average of $10 comes back for every dollar spent on direct mail pitches. This chapter will introduce you to the concepts of direct marketing. However, it's not meant to be the definitive how-to for this growing field.

Direct marketing can be defined as the interactive method for consumers to access buying information and to make purchases of goods and services through a variety of media. Its potential application with new media convergence has not been maximized. The latest technology advances not only affect advertising, but journalism, public relations, broadcasting, and communication departments. Any book trying to keep pace with the latest trends in new technology is out of date before it's printed. Uses for direct marketing are varied and widespread. It's targeted and measurable. Moreover, savvy marketers know what products customers like to buy, so they can target their offerings based on past purchases, which is why it often provides a higher return on investment than other media.

Unlike magazine or newspaper subscriptions, everyone has a mailbox or post office box, and almost everyone has Internet access and a cell phone. Direct marketing creates a lot of revenue for many retailers, both large and small. Nonprofit groups rely on it for fund solicitation, associations draw on it for membership recruitment and retention, political groups apply it for causes and candidates, and manufacturers draw on it for new product promotions and to support sales of mature products and services. Direct marketing can be used for a national campaign or a local cause.

Direct Mail

More than one billion pieces of promotion-oriented mail were delivered to consumers at work and home in 2007. Consumers have mixed feelings about receiving unsolicited mail, much of it negative. Direct mail greatly contributes to the clutter of message bombardment facing every man, woman, and child in North America. The growing antagonism toward advertising overload takes aim at all media, including the direct mail industry. Despite the junk mail label, much of it tends to be opened, based on various studies.

Unlike the limited time or space allocated for other advertising messages, direct mail can provide details, color photographs, testimonials, free samples, and other convincing arguments for products and services. Marketers wouldn't be pouring money into direct mail pitches if they thought such endeavors were worthless, especially with the measurement tools that tell how effective each mailing is.

Consider what David Whitman, in the Nov. 10, 2006, edition of *Bulldog Reporter's Daily 'Dog,* had to say:

> The mere fact that the amount of mail sent by marketers has increased despite the popularity of online advertising is a paradoxical recent market trend. Advertisers and media relations specialists are discovering that a combination of online marketing and corporeal materials are the most effective marketing package for selling products and services. Furthermore, there are no spam blockers on traditional mail, which allows for more consumers to receive the promotional materials sent out.
>
> While email promotions are in no way on their way out, marketers are finding more opportunities to target specific audiences more efficiently through standard mail delivery. Peter Johnson of the Direct Marketing Association added, 'The Internet has actually been a trigger of direct mail. With every company now basically having a customer-facing Web site, suddenly they're having interactivity with their customers that is much more real to them.' Rob Bagot of international marketing firm Interpublic Group told *The Times,* 'As the world becomes more digital, there is a need for tangible experiences. And there's nothing like a piece of paper.'

The national average for direct mail success has hovered around the 2 percent **response rate** (percentage of individuals who respond to a solicitation) for the past few decades. So if you think those appealing ads for Elvis plates in your mailbox aren't working, think again. If only two out of 100 readers place an order, profits roll in.

One of direct mail's major advantages is that it serves as a personal appeal to a consumer, rather than that delivered through the mass media. Unlike the dozens of ads in other media, direct mail occupies an uncluttered arena. Nonpersonal messages strew the consumer landscape. Getting a letter from an organization, product, or service for which the recipient has some kind of a connection can be a welcome relief from that anonymous muddle. Even though it's computer-generated, direct mail correspondence often uses the person's name and address, unlike broadcast commercials or print ads.

Another obvious benefit of direct mail is that it can be measured, more so than other ad vehicles. Using different Web sites, post office boxes, or toll-free phone numbers for responses, direct marketing can pinpoint what pitches are more successful and what ones need modifications. Tracking sales and orders from specific appeals can help marketers improve their next effort. Testing is especially important for this method because you want the optimal appeal reaching the ideal respondent.

Research sponsored by the direct marketing industry claims that three out of four adults read direct mail advertising. And half of them read it immediately. In the long run, 10 times as many customers respond to direct mail versus newspaper ads. The industry maintains that the record is even more impressive against television. Despite numerous shopping channels, abundant infomercials and endless other TV pitches, direct mail claims its response rate is 100 times more effective than television.

How can it be even half that successful?

Whether tossed aside or thoroughly read, the solicitations tempt addressees with special offers, special prices and special announcements. Simple logic dic-

Notepad

The "J" Word

Arguments against direct mail often come from the newspaper and magazine industries, in their quest for lucrative but limited ad dollars. House ads in various dailies have even shown a sketch of a man opening his mailbox with his trash can nearby. Among typical headlines for such ads is one that reads: "Now You Know Why It's Called Junk Mail."

The "j" word is not supposed to be uttered, of course, among direct marketing industry professionals. They are aware of its sometimes tarnished image, especially every two years when local, state and national political ads overflow the average household mail slot.

tates that the difference between unwarranted correspondence and welcomed letters is the perception of the addressee.

Manufacturers, nonprofits, small businesses, and associations must convincingly appeal to their recipients. That's why every guideline for direct mail success starts with the obvious: send your message to the right audience.

Mailing Lists

No matter how great an offer is being sent to consumers in a wonderfully packaged mailing, it's totally wasted if the correspondence has been incorrectly targeted to the wrong individuals. The proper, updated mailing list holds the key to success in direct mail campaigns.

To highlight this point, you may have seen the large print ad that shows a bald man opening a direct mail package with a free sample of shampoo. Similarly, a deliciously enticing mail solicitation from Omaha Steaks will pull negligible orders, at best, among vegetarians. You're wasting your time and that of the nonprospects.

Many direct marketers refer to a 60-30-10 rule. The 60 represents the percentage of your direct mail success that relies on the proper mailing list. The sales offer itself reflects 30 percent of your success. Sorry, but only 10 percent rests with the creative process.

Business-to-business firms especially often use the services of a list broker to specify exactly the type of client they need to pitch. "Hot" prospects, those who have ordered products or services within the past six months, for example, will cost more to rent than a generic list of names within your targeted market. But it will be more productive than a list of nonspecific addressees.

Contrary to popular belief, you don't buy a mailing list. You rent it. You don't even get to see the names and addresses on your one-time rental arrangement. It makes sense, therefore, for companies to develop their own customer information so they can eliminate the costly and constant renting of lists. And their own clients are already on the more expensive hot lists. Be sure to use correctly spelled names, rather than mere occupational titles to get a higher readership. It's hard to build customer loyalty if you misspell the person's name. A computer program that personalizes each message will score points with readers—and win orders—despite its extra cost.

Keeping a list updated is a constant but necessary battle. Americans move

Direct Mail Drives Traffic Directly to Web Sites

Direct mail, even more direct response?

Increasingly, the line between direct marketing and online marketing is blurring.

"True 'relevance' lies in the content and context of a marketing message, not in the mere strategic placement of a recipient's name or other customer data in a marketing solicitation," Bruce Biegel of Winterberry Group told attendees at the DMA 2006 Conference in San Francisco. "If marketers expect results, they must tailor relevant messages by utilizing data and analytics programs that react to geo-, demo- and psychographic information to enhance behavioral targeting and measurement."

US Consumers* Who Visited a Retail Web Site within 30 Days of Receiving Direct Mail, 2003 & 2006 (% of respondents)

2003	14%
2006	21%

Note: *among those consumers who responded to a direct mail piece
Source: The Winterberry Group, October 2006; Internet Retailer, October 2006

077688   www.eMarketer.com

In the "What's in the Mailbox?" survey, meant to find how to stand apart in a crowded marketing landscape, researchers found that 21% of respondents visited a corresponding Web site within 30 days of receiving direct mail, up from 14% in 2003.

According to *Internet Retailer*, the results indicate that direct-mail-influenced Web traffic grew 50% over the past three years. Though that may be putting the case a little strongly, the trend is definitely up.

Direct marketers are doing a number of things to make their mailings more effective.

Though over 80% of them only modify the salutation and a few basic content elements, the survey shows that 44% of marketers are now using some form of personalization in every e-mail campaign they send.

October 20, 2006
eMarketer.com

frequently. On average, almost 20 percent of the population uproots every year. But for those under 30, 57 percent of them changed addresses in the prior year. Consider a university's alumni office and its ongoing efforts to keep names (because of marriage) and addresses (because of moves and employment opportunities) up to date.

Envelope

According to direct marketing expert Herschell Gordon Lewis in *Open Me Now*, an envelope has only one purpose: to carry the contents of the mailing and get opened. Just as advertisements need to break through the clutter of the printed page to get a reader to stop and look, a direct mail piece needs to encourage the recipient to open the envelope rather than discard it. Many direct marketing pros suggest enticing the customer right away with teaser copy on the envelope. If you're offering a limited-time special, then the sense of urgency can be an added inducement to open the packet to get to the message. It could be a bigger discount, a free gift or free shipping if a response is given or a customer visits a retail store by a certain date. Test mailings are often used to determine what teaser copy is most effective.

However, steer clear of scare tactics or other unethical means to unnerve the recipient. Many people have been frightened by fake exterior messages urgently talking about their facing federal tax penalties or vehicle registration violations. Upon ripping open the parcel, the distressed customers feel duped by correspondence from income tax preparation centers or car dealerships. Few things can kill the possibility of a sale like a hostile, alienated prospect.

The envelope itself should have the same quality as company letterhead. That typically means off-white in color and thicker paper with a high rag content. Cheap, discount-store white envelopes shout "junk mail" to most residents. Likewise, another telltale sign is a mailing label, whether white or clear. It takes more time and money to personally print each envelope, but the higher response will be worth the extra effort. A secondary option, if one must go another route, is the envelope with the see-through window for the recipient's name and address. Oversized envelopes get higher response rates, perhaps because they contain more helpful information as well as an occasional freebie for the addressee, but especially because they stand out in a typical stack of envelopes.

One ploy to get that envelope opened is the use of what the industry calls lumpy mail or, more properly, dimensional mail. The shape is not flat like a sales letter, so it intrigues the curious child in all of us to see what's inside. It could be a small box with product samples and sales materials. It might be a desktop item or conversation starter that will remind the person about the product or service being featured in the mailing. Dimensional mail, based on a Direct Marketing Association survey from October 2004, has a better-than-average 2.3 percent response rate. But it is important to consider the specific package you plan to use; 2007 postal regulations may impose higher postage costs if the mailing is too lumpy.

According to Vertis Customer Focus research findings, six out of 10 Gen Xers and Gen Yers indicate they are more apt to open a direct mailing that "looks interesting." Give them a reason to read your letter. Make the package inviting to the eyes, or even lumpy.

Postage

Another negative sign tipping off residents that their mailbox content is not crucial is a preprinted, presorted postage mark announcing the arrival of more direct mail. A Fortune 500 survey indicated that about one-third of such envelopes are routed directly to the recycle bin by internal postal gatekeepers.

Some direct mail experts feel that a postage stamp is crucial for giving a letter first-class appeal. Others feel that metered letters, now typical for a majority of normal business correspondence anyway, are suitable for such appeals, especially when they are sent first class. Money can be saved using cheaper delivery rates. But who wants to tell current or potential customers that they're not worth first-class postage?

Make friends at the local post office. Its official scale will inform you that the one extra half-sheet of paper in your proposed mailing just upped your postage costs considerably. With stricter regulations in force starting in 2007, you may find extra charges because your post card was a mere one-fourth of an inch too wide. Or postal officials can tell you that you can add eight more pages to your catalog and not pay a penny more in postage. Nonprofits benefit from USPS discounts. Presorted letters up to 3.3 ounces could be sent for about 17 cents during 2008. Consumers don't expect nonprofits to waste precious funds on first-class stamps, so there's much less stigma for such groups to use cheaper postage.

Letter

Your message, if you can get that far, must grab the reader's attention quickly. The opening probably contains the most important words you can craft. Many letters will continue the urgency from the envelope onto the letter with a headline just beneath the company letterhead. Using key words (such as you, new, free, save, easy), this grabber will help direct the prospect into the body of the sales pitch, much like a print headline will draw readers into the ad copy.

Another tested method of getting more responses is to use what has been called a "Johnson Box," named after Frank Johnson, who used the tool to increase the pulling power of his own sales letters. Rather than wading through the entire letter, readers would prefer to get to the bottom line at the top. So Johnson put a box at the top of his first page, with two or three phrases or, maybe, sentences containing vital details about the offer there. It could be the key benefit for the consumer, a money-back guarantee, a toll-free number, or a Web site.

Since you've already targeted your letter to someone with whom you may have a previous relationship (or who at least has indicated by past action some interest in your offer), it's best to come right to the point. Talk about benefits, probably right away in your headline or Johnson box. And direct mail headlines could also have smaller, subordinate headlines as well. Some even suggest that the headline should go at the top of the page and the letterhead at the bottom of the first page. That may be especially good advice if your company name is not a universal synonym for quality—yet.

Don't waste previous space in the headline or opener telling readers how old your company is or how good you think your service is. Product features are not as important as how using this service or item will benefit the recipient (e.g., make them more productive, etc.). Recall the concept of the Unique Buying Proposition. Determine what the consumer needs to hear in your ad. Try to translate features into benefits at all times. "Talk about my lawn, not your grass seed!" admonishes George Duncan of Duncan Direct Associates.

Your goal from the start is to establish trust and credibility with your audience. Think of it as a one-to-one correspondence. You want the individual to keep reading. Many letters will cite statistics, use testimonials or present case studies, all of which should be meaningful to your target audience. Compel them to desire your offerings. Give them incentives, such as bulk discounts, complimentary shipping or free trials.

Letters should be written in a conversational tone to that individual reader, using contractions, personal pronouns (you rather than me), and short, simple words. Sentences and paragraphs, likewise, should be brief for reading ease. The length of the ideal letter has been debated for decades. Some feel that a one-page missive is a must. Others realize that the advantage of direct mail is delivering lots of detailed information in a format that would be cost prohibitive through other advertising channels. Most broadcast commercials, for example, can only deliver headlines. So four or more pages are recommended with that argument.

Many studies indicate that two pages, or both sides of one sheet of paper, give the copywriter adequate space to present convincing material to the intended customer. Longer than two or three pages and reading the letter becomes a burden for the hurried consumer. *USA Today* format has taught copywriters that Americans typically prefer shorter copy over long stories. The bottom line regarding the issue might be summed up in two old sayings: (1) How ever much copy you write, the reader should feel that it was worth reading; (2) Know when to stop—when you've made the sale, stop selling.

One of the crucial aspects of the letter, although fairly obvious, is labeled the call to action. In other words, don't present convincing copy and neglect to ask for the sale. Make it easy for the customer to complete the transaction. Go online? Call a toll-free number? Return a postage-paid envelope or postcard? Encourage the action to take place immediately, before the letter is set aside and perhaps forgotten. That's a major advantage of the Internet. Your store can accept worldwide orders 24/7, even on holidays or during stormy weather.

A final concern is whether to include a postscript following the signature at the bottom of your letter. Most direct mailers use one. Readership scores indicate that a majority of readers scan the page, read the P.S., and then decide if the offer sounds tempting enough to dive into the copy. The typical postscript is a summary of your best selling point. It's a reminder that this fantastic offer will only last so long. (Deadlines do enhance response rates.) The P.S. reminds the reader that this is a great deal. You might even rephrase your call to action here. Aside from the headline (or Johnson box) and opening sentence, the P.S. gets the highest readership scores in your mailing.

Yet a few direct-response practitioners sense the P.S. is passé. Back in the days when correspondence was written on a manual typewriter with carbon paper (recall Klinger or Radar doing that on *M*A*S*H* reruns?), one did not have the time or patience to rewrite a letter if a crucial piece of information was overlooked. So the postscript was the ideal location to add what you forgot. With 21st-century technology, it's easy to cut and paste insertions anywhere we want them.

Over the decades, however, we've trained people to look for a P.S. It's where lovers put their vital reminder message of "I love you." And it's where most direct mailers put their bottom-line benefit for their prospects. Its high readership warrants the inclusion of a P.S. in your direct mail package.

Collateral

As we all know from personal experience, the direct mail piece rarely consists of just a letter. Along with that are other support materials called **collateral**. A typical staple among them is the postage-paid reply card or envelope. If you want a mailed response, you should provide those for your readers. Having to scrounge around the house or apartment for an envelope plus a stamp is enough of a turnoff for many busy consumers. And business-reply envelopes cost you nothing in postage if they're not returned. Why blow a $100 sale over pennies?

Other sales collateral items found in direct mailings might include newsletters, DVDs, brochures, article reprints, testimonial letters, stickers, photographs and technical data sheets. They should complement your sales letter. (Make sure you have signed authorization for those often-persuasive testimonials and photographs of endorsers.) All of these materials can engage the reader with your product or service and be useful in convincing the person to buy. Just make sure you don't insert them all in the same mailing. Having too many loose objects fall out of an envelope can create a negative impression.

Sending such complementary extras is a plus not available through other advertising alternatives. A magazine ad could have a tear-off reply card, but other insert options such as those listed above are ideal only for direct-response mailings.

Promotional products are often inserted as free gifts for direct mail recipients, hoping to remind them to think of the company when making the next purchase decision. Such items might include colorful magnets, small desk calendars, or pens. These inexpensive items, imprinted with the organization's name, Web site, or phone number, are gentle nudges to remind you who you need to contact for your products or services.

The promotional products industry (www.ppa.org) has documented studies where adding such items has increased the response rates by 50 percent. Even higher numbers are reported when a desired specialty product becomes an incentive for placing an order.

Timing

One university's communications department was somewhat surprised when its latest alumni questionnaire generated less than a 20 percent response rate, much below previous surveys of that active population group. When searching for the reasons, a consultant asked when the recent mailing was sent out. After it was determined that the survey went to the post office on Dec. 11, everyone understood why the return numbers were so low. If only other examples could be determined so easily.

December is probably the worst month for overall direct mail pitches. It's typically too late for ordering Christmas presents, for example, when you factor in delivery times. Moreover, mail campaigns get lost in the mountain of holiday cards, overstuffed newspaper supplements, retail store mailings, etc. On top of that, people frequently are vacationing from work or school, traveling more, attending special Christmas or Hanukkah events, shopping at malls, wrapping gifts, decorating the home and entertaining during the month. They don't have the time—nor are they in the proper mood—to consider your offer during the busyness of the holidays. The same typically holds true for shorter periods around other major holidays, such as Thanksgiving or the week of July 4.

Much of the timing decision for direct mail is determined by the product or service being advertised, of course. Chemicals for swimming pools attract more attention in early spring, when homeowners needing such supplies are getting ready for the outdoor swimming season. The latest gadgets for clearing your windshield of snow and ice would be appropriate in the early fall for most parts of the country. Minnesota and North Dakota may be on a mid-September mailing cycle, for example. Tennessee and North Carolina, meanwhile, might receive the same offer in mid-October. Other direct mail pitches are timed for special events in people's lives. They get offers when they graduate from college, get married, have a child, buy a car, purchase a new home, etc.

Although it varies by market, January and February, when normal routines return following the holidays, are considered the best months for most direct mail campaigns, and September and October for the same reason after summer break. June and July are often suggested as taboo months—along with December—because of longer vacations. (August is *the* month for vacationing among many Europeans.) Many residents merely stop their mail delivery while they are away for extended periods of time. Dated offers would be useless once finally picked up by the recipients.

The verdict is still out on days of the week. Mail delivery to businesses is usually higher on Mondays, Tuesdays, and the days after holidays. So it's often considered wise to avoid the massive piles of incoming parcels. If and when the post office halts Saturday home delivery, the problem of crowded Mondays would occur for residences as well as the after-holiday glut. You want to avoid as much competition for your letter as possible.

So it makes good sense to find out about floating religious holidays, as well, such as Yom Kippur and Easter, and spring break dates if you're targeting college students. Most college students start getting their beach offers in January when they return to campus, although some are sent out well before Thanksgiving. Because spring break dates vary from early March to late April, check with individual schools before embarking on a college campaign.

Unlike buying a network TV spot to air during a specific 9 p.m. Thursday program, less control is available for direct mail. The post office can cooperate, but not guarantee exact delivery dates.

Catalogs

Successful copywriters for catalogs are in high demand. They have to overcome a slew of challenges. As one female baby boomer shopper said:

> I don't do catalog shopping for clothes or anything wearable because all manufacturers' sizes are different. I need to feel and see things, and to be able to ponder if I want it. Returning things through the mail is a hassle. I like quick action.

It doesn't take a rocket scientist to conclude that catalog and online shopping can be riskier than in-store purchases. Even a warranty from an unknown company for a new product could be worthless if either the company or the cataloger goes under. Despite that, catalog sales have increased for a number of reasons.

Naturally, most people despise crowds, higher gas prices, congested parking lots, unpleasant weather, and rude salespersons. Marketers have used the phrase "cocooning," coined by Faith Popcorn, to describe how people return home after work and want to stay inside their comfortable surroundings. There's increasingly more confidence by shoppers in receiving proven-quality merchandise at a good price in a timely manner. And return policies have improved for the consumer as well. Great copy may determine, however, where the shopper (from the convenience of the living room) is going to be making those purchases.

Herschell Gordon Lewis, catalog guru, suggests in his writings and workshops that catalog copy can be improved to entice sales. One of his simple tips is to create confidence in the company by eliminating typographical errors and misspellings. Another suggestion is to take advantage of what he terms the catalog's "five hot spots"—spaces where new products, clearance goods, and best-selling items can be displayed for maximum exposure. These locations are the front cover, inside front cover, back cover, center spread and pages next to the order form. An additional maxim is to consider each word in your copy. "You're in command of the reaction to your words," Lewis once said. "Check each noun and verb to be sure it's as colorful, specific and dynamic as it can be."

Just as consumer magazines effectively use front cover teaser headlines about a variety of inside topics (recipes, travel, fitness, business) to entice a range of readers, catalogs can also employ teasers for the same purpose. Unlike magazines, however, smart catalog copywriters can also use back cover teasers in the same way.

Typically, longer copy may be necessary for complex or expensive products. Business-to-business ads, for example, may need to extol the virtues of buying color copiers for the office. Not only do you explain the cost-savings and fancy features, but you push the benefits for the buyer. Copy provides technical details without using jargon for those who have to justify the purchase to their superiors. Some of that longer copy could be set off in a box or identified with subheads. Even if long copy is necessary, don't waste words.

Another key reason catalog sales are increasing today is that the mailings have become more targeted. And more numerous. The *National Directory of Catalogs* claims more than 13,000 U.S. and Canadian consumer and business catalogs are distributed in 232 categories. Long gone is the massive, generic Sears book, which started back in 1888 on a smaller scale. Now anyone can request specialized catalogs for cabinets, cameras, camping gear, candles, ceramics, church supplies, cleaning products, clothing, coffee, coins, comic books, computers, cosmetics, crafts, or cushions.

Exhibit 9.1 Typical Catalogers

Talbots, Victoria's Secret, Lands' End, and Coldwater Creek (see Exhibit 9.1) are among several retailers that issue catalogs frequently, often to supplement online shopping. With a proven name, these outlets have overcome shopper hesitancy. Catalog copy often promises discounts, free shipping and money-back guarantees. Coldwater Creek, for example, sometimes inserts peel-off plastic "credit cards" in some of its magazine ads for $25 off a catalog purchase of $100 or more.

One of the secrets for successful copy is to attract attention quickly. Veteran copywriter Bob Stone said, "Your first 15 words count more than the 15,000 words that follow." So your words have to speak quickly to the audience, which might include newcomers to your catalog as well as the loyal shopper back for three more L.L. Bean polo shirts.

E-Mail

Considerably faster and cheaper than so-called snail mail, the electronic route has been adopted by a majority of marketers for their direct marketing campaigns. After all, online growth has seen the Internet become as pervasive as newspapers and Yellow Pages for consumer shopping decisions. Three out of four households now have home Internet access, and that figure continues to climb, as does the double-digit percentage increase in Internet advertising.

For 2006, Internet ad revenue was $16.8 billion, a 34 percent jump over 2005. As noted in the Notepad "Direct Marketing Drives Business…," there has been much blurring, as direct mail often drives consumers onto Web sites. E-mail, in turn, often precedes personalized direct mail appeals. Based on that research, more than one in five letter recipients in 2006 visited a retail Web store within 30 days of being targeted by direct mail.

Land Rover is one of many corporations that placed added emphasis on its e-mail solicitations starting around the middle of this decade. Aiming at current and prospective customers, the campaign includes invitations to test drive the new models. "We found that follow-up e-mails, in particular, generated a significant positive uplift in response rates and sales where they supported direct marketing campaigns," says Land Rover Internet Manager Serge Sergiou.

Just as the original direct mail campaigns determined that higher response is achieved with personalization of appeals, that feature is being used for almost half of e-solicitations as well. Research originally concluded that Monday may be the best day to conduct e-mail marketing, but others are saying Wednesday seems to be a peak time. (Your corporate target is probably swamped with piles of e-mail to sort through on Monday.) Weekends could even be efficient with little competition and most individuals having more time to digest online messages.

Research by DoubleClick showed that about 6 out of 10 employees admit to checking personal e-mail during the day and view their work e-mail during the evenings or weekends at home. Another study, AOL's third annual e-mail addiction survey, released during July 2007, found that e-mail use via portable devices doubled from 2004. About 6 out of 10 individuals said they check e-mail every time one arrives. More than half said they e-mail while in the bathroom.

Other timing issues—such as holidays—are similar in both types of mail. Months to avoid generally are June, July and December. However, the offer itself still dictates when your appeal should be delivered. If a major hurricane hits the Caribbean Islands, as Felix did in September 2007, tourism destinations will want to postpone both e-mail as well as regular mail appeals and other ads to visit the area too soon, of course.

E-mails are less disturbing than telephone calls at work or home. Yet, one of the major problems with e-mail solicitations is the intrusion factor. People go to their physical mailboxes with the express intent to pick up three or four pieces of correspondence. But individuals often go to their electronic mailboxes and get inundated with unwanted, bothersome e-mails selling things or services they have no interest in buying. Because of the low costs involved, marketers often send out electronic appeals to every name they have accumulated, despite having no prior relationship or knowledge of the recipient. This negative image is perhaps worsened when spam filters don't perform up to expectations and allow unsolicited messages to fill incoming boxes. But even spam underwent a facelift, according to a Dec. 21, 2005, DoubleClick Email Solutions news release:

While spam still constitutes the largest portion of email that consumers receive, the overall percentage has dropped every year since 2002 (from 45.5 percent in 2002 to 30.3 percent in 2005), and while spam is still an issue that concerns a large number of consumers (55 percent are very concerned), viruses (75 percent), identity theft (67 percent), spyware (66 percent) and scams (61 percent) are of greater concern.

Consumers have consistent views of what constitutes spam, most of which match industry definitions, although almost half of respondents also consider permission-based email that comes too frequently or that is no longer relevant as spam. With regards to dealing with spam, almost half of respondents check their bulk mail frequently, usually to confirm that no wanted messages have been incorrectly filtered into their bulk folder. More than forty percent report finding legitimate email in their bulk folders.

However, a newer global study of International Association of Business Communicators members indicates spam is still a major problem in the workplace. An overwhelming 85 percent said that e-mail overload creates a negative impact on their productivity. "Too Much E-mail!" in the organization's November 2006 publication, *Communication World*, revealed that the figure was even higher (93 percent) for respondents with BlackBerry or personal digital assistant devices. Of course, these IABC participants are in the communications field and admit that 61 percent of the overload stemmed from external news sources and professional subscriptions.

For successful e-mail results, many of the same tips for direct mail are applicable. The mailing list, for example, should be targeted to those with whom the company has a relationship or permission. It, too, needs to be updated regularly. People keep their same personal e-mail typically when moving, but they may be in a different occupation or career and not need the same offerings as before. Ask for customers' e-mail addresses. Put your own and a request for others on all forms that ask for information. Developing your own lists now saves rental fees in the future.

Rather than the envelope carrying your hope for consumers reading a message, the burden now rests on an appropriate subject line. This is not the time to be generic with a "Hello Customers." An envelope teaser gives a hint about what's inside a direct mail pitch. You have to do that much at least. Simply stated, give a brief summary of the main point you want delivered to your customer. "Test Drive a Saab and Get $50" will create a certain level of excitement among most car enthusiasts, as well as those looking for some extra cash. But notice the absence of an exclamation mark at the end of that statement. Just as its use is deplored for ad copy, such punctuations should be avoided in e-mails as well.

If your brand is relevant, play it up in your topic line if it's not in your "from" space. If the sender is not familiar to the receiver, chances increase that the delete key will get stroked. The most effective subject lines tend to be short, personal and meaningful for the recipients.

Instead of delivering a three-page direct mail letter, your e-mail message should ideally stay within one computer screen. (Exceptions are always allowed when needed.) Therefore, even more stress should be placed on quality, conversational copywriting in a limited space. A clear subject line is essential. You can—and probably should—offer a click-through URL for additional details. Your emphasis again should be on benefits for the consumer, rather than product features. As in direct mail, suggesting a limited-time offer with a call to action should enhance responses.

E-mail advertising continues to grow as a cost-effective way to establish meaningful, two-way communication with customers and prospects. Coupled with the Internet's 24-hour open shopping center, e-commerce will continue to rake in dollars. Taken as a whole, online advertising expenditures increased about 30 percent between 2005 and 2006, to $16.6 billion. Growth continued in the 20-plus percentage range for 2006.

Online Advertising

More ad budgets are shifting to the digital revolution. Apple's iTunes had sold 3 billion songs by August 2007, for example, ranking it as the third-largest music retailer, behind only Wal-Mart and Best Buy. Companies, of course, have long realized the importance of a 24/7 Web store that's available worldwide. Many of them use one ad agency for traditional media and another for digital marketing expenditures.

Internet advertising continues to grow at a pace faster than other media, partly because of the declining numbers of network TV viewers. Commercial radio advertising is also showing declines because of the growth of satellite radio, enhanced by auto manufacturers offering it for free with new car purchases. And print is contributing to this increase. Based on a 2007 study by the Center for Media Research, 42.3 percent of respondents indicated they were most motivated to visit an online site after seeing an ad in a newspaper. However, the unwanted nature of pop-ups and other intrusive ads on the Internet have caused negative feelings toward this form of advertising.

Google and Yahoo have thus far dominated the Internet market. Search engines are simple tools used to locate Web sites by seeking out key words. Search engine optimization, as the name implies, is a way to enhance the volume of that flow to a Web site. One simple way to do this beyond using key words may be to insert unique content to a company's site.

About 40 percent of current ad spending relates to paid search, when a computer user clicks on a site to view its contents. But competition is expected to increase, especially with the growth of personalized mobile ads delivered via the ubiquitous cell phone. If you can get permission to send such messages, it is not considered spam. (This is where the phrase permission marketing gets bantered around.)

CBS signed a contract with four mobile-advertising firms back in August 2007 in order to promote itself via mobile devices. The ads tout the network's news, sports and entertainment programs. Options include banners, text ads and video commercials for airing on mobile units. A recent mobile messaging unit called "brand2hand" enables companies to send and receive text messages around the globe. One of the leading marketers with a mobile presence has been Budweiser. It offered Bud wallpaper and ringtones five years ago. It also has a separate cell phone presence on its Web site, much earlier than any of its competitors.

Based on an August 2007 article in *The Wall Street Journal*, many universities are finding revenue by selling case studies via the Web to other schools. The University of Western Ontario, for example, sells over one million copies of case studies per year. Harvard is garnering online sales of over seven million a year. George Anders writes: "Well-crafted Web sites win unexpected orders from China and Brazil. Clumsy Web sites lose business."[1]

Apple's long-anticipated—and expensive—iPhone was predicted to have

10 million users by the end of 2008. Total online spending is projected to top $30 billion by 2010.

No matter how clever and exciting an Internet ad looks, the content still has to convince the viewers that the product or service is worth their time. And writing online ad copy still requires the same skill techniques mentioned throughout this book. About ten years ago, for example, one major manufacturer decided to create a Web site. In proofing the 12 pages of content to be displayed online, one of your authors found 58 typos, misspellings, and punctuation mistakes. Imagine how much confidence you would have in the quality of such products, if this national company's work crews reflect the same care and precision on the assembly line.

A June 12, 2007, article in *The Wall Street Journal* echoed this sentiment. "In a recent report, the research outfit (Forrester Research) says that Web-site design for businesses trying to attract consumers still has a long way to go."

Notepad

Online Ads Get Clever

"Rich media" is the phrase describing the recent trend in online advertising. Those unexpected ads that shimmy and shake and even follow your cursor as you try to outrun them became the rage during 2007.

Another trick resurfacing is to break copy content onto multiple pages in order to force the viewer to see more ads. Going to a print version format usually can circumvent the ploy.

Recap

Direct marketing consumes half of all advertising dollars.

Properly used, direct mail can deliver an individualized appeal to its recipient, rather than the impersonal delivery via the mass media. It's often used in tandem with the Web. A secret for direct mail success is using the proper, updated mailing list. Equally crucial is an enticing envelope and a postage stamp. The letter needs to be personal, credible and persuasive; a Johnson box and the postscript are among the first things read. Collateral materials can provide extra incentive to read and take action. Sending the piece at the appropriate time (avoiding June, July and December in most cases) enhances reading and response.

Catalogs continue to rack up sales. Specialized offerings, teasers on the cover, and clever copy are effective hooks to catch readers.

The ever-present and economical e-mail can have success if an effective subject line gets recipients to open the electronic communication. Targeted mailings often team with direct mail.

Online advertising is one way to support or replace a brick-and-mortar store. New technology is seeing a growth in mobile marketing. Quality copy is still crucial, however, no matter what the delivery vehicle is.

Notes

1. "Case Studies Adapt to the Web: Schools Win Customers, Revenue By Selling Teaching Tools Online," *The Wall Street Journal*, Aug. 6, 2007.

For Further Reading

Matt Haig, *Mobile Marketing: The Message Revolution*. London: Kogan Page, 2002.

Herschell Gordon Lewis, *Catalog Copy That Sizzles: All the Hints, Tips, and Tricks of the Trade You'll Ever Need to Write Copy that Sells*. Lincolnwood, IL: NTC Business Books, 2000.

Chapter 10

Out-of-Home

> "*I think that I shall never see a billboard lovely as a tree. Indeed, unless the billboards fall, I'll never see a tree at all.*"
>
> Ogden Nash
> Poet

In Focus

★ How does the billboard industry operate?

★ What has driven the growth of transit ads?

★ Why are inflatables still afloat?

★ What other opportunities are there in outdoor advertising?

T he out-of-home advertising industry has undergone tremendous growth and changes over the past couple of decades. Originally defined as billboards, the outdoor industry has expanded to include transit and shelter ads, inflatables, logos on store floors, and stadium turnstiles as well as bases.

Total spending on out-of-home advertising continues to be among the highest percentage increases in this decade. It jumped 91 percent, for example, between 1994 and 2004. For 2007, outdoor advertising revenue soared to about $7 billion, growing faster than all advertising categories except the Internet. Not as intrusive as volume-enhanced commercials, out-of-home media are noticed by key demographics that advertisers seek.

WPP Group's Mediaedge:cia researched outdoor's growing reception. Joe Abruzzo directed the study, which predicted growth but difficulty in effective measurement: "Historically, it's been harder to capture the impact of outdoor media than other forms, such as TV, radio, magazine—mainly because its audience is defined while on the move."[1]

Billboards

Critics of billboards, the oldest form of advertising, are easy to find. From the poet Ogden Nash early in the 20th century to the White House's Lady Bird Johnson in the 1960s, calls for their removal continue into the 21st century. Despite claims of their destroying the landscape and promoting unhealthy choices (alcohol and tobacco), billboards have ardent supporters—the motoring public. Americans, especially, are spending more time on the go, despite high gas prices. The country's 168,000 billboards can't be ignored by traveling consumers.

A traffic study by the Virginia Tech Transportation Institute revealed that billboards were no more of a distraction to motorists than cell phones, loud passengers, or even clear countryside. For drivers seeking fuel, food, or a place to sleep, signs telling them where they can find such refuge are a welcome sight.

Companies are drawn to the economical expenditures of outdoor, usually listed along with radio as having the lowest cost-per-thousand (CPM) of any media. Estimates place out-of-home CPM between $1 and $5—depending on location—with network television averaging a CPM of $25. The large canvas—12 by 25 feet is the standard poster—with 24-hour exposure can present a pretty picture to commuters, who can be targeted geographically. Illuminated electronic boards that change scenes and advertisers every 6 to 10 seconds present an additional option for those seeking the motoring public.

Another reason for outdoor's continued popularity is its proximity to venues for consumer use of their debit or credit cards. The billboard is often the last visual reminder of a product or service before the motorist pulls into a retail establishment or grocery store. In this day of segmented audiences, outdoor companies often refer to their posters as the last remaining mass medium.

So popular are key locations that by early fall of 2005 prime spots in Chicago, San Francisco, and Los Angeles were sold out into 2006. Such examples continue to be the case today in many metropolitan areas, especially New York City.

In celebration of its 100th issue in April 2006, *Maxim* constructed a 75-foot by 110-foot billboard in the desert outside Las Vegas. It depicts its January 2005 cover of Eva Longoria—in a bikini, of course. The vinyl mesh landmark could be viewed from outer space via Google Earth.

That's far from the record for the world's largest outdoor advertisement. That honor belongs to another publication, the *Financial Times*. Documented by the Guinness Book of World Records, the ad promoted the Asian edition of the newspaper. It consisted of a 209,401 square-foot wrap of the paper's front page onto 50 floors of the 88-floor IFC 2 building, the largest in Hong Kong.

Exhibit 10.1 Multistory Billboard

This multistory billboard helped kick off the November 2006 launch of Enviga, a joint beverage venture by Coca-Cola and Nestle, in the Northeast U.S. This one was near Times Square in New York City. Other test markets were Boston and Philadelphia before Enviga's national launch occurred during 2007.

Special kinds of billboards, called *spectaculars*, include special features that draw attention to them. It could be a 3-D effect (e.g., a car seemingly smashed through the billboard) or extensions beyond the side or top. Calvin Klein's cosmetics division even hired 40 models to party nonstop (working in shifts, of course) on the side of a New York City building. Pedestrians could view their activities on the live billboard and listen to the music being played.

Another unusual billboard appeared in 15 major markets across the U.S. during 2006 when Honda Element ads posed unusual questions, such as "What do an Element and a platypus have in common?" The next line said, "Find out at AM 1640 now." The radio frequency—good for about a two-mile radius—gave motorists answers to the questions asked on the billboard.

Always a challenge for the creative department, billboard space limitations eliminate verbosity. With speeding motorists having only a few seconds to catch the message, they need to read a sharp, to-the-point message. Often called a reminder medium, billboards typically employ a short phrase with a logo ("I'm loving it" with McDonald's golden arches). Sometimes they make their debut after a television campaign has saturated the market for a few months. Then the short punch line on the billboard helps viewers recall the commercial they previously viewed.

The test for skilled copywriters is to create a terse expression that can be scanned quickly at a distance, clearly understood, and remembered for its shrewdness or humor. Advertising books usually suggest a word limit for billboard copy. Some say 6, others declare 10 or 12 as the absolute maximum. Much depends on location, of course. A distant poster along an Interstate won't have the luxury of using many words or smaller print, but an urban billboard, such as Exhibit 10.1, can be read more leisurely by mass transit riders, pedestrians, office workers, and traffic-clogged motorists.

Have you seen any billboards for universities? Many admission staffs, trying to create awareness, have used this tool to get their schools noticed by potential enrollees. What copy would a local university use to attract high school seniors or adult learners to attend its classes? What would be a few ideal locations to place such a billboard? What about a small business owner? Should her one or two boards be placed as reminder advertising where current customers live or farther away to attract new revenue?

Transit Advertising

Primarily found in metropolitan areas, transit ads include signs placed inside and outside of public transit vehicles and at related terminals, stations, and shelters. More recently, the trend has spread even into rural and suburban areas as cash-strapped school districts are selling advertising on the backs, sides, or even interiors of their school buses. A few consumer groups and parents are upset with this sales technique, but advocates point out the extra income and the fact that ads on the backs of the buses are targeted at other motorists, not the children inside. Many districts refuse to run bus ads for fast food restaurants or snack foods to avoid even more criticism.

The location of transit advertising dictates its copy content. Those inside buses and subways, for example, will have a captive audience with enough time to read plenty of words. However, a copywriter for interior signs needs to keep in mind the distance of the reader from the message, so print and graphics are large enough to be clearly seen to convey their messages. The usual inside ad size is about 11 inches high by 14 to 28 inches wide.

Transit ads have several benefits compared to other media. They can't be zapped or turned off. They reach a variety of consumers, usually without other ad competition. Additionally, transit advertising has the advantage of being targeted geographically (see Exhibit 10.2). A small retailer may want to reach residents who live within a 5- or 10-mile drive of that store, for example. So ads are placed on bus routes and shelters close to that neighborhood. Not only do bus riders see such ads, they are also viewed by other motorists and pedestrians. Shelter advertising can also adopt this proximity function as well for office workers, pedestrians, passing motorists, and riders waiting for and getting off or on mass transit vehicles.

But the ads also have their problems. San Francisco experimented with five bus shelters scented with chocolate chip cookies for a "Got Milk?" outdoor campaign during December 2006. The new posters were yanked along with their scent strips after only one day. Protesters claimed that some individuals could be allergic to the odor. Others said it was a slap in the face of homeless people who could not afford to buy cookies or milk.

Yet transit ads continue to proliferate. In an effort to build brand equity, Geico used Monster Media's patented Turnstile Adsleeves in Chicago for the

Exhibit 10.2 Sample Transit Ad

This eye-catching billboard promoting lingerie at a major department store appeared in the Paris subway system. It may be slightly risqué for a U.S. audience, but it certainly catches the attention of many Parisian commuters, along with tourists. (You may have noticed that either the model is a 6-foot, 11-inch woman, or someone played with the original photo for her feet to show.)

first-ever transit system function. Sports stadiums and convention centers have used the concept for more than 10 years.

Taxis have been a popular vehicle for transit advertising for decades. Cabs in Houston experimented with a new ad location: their hubcaps. "We love them," says Raymond Turner, president of Texas Taxi, parent of Yellow Cab. "They're a novelty. We think it's an innovative way to advertise." Several colleges started that trend back in the 1990s to promote their sports teams.

A practice fairly common among some metro bus companies is to vinyl wrap an entire bus with a company logo or product. Larger-than-life cars and athletic shoes have appeared on the sides of participating buses.

Such wraps are appearing more frequently on automobiles, both corporate fleets and single-vehicle small businesses that want to promote their stores and

Exhibit 10.3 Vehicle Wrap: A "Moving Target"

services. Many of these cars are parked at high-traffic locations for significant exposure. The wraps are temporary and do not harm the vehicle's original paint. The Smart car pictured in Exhibit 10.3 was parked at a popular restaurant in central Pennsylvania. The same company wrapped an older station wagon (Exhibit 10.4) and parked it near a busy intersection a few miles from this restaurant. After a few days the locations change, even to neighboring cities, thus exposing the message to a new set of motorists.

Subway riders in many cities recently have been entertained with what appears to be a moving billboard. Painted along the tunnel walls are flipbook pictures that appear to subway passengers to be lively motion-picture ads. SideTrack and Submedia are two companies that offer such services. Automotive ads and movie trailers have been displayed this way in the U.S., Hong Kong, Tokyo, and London.

Metropolitan and suburban commuters are considered an ideal target market for advertisers, hence the importance of the transit signage, whether on subways, trains or buses. For example, 80 percent of urban Japanese workers commute to their employment by train and subway. More than 4 million people use mass transit in Beijing every day.

Exhibit 10.4 Another Vehicle Wrap

Airport advertising also reaches a highly sought audience. Airport kiosks, walkways, and lobbies provide plenty of space for transit ads. Alternate locations will continue to be found to break through the ad clutter.

> Electrical outlets might not seem the ideal location for an out-of-home advertising campaign, but don't tell that to JPMorgan Chase. A commercial-banking unit of the financial services marketer has placed 90 two-foot-long stickers containing its name and various slogans on outlets at Indianapolis International Airport, hoping to catch the attention of business travelers plugging in their laptops while waiting for flights.[2]

Airplanes are getting in on the act also. Ads appear on the headrest covers, trays and tray liners, and air sickness bags. Now Fiat (in Exhibit 10.5.) has even printed promotions on the jet's interior window shades in honor of its Sky-Dome model.

Inflatables

When you hear the word *inflatable*, thoughts usually turn to the Goodyear blimp. Actually it's *blimps*, plural. Goodyear currently has three airships aloft, after

Exhibit 10.5 New Airline Advertising

launching its latest during 2006. The tire company frequently displays product messages along its sides, making it a flashing billboard for nighttime viewers.

The blimp you see in Exhibit 10.6 was frequently seen flying between the Swiss and German borders. It's advertising the European firm Vaude, Spirit of Mountain Sports, while creating substantial revenue by offering passengers expensive rides in its cabin.

Once the only game in town, Goodyear has faced stiff competition in the U.S. lighter-than-air category. Fujifilm, MetLife, Outback, SeaWorld, and Bud-

Exhibit 10.6 Inflatable Advertising

Exhibit 10.7 Ron Paul Blimp

GOP candidate Ron Paul became the first presidential hopeful in U.S. history to promote his campaign via a blimp in mid-December 2007.

weiser, among others, also fly them for promotional purposes and for providing video shots of North American sporting events in exchange for a glimpse of the sponsoring blimp and its large colorful logo. Mobile Airships in Ontario, Canada, is one of many companies that provides toy blimps that can be tethered at a business location or flown indoors by remote control at a stadium, concert hall or trade show.

Available in all shapes and sizes, advertising balloons are used to attract crowds to a store's location. Some inflatables are shaped like animals or birds— such as giant apes or eagles—and are kept upright and moving by a fan at the base. Auto dealerships are among the leaders in using this particular type of inflatable.

Miscellaneous

Other examples of out-of-home advertising are too varied to classify by category. For example, what would you call the growing collection of bathroom ads? (No, we're not talking about graffiti.) Found in both men's and women's

Exhibit 10.8 Advertising "On the Hoof": Blanket Ads

public restrooms, the colorful ads, usually framed, appear anywhere from upscale boutiques, to sports bars to highway rest stops. They may feature a product to purchase, a fast food menu item or a regional travel destination. One company actually installed a small video screen that displayed ads in the bottom of urinals during December 2006.

Although still rare, one company in the Netherlands decided to advertise along a highway with its logo on blankets placed on sheep (see Exhibit 10.8). Hotels.nl, a Dutch reservations service, thought the 1 euro per day per sheep charge was worth the exposure to passing traffic. It "hired" 144 sheep for its low-tech efforts. However, the authorities in Skarsterlan fined Hotels.nl 1,000 euros per day for violating the town's ban on high-

Notepad

Exercise

Can you imagine the golden arches on cows along U.S. highways? Or that Chick-fil-A might resort to blankets instead of billboards for its successful campaign efforts? In such cases, does the publicity for such a stunt give added return on investment for the costs? What could be other possible outlets for this unusual type of advertising? Would products or services be the best targets for such attempts?

way advertising. The online reservations company appealed the fines while seeking out other congested areas for its blanketing efforts. Easy Green Promotions owns the blankets and plans to expand to Europe with attire for cows and horses.

Many companies have discovered the advantage of placing their logos or names in large lettering on top of buildings near busy airports. Passengers—always considered a lucrative audience—can view the message on takeoffs and landings. Target, with its trademarked bulls-eye, has been one of many businesses that advertises this way.

Already in place at Newark International Airport and in London are ads on staircases, often for nonprofit health and fitness messages. Similarly, Reactrix of Foster City, California, developed an interactive floor ad. Located in malls, movie theaters, and retail stores, the ads become animated as people step on them. Orville Redenbacher kernels, for example, will explode into large white pieces of popcorn.

Another out-of-home version is the point-of-purchase ad, popularized by retail stores. Some studies are suggesting that up to 70 percent of buying decisions are made in or near the retail establishment, often called "the last mile." Many crowded grocery stores have resorted to placing ads on the floors of their aisles, usually where such products are on shelves. Whether a small shelf sign or a life-size cutout of the Country Music Association's Female Vocalist of the Year, these POPs draw attention and often result in higher sales for the related products.

One more entry into the out-of-home miscellaneous category is the coat hanger. In an effort to reduce landfills of the plastic and metal hangers, at least one ad firm started marketing biodegradable, recycled, paperboard hangers free to dry cleaning establishments. The hangers have ads for clothing manufacturers and other establishments.

Many companies throughout the world have conducted guerilla tactics by placing multiple posters illegally just to grab the attention of passersby. Sometimes the placards appear on construction site fences or in subway areas. Businesses are even willing to pay fines imposed by the authorities just to get their timely messages out to the targeted public. Both London and New York City during 2007 vowed a crackdown on such efforts. A potentially tragic event occurred in early 2007. Boston authorities, thinking the strange Cartoon Network's electronic light boards around town were bombs, put major sections of

Starting at Second Base—Spider-Man

Advertisers today are looking beyond traditional print media such as newspapers, magazines and billboards—and are instead seeking new, untapped places where they can display promotional images and messages. This move into new territory has not come without controversy, however. Case and point: Major League Baseball's plan to put Spider-Man 2 movie ads on bases in big league ballparks.

As part of a deal between Major League Baseball Properties, Columbia Pictures and Marvel Studios, MLB reportedly would have received more than $2 million in exchange for allowing webbed Spider-Man logos to be placed on and around Major League playing fields—most notably on the bases—in anticipation of the movie's release in June 2004.

Even though the ads on the bases would have measured just six-by-six inches and would have been removed after only one weekend, the plan sparked such outrage among baseball fans that it was scrapped within 24 hours of being announced. Polls, including one by ESPN.com, showed more than three-quarters of fans were opposed to the ads, which were derided as a slap in the face to baseball tradition. Fans who spoke out characterized the planned ads as tasteless and tacky. According to these critics, the ads would have been an unwelcome encroachment on hallowed ground. (Yes, baseball ads for years have been plastered on outfield walls, but at no point in history had they ever crossed over the foul lines, into the actual field of play.)

Criticism of the Spider-Man promotion came from all directions. National sports columnists and broadcasters were particularly vocal, while former MLB commissioners Fay Vincent and Peter Ueberroth—men who had been entrusted to watch over the game in the 1980s and '90s—expressed reservations about the sport's plan to turn bases into billboards.

Ironically, all of the negative reaction created such a buzz about Spider-Man 2 that the movie probably wound up receiving more publicity than had the ad campaign gone off without incident.

What's more, the Atlantic City Surf—an independent minor league baseball team not affiliated with Major League Baseball—capitalized on the brouhaha by holding its own Spider-Man Day. Team personnel painted Spider Man images on bases at the Surf's stadium, then auctioned off the bases after the game to raise money for charity. Spider-Man bobbleheads were also distributed to children in attendance.

Even though the marriage of Spider-Man and baseball seems to have ended there, the relationship between advertising and the national pastime raised eyebrows on another occasion when, just three months before the Spider-Man flap, MLB allowed advertising on player uniforms for the first time in modern history. With the New York Yankees and Tampa Bay Devil Rays opening the 2004 Major League season with a special two-game series in Japan, MLB granted a temporary, two-game exemption that allowed Ricoh—a tremendously successful company in Japan and elsewhere—to affix its logo to the side of the players' batting helmets. The exemption was granted in order

Exhibit 10.9

to conform to the practices of Japan's professional baseball league, which does allow advertising to appear on players' helmets.

Despite MLB's refusal to allow any advertising on player uniforms when the games shifted back to the United States, cynics suggest it's only a matter of time before ads find a permanent home on the jerseys and helmets of Major League Baseball players. Until such time, though, MLB stands as one of the few major professional sports that has kept its uniforms and playing surfaces free of advertising. The flack over the Spider-Man proposal notwithstanding, baseball has actually restricted advertising more sharply than other sports. Consider:

- NASCAR drivers wear jumpsuits plastered in ads, and their cars are brightly painted with sponsors' colors and logos as well.
- Some jockeys in the Kentucky Derby have begun wearing patches that bear the logos of corporate sponsors.
- Professional soccer players throughout the world regularly wear jerseys featuring the name of a corporate team sponsor, even during the 2006 World Cup in Germany.
- The National Football League and National Basketball Association have had contracts with shoe companies to outfit their teams with uniforms and other team personnel apparel. Consequently, much of the game-day and practice clothing used by players and coaches features shoe company logos.
- College football bowl games are frequently named after corporate sponsors (the Tostitos Fiesta Bowl, the FedEx Orange Bowl, Allstate Sugar Bowl, etc.), with the logos of those sponsors appearing on the middle of the playing field and elsewhere.
- Similarly, the National Hockey League has allowed ads at center ice of its playing arenas.

What's more, the trend is steadily moving toward more—not less—advertising in sports. Given that, will baseball's bases really remain lily white all that much longer? Our Spidey Sense tells us no.

by Dr. Dave Kaszuba, Yankees fan and
Susquehanna University faculty member

Exhibit 10.9 (continued)

the city on a virtual lockdown. The ensuing nightmare and embarrassment cost owner Ted Turner $2 million, half of which covered emergency security costs, the other half serving as an apology payment.

A recent form of out-of-home advertising—that eventually winds up in the home or office—is the U.S. postage stamp. The May 2006 repeal of a 19th-century postal law barring advertising opened up another avenue for marketers to promote their wares. For about 10 cents per stamp, businesses can personalize their mailings with small images of logos or products. Hewlett-Packard was the first advertiser to take advantage of this outlet. Its early branded postage efforts included the HP logo, a 1960 head shot of its two founders, and a photo of a California garage that served as HP's research lab in 1939.

Would high school students be impressed to receive a letter with a nearby university's individualized postage stamp on the outer envelope? Do you think they would even notice the special stamp? What would you design for such a stamp for that particular university? How many varieties would be effective for recruiting purposes? Do you think an established company or a newer one would benefit the most from such a personalized stamp? Would a unique stamp be worthwhile for a company's major anniversary?

Sidewalk chalk is not new, yet Verizon found out in 2006 that sidewalk chalk ads are illegal in Washington, D.C. The second-largest phone company was fined $1,050 for water-soluble chalk ads sprayed on D.C. sidewalks. Verizon spokeswoman Vanessa Banks said this was the first time Verizon had attempted such an ad campaign. "It's harder and harder to catch consumers' attention, so many companies, including us, are turning to nontraditional advertisements," she added.[3] It's naturally wise to check with the relevant authorities before attempting such chalk-art ads.

City benches often have company names or products painted on them. The newspaper industry, always looking for additional revenue, has sought advertisers for the sides of its metal sales racks for decades.

Recap

Outdoor's percentage growth is surpassed only by the Internet. Billboards are criticized by many as eyesores, but motorists love them. Advertisers enjoy their low costs and strategic locations. Although their wording is succinct, they effectively serve as reminder messages.

Transit ads are ubiquitous in urban areas, found in and outside mass transit vehicles, bus shelters, subway property, and airports.

Inflatable used to mean the Goodyear blimp, but competition is in the sky, as well as inside indoor facilities and above retail stores.

The catch-all category for everything else includes bathroom ads, point-of-purchase ads in and near retail establishments, posters, postage stamps, and even sidewalk chalk.

Notes

1. "Agency Finds Outdoor One of the Fastest Growing Media," by David Kaplan, *Media Daily News*, March 21, 2005.
2. "Chase Targets Business Travelers With Wall Outlet Stickers," *The Wall Street Journal*, Feb. 22, 2006.
3. "Verizon Fined by District for Chalk-on-Sidewalk Advertising," by Arshad Mohammed, *Washington Post*, April 1, 2006.

Chapter 11

Ad Campaigns

> "With repetition, even imperceptibly small effects can build into larger perceived differences between brands."
>
> Dr. Max Sutherland
> Independent marketing psychologist

In Focus

- How have ad campaigns changed over the years?
- How did the International Paper campaign operate to fill its goals and objectives?
- What are the different types of campaigns?
- What are the key elements of a campaign?
- Why is integrated marketing communications important?

What is an advertising campaign? Twenty years ago that question probably would have gotten a response roughly equivalent to today's "Duh!" A campaign was a series of at least three ads, basically multiple executions of a single theme, almost always with a strong print component if not primarily in print. We looked at International Paper's Power of the Printed Word campaign in Chapter 6—16 two-page spread ads in a nearly identical format developed at a rate of three or four per year to position International Paper as a "defender of the faith," an apostle of print. (See Appendix B.)

You may be surprised, however, when you hear what the real underlying objective of the campaign was. That's one of the things we'll discuss in this chapter: What kinds of campaigns are there? What are some of the purposes companies have for campaigns? What are the elements that make up a campaign? What media are used? How do writers both maintain continuity and keep the campaign fresh at the same time?

What Are You Trying to Accomplish?

Let's start with what the International Paper campaign was all about. In the 1980s, when the campaign was developed, publishers of books, magazines, and newspapers perceived themselves to be under siege. People, particularly young people (the publishers' future customers), seemed to be reading less and turning more to TV and other electronic media of the day. Please keep in mind what we said earlier: If you can write to what wakes somebody up at three o'clock in the morning, you'll be pretty sure to get their attention.

What was waking up publishers in the middle of the night was the overwhelming fear that their companies might become irrelevant. IP was at the time the largest single supplier of paper for books, magazines, and newspapers (taken as a category), but the competitive situation was very difficult. Besides the specter of a potentially declining market, there was perceived parity among the paper companies, their products were perceived as commodities, and IP didn't lead in any specific segment. Someone else was the leading supplier for magazine paper, another company led in newsprint (the term for the paper most newspapers use), and still another was the biggest seller to book publishers.

There was great pressure on pricing, as publishers played the paper companies off against one another, and International Paper even had some quality

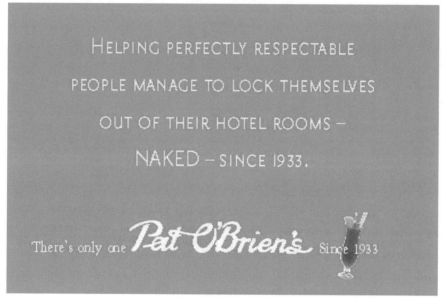

HELPING PERFECTLY RESPECTABLE

PEOPLE MANAGE TO LOCK THEMSELVES

OUT OF THEIR HOTEL ROOMS –

NAKED – SINCE 1933.

There's only one *Pat O'Brien's* Since 1933

Exhibit 11.1A One Ad from Pat O'Brien's Campaign

Pat O'Brien's Bar has had success with more than a dozen similar ads in its campaign to promote its establishments in New Orleans, Memphis, Orlando, San Antonio, and Cancun.

problems. To top it off, magazine publishers in particular needed a new, lighter-weight paper to offset postal rate increases (if they could reduce the heft of magazines, they could cut mailing costs), but that was going to require IP to build a new mill—an investment of a billion dollars—which the company wouldn't be able to put into operation for five years. A bleak situation.

So how could an advertising campaign overcome that big a litany of problems? Well, we've talked again and again about the importance of having specific, measurable objectives for your work. Here was the specific, measurable objective International Paper challenged its advertising agency, Ogilvy & Mather (now simply Ogilvy), to achieve: Create a campaign that would keep IP's printing and publishing customers loyal by giving them a reason to prefer to do business with the company that transcends the product problems until IP could build the new mill that would solve them.

All good advertising begins with a fundamental understanding of the prototypical person whose behavior you want to affect, the potential reader of your advertising. (Recall Chapter 3's explanation of segmenting people into groups

GUILT-TRIPPING BOYFRIENDS INTO BUYING CRAPPY OVER-PRICED ROSES SINCE 1933.

There's only one *Pat O'Brien's* Since 1933

NEW ORLEANS | CANCUN | MEMPHIS | ORLANDO | SAN ANTONIO | PATOBRIENS.COM

Exhibit 11.1B Sample Ad from Pat Brien's Campaign

All of the ads in the complete set from this Pat O'Brien's campaign except this example are vertical full-page ads (such as Exhibit 11.1B) and list the locations along the bottom. You'll notice such similarities as the same color background, the same font and the same signature at the bottom. Even though it's reverse type, notice the effective use of large white print, extra spacing between lines, and limited copy. When designing a campaign, you want the series of ads to be readily identified, yet to be viewed as a different effort from the latest one. You want customers looking forward to the next installment. What copy would you produce for the next two ads in this successful series?

Award-winning copywriter Richard Sullivan, Jr., president of Red Square, formerly Sullivan-St. Clair Marketing/Public Relations in Mobile, Alabama, was responsible for the effort to refresh Pat O'Brien's image. Ads ran in tourism publications and *Travel Host*. Exhibit 11.1A was used quite appropriately on hotel keys in the French Quarter of New Orleans.

and the Hierarchy of Customers.) IP and the agency commissioned third-party research among publishers. ("Third-party" research is that done by an outside professional research company so that the respondents—the individuals being interviewed—don't know who's really asking the questions and so won't bias their answers.) As IP and the agency expected, the news wasn't encouraging.

Publishers thought all paper companies were alike: rapists of the forest, price-gougers, and crass people interested only in their own businesses, not their customers' concerns. Moreover, what the publishers wanted to hear from paper companies was that paper prices were going down, quality was going up, and all the kinds of paper they needed would be readily available—none of which IP could say.

However, buried in the research (consisting primarily of personal interviews with publishing company top executives and paper buyers) was a nugget of insight. At a deeper level, nearly all the publishing people expressed a concern that young people in particular were turning away from print as their primary source of news, information, and entertainment. (Yes, this was even before the rise of the PC.) That was the "Aha!" moment that led to the PPW campaign. If IP could somehow position itself in publishers' minds as the one company addressing that concern in a positive way, the company could separate itself from its competitors and gain brand loyalty, thus accomplishing the five-year, maintain share-of-market objective. Done really well, the campaign might even enable IP to earn a premium price for its paper.

Let's look at the thinking process the writer went through. There were several possible ways to approach the opportunity. For example, IP could have run a series of "issue" ads that cited the statistics and sympathized. However, that would have been what somebody called "the politician's solution"—point with alarm at the problem, but don't do anything to solve it.

Or the company could have contracted with celebrities to tell young people how important it is to develop reading and writing skills; but that approach would have been similarly empty. Instead, the writer thought IP should try to make a real difference, that the company could actually try to help young people learn to read and write better. His first thought was a series of instructional essays by educators with academic credentials in reading, writing and so on, but it would have been unlikely that young people would have read anything like that. Can't you just hear the chorus? "Bor-ing!"

One definition of creativity is the juxtaposition of two previously unrelated ideas, and that's exactly what the writer (who worked at Ogilvy, IP's advertising agency) did next. He combined the latter two concepts, conceiving the idea of famous people with credibility writing how-to articles, with the help of educational experts, if necessary.

How do you decide which celebrities you should use? It doesn't matter what you think. The question is what do your potential readers think? Check out this Web site: http://www.qscores.com. A research company named Marketing Evaluations assigns what it calls Q-ratings to sports celebrities, entertainment figures and others in the public eye. Such ratings tell you how familiar a given person may be to a particular demographic cohort, how well-liked that person is, how credible, etc. What the Ogilvy researchers looked for were people who were not only known to the target audience, but liked, and even more important, were considered believable. (Ty Pennington from the TV show "Extreme Makeover: Home Edition" ranked as one of 2007's top Q-score leaders along with golfer Tiger Woods.)

Notepad

UK Campaign Aims at Smokers

A $17.3 million, six-month campaign in the United Kingdom in 2007 reminded smokers that their habit was now illegal that summer in pubs, restaurants and enclosed work spaces.

TV spots, billboards, newspaper ads, posters, transit ads, brochures and stickers were used in the widespread effort to warn citizens about the new law and subsequent fines. A big reason for such a major campaign? About 25 percent of Brits smoked at the time.

The designated audience for the IP campaign (the potential Receivers, in FOCUS-speak) was young people in high school who were likely to go to college, people in college now and recent college graduates. (That just happened to be the most promising future market for publishers of books, magazines and newspapers—a highly merchandisable fact for IP.) At that time, a comedian/television sitcom star named Bill Cosby was known and liked by virtually everyone IP sought to reach. What also made him credible on the subject "How to read faster" was something most people didn't know. He had recently earned a doctorate in education from the University of Massachusetts. Perfect choice, huh? Similar analyses were done for authors proposed for each of the subjects the campaign proposed to tackle—writing, spelling and so on.

So did the copywriter write the pieces or did the celebrity? A bit of both. It's necessary for a good print advertising copywriter to be able to work in various ways, depending on the situation. In some cases, the celebrity author would write a draft that the writer would then edit for length and adapt to the campaign format. In other cases, the copywriter would research educational thinking on the subject and supply the information to the celebrity author who would then produce a draft. In still other cases, the copywriter would produce the first draft that the celebrity author would then adapt to his or her style and add his or her thoughts. You can see how important it is for copywriters to be flexible and multitalented.

There are several kinds of campaigns, often calling for different kinds of writing.

Corporate Advertising

The International Paper example we've been examining is called a **Corporate Advertising** campaign. Its purpose is to position the company in a certain way in the eyes of a particular audience. Oil companies such as BP may want to be perceived as concerned about the environment to counteract any less-favorable impressions people may have. Chrysler kicked off its new corporate campaign, "Get Ready for the Next Hundred Years," in August 2007 after being sold to a private equity group. Companies without familiar consumer products, such as BASF, may seek to explain their businesses to potential investors through this kind of campaign, also called "Institutional Advertising."

Issue Advertising (or Advocacy Advertising)

An offshoot of Corporate Advertising is **Issue Advertising** or **Advocacy Advertising**. Companies may use this kind of a campaign to argue for or against legislation or government policies. A famous venue for this kind of advertising is the Op-Ed page (short for opinion and editorial) of *The New York Times* and other major dailies.

The first advertiser to use this space was Mobil (half of Mobil-Exxon, then two independent companies that later merged). During the first oil crisis in the early 1970s, the company and its industry were under constant attack in the national media. They perceived some of the reporting as uninformed at best, perhaps even irresponsible, and undertook to correct the record with an issue advertising campaign placed in the most visible, credible forums they could find. The ads ran on the inside front covers of *Editor & Publisher*, *Columbia Journalism Review*, and *Washington Journalism Review*—places where publishers, editors, and news show producers would be sure to see them—and sought to reach other influential segments of the public by contracting with *The New York Times* to place the same ads on its Op-Ed page. (Perhaps you've noticed that the ads they and other companies run in that space today are the same size as a magazine page; now you know why.) Credibility, factual accuracy, and a calm, explanatory style are the hallmarks of this kind of copywriting.

Consumer Advertising

The campaigns you are probably most familiar with—besides political contests—are for consumer products and services, particularly those purchased frequently. (The British call products such as soap, shampoo, crackers, etc., "FMCG"—**fast-moving consumer goods**—while Americans are most likely to call them **packaged goods**.)

When you accessed the Magazine Publishers Association Web site—www.magazine.org—and looked up the Kelly Award winners, you saw a lot of campaigns for products such as Altoids breath mints, a perennial contender for Kelly honors produced by Leo Burnett.

Looking at that particular campaign, you'll notice that it's very visual, with only a word or two of copy—basically a headline, which functions as the caption for the illustration. Does that mean the copywriter has little or nothing to do? Certainly not. A hallmark of great copywriter/art director "marriages" is that often they themselves cannot say for sure which one of them came up with the visual idea or the words. Great copywriters think visually; great art directors have a solid command of the language. Sometimes those unrelated ideas are in two different heads, and the best partnerships are characterized by the ability of the creative team to stimulate each other to generate relevant ideas, pull them out and connect them, sometimes visually, sometimes in words.

Gap decided to forego its customary television commercials in favor of a print campaign in magazines, billboards, and bus shelters that began in fall 2007. It was targeted primarily for consumers in their late twenties and early thirties. To help it stand out, the effort used black and white shots of known and lesser-known celebrities.

What makes a campaign a campaign?

1. **Visual continuity**. Notice how an Altoid ad from several years ago is virtually indistinguishable from one that runs today. The illustrations are in the same style, the color palette is the same, the type is the same, the elements are in the same relationship to each other, and the logo is in the same place.

2. **A verbal "attitude."** There's a style to the writing in every great campaign—flip, serious, trendy, humorous, whatever. It always sounds like the same person is talking to you, which, of course, is true. It's the voice of the brand that you hear.

Trade Advertising

Most of us only see consumer advertising campaigns, but a broad range of campaigns run in trade magazines, publications rarely found on newsstands. **Trade Advertising** is advertising of products and services from one business to another—*B2B*, it's called, as contrasted to *B2C*, business advertising to consumers. Telephone companies, for example, do both. They run campaigns to try to persuade you to buy their service and equipment for yourself or your home, and they also run campaigns to try to persuade business owners or corporate users to install their brand of phone systems throughout a company.

Some of the equipment and even the service offerings may differ only in scale—you'll buy one or two phones, a business may buy hundreds or thousands—but the copywriter's job can be much more complicated.

The fundamental principles we've been discussing still apply, of course. All good advertising begins with a fundamental understanding of the person whose behavior you're trying to affect, and you're still going to talk *to someone*, not just *about something*. Good design is still good design; good writing is still good writing.

What's different, however, is the buying decision process. What do you want when you are buying a phone? The ability to make clear calls, of course, and good coverage in the areas where you'll be using the phone the most. Maybe certain features are more important to you than others—the ease of text messaging, perhaps. And certainly cost matters.

But on a functional level (remember the David Aaker litany?), most phones probably work pretty much the same, don't they? So what else figures into your thinking? What emotional needs does the phone satisfy? Keeping in touch with your friends, of course. And maybe an awesome design matters. Maybe you have a well-developed aesthetic sensibility. You want a slim, smart phone that makes you feel good when you look at it. Finally, on a self-expressive level, what needs can a phone help satisfy? Maybe you want to be seen by your friends as techno-savvy, the person who camped out to be among the first to purchase Apple's iPhone or the follow-up versions. So your latest phone high-tech gadget can take pictures and videos, download tons of music, get online, and send unlimited text and e-mail messages. And it even makes phone calls, too, of course.

In any case, when the copywriters are talking to you as a consumer, all they have to do is learn all they can about you and your lifestyle, how and where you use a phone and what you use it for, figure out your priorities, and focus on persuading you that there is no completely satisfactory substitute for their client's phone relative to your needs and wants.

Not a simple task, but a whole lot easier than the job the same copywriter would have to do to sell you if you were a person in charge of buying a phone system for a company.

Here's why. When you're buying a phone for yourself, you're the only person you have to satisfy. And even if you make a mistake, so what? You'll kick yourself, and it'll cost you a little money, and maybe you'll have to live with something less than perfect for a little while until you can get out of a two-year contract or replace the phone, but no biggie.

Now imagine you're in charge of buying phones for a company. The decision isn't just yours anymore. You have to make all the users happy, from the receptionists to the denizens of the executive suite to the sales force out in the field. You have to make sure the phone system meets the IT people's specifications technically and that they're able to install and maintain it. You have to justify the purchase price to the finance types. And if you make a mistake…well, maybe you were thinking about changing companies anyway.

So what does the copywriter have to talk to you about? Well, he or she still needs to give you the functional information about how the phone works. But what are your emotional needs now? What wakes you up at three o'clock in the morning screaming? You're afraid of making a mistake. You're afraid of looking foolish in front of peers and superiors. You're afraid of losing your job, for goodness' sake. So it's not just about a cool design anymore. You need to feel *safe*. The copywriter has to persuade you that no other company would do more to help you win over the others in the company who need to agree with your decision, that no other company would do more to back you up and keep you out of trouble if something were to go wrong.

In the first few decades of the computer industry, when people who had to make computer-buying decisions for their companies had the same sort of fears, IBM's trade advertising strongly implied that "Nobody ever got fired for buying IBM." They knew that to these people, it wasn't about the bits and bytes, it was about sleeping nights.

With that Maslow safety and security level secure, the copywriters can go on to speak to your self-expressive need. You want to be perceived as a smart guy, maybe the guy who knows all about phone systems, the expert. If they can show you how their client can help you achieve that status, the sale is made, isn't it?

Trade advertising can be a bigger challenge than consumer advertising, as you can see. You have to understand how multiple people interact to make a buying decision and know what motivates all of them. If you have the kind of mind that thrives on complexity and you're interested in how things work—in other words, if you're a writer with an engineering mind—maybe this is a career you should look into.

See if there's a Business Marketing Association chapter in the city where you live—you'll find the national headquarters at *www.marketing.org*—and if so, see if they'll let you attend a meeting. That would be a great place to start. You can also access award-winning B2B advertising campaigns at that site.

Integrated Marketing Communications

Another version of an advertising campaign is more complicated for a copywriter. Perhaps you've heard of IMC—Integrated Marketing Communications. A 2007 survey done by the Association of National Advertisers found that IMC was the number-one concern of chief marketing officers in advertising companies. At the beginning of this chapter, we talked about what a campaign used to mean—some print ads backed up by other media, maybe TV or radio commercials, direct mail, some point of sale material, or whatever. Advertising people thought more about the product than about the people whose behavior they were presumably charged to change. They perceived their mission as "to get the word out" and their media choices were relatively limited.

It's not that easy any more, for a lot of reasons. The population is less homogenous, their media options seem almost infinite, their media use patterns differ greatly and they perceive most products as commodities. IMC involves all aspects of an organization—advertising, public relations, marketing, and sales, for example—that complement one another to distribute a unified message to intended audiences.

What's a writer to do? Think at least as much about the people as the product. Understand how they make decisions, know which media they turn to during the decision process and when, and figure out how to carry on a consistent conversation with them over time. Since we're

Notepad

The phrase *integrated marketing communications*—in whole or in parts—has appeared on a lot of books since the early 1990s. Don Schultz, Stanley Tannenbaum, and Bob Lauterborn published the first edition of the text by that title in 1993. *Integrated Marketing Communications* has seen six editions in five languages. Do an Internet search to see how publishers have used the title in a variety of ways since then.

More than two dozen recent titles or subtitles are in use today in advertising and marketing courses across North America.

talking about print, what's the role of print advertising in the process? What do you want the print ads to do, relative to the rest of the integrated marketing campaign? Once, print was expected to do everything, but that's seldom true anymore.

Maybe the print explains in more detail something the audience has heard about on TV and makes that message more credible. Or perhaps the job of the print is to get people excited about a direct mail solicitation they're going to receive and thus increase the rate of response. Or maybe it's to get people to go to a dealership or a store or, as is often true today, maybe print's mission is to drive people to the advertiser's Web site where the sale will take place. It's the writer's job to understand all that and integrate it seamlessly.

Another characteristic of an IMC campaign is that it involves communicating with multiple people who can influence a consumer's decision—employees of the advertiser's company, salespeople on the retail floor or anyone to whom the consumer might turn for advice.

What further complicates the writer's job today is that the same person who is a potential consumer may also be a shareowner of the company that makes the product or work for the company or both. The person may live in a community where the manufacturer has a presence or may be an activist keenly conscious of the company's environmental record. In all its communications with all its many "stakeholders," a company must present one face and speak with one voice. An advertising copywriter may find himself or herself working across multiple media with multiple missions, very much concerned with keeping that integrated message consistent.

Notepad

Campaigns Use Various Media

A typical IMC campaign may start in one medium, but it's almost always more effective when spread to others, especially print. For example, a 30-second TV commercial—after airing for three months—is able to carry the visuals into the less expensive radio listener's memory with identical music, narration or sound effects.

Key graphic images can then be used effectively for magazine and newspaper ads as well as out-of-home campaigns. The original TV spot might be edited later and run in shorter versions, perhaps 15 seconds, to tell the original story line in an abbreviated (and cheaper) format. Integrated marketing communications—when a company's efforts are all on the same focus—can even incorporate the use of promotional products, special events, sales incentives and PR.

Advertising Age's Top Advertising Campaigns of the 20th Century

1. Volkswagen, "Think Small," Doyle Dane Bernbach, 1959
2. Coca-Cola, "The pause that refreshes," D'Arcy Co., 1929
3. Marlboro, "The Marlboro Man," Leo Burnett Co., 1955
4. Nike, "Just do it," Wieden & Kennedy, 1988
5. McDonald's, "You deserve a break today," Needham, Harper & Steers, 1971
6. DeBeers, "A diamond is forever," N.W. Ayer & Son, 1948
7. Absolut Vodka, The Absolut Bottle, TBWA, 1981
8. Miller Lite, "Tastes great, less filling," McCann-Erickson Worldwide, 1974
9. Clairol, "Does she . . . or doesn't she?" Foote, Cone & Belding, 1957
10. Avis, "We try harder," Doyle Dane Bernbach, 1963

For the complete list of *Advertising Age*'s Top 100 Campaigns, log on to adage.com/century/campaigns.

Exhibit 11.2

Recap

Campaigns used to be fairly simple, with a series of at least three ads, usually print dominated. International Paper's Power of the Printed Word is an award-winning print campaign aimed at high school and college students.

Common types of advertising campaigns include corporate, issue (or advocacy), the more common consumer goods and services, and trade (or B2B).

All campaigns need a visual continuity and a verbal continuity, so they look different but with similar elements.

Integrated marketing communications is a method to put all of an organization's interaction tools on the same page to send a unified, consistent message to a targeted public. Advertising, PR, sales, marketing and so on work in sync to harmonize what consumers see and hear.

For Further Reading

Barry H. Cohen, *10 Ways to Screw Up an Ad Campaign*. Avon, MA: Adams Media Corporation, 2006.

Chip Heath and Dan Heath, *Made to Stick: Why Some Ideas Survive and Others Die*. New York, NY: Random House, 2007.

Donald E. Parente, *Advertising Campaign Strategy: A Guide to Marketing Communication Plans*. Belmont, CA: South-Western Publishing, 2005.

Max Sutherland and Alice K. Sylvester, *Advertising and the Mind of the Consumer: What Works, What Doesn't, and Why*. Melbourne, Australia: Allen & Unwin, 2000.

Chapter 12

Selling the Work

> *"Everyone lives by selling something."*
>
> Robert Louis Stevenson
> Scottish author

In Focus

- At what point must an ad be "sold" for approval before it appears?
- What are speculative ads and co-op advertising?
- How should an ad agency (or in-house ad group) make presentations to its clients?
- How can advertising content analysis be used more competitively?

OK, you've done a terrific job. You did your research, developed a deeper understanding of the designated recipient than you may have of your own sister, found a bit of insight that led you to exactly the right UBP, dramatized the proposition with the perfect visual and headline, and wrote urgent, compelling copy. Congratulations!

Selling in Print

But wait. There's more. No one will ever have the chance to be inspired and driven to action by your masterpiece, no hordes of people will surge to buy your client's product or service, no creative judges will hand you a check for $100,000 and a Kelly Award unless you do one more thing equally well: sell it. Yes, at times, the person who creates the ad has to then persuasively convince others it's a good idea. So please read on.

How do you do that? Apply the same process you did in developing the work in the first place. Figure out exactly who will have to say "yes" for the work to go forward and just as important, exactly who could say "no" and (shudder) send you back to the drawing board or computer screen.

Determine what each person wants most—and fears most. Remember the part about what wakes someone up screaming at three o'clock in the morning? Strategize a UBP for each of those people; then build a presentation(s) around that insight that will make it inconceivable for any of them to do anything but bless your work (and you) and move forward. (Yes, you may need to present your work to different people in different ways, just as you present yourself to your friends differently from how you present yourself to your parents or relatives.)

So who are these people who potentially have so much of an influence on whether your work actually runs?

If you're a copywriter, the first gauntlet you have to run will probably be within your own agency. Most agencies have a "plans board" or something similar, a senior group of executives who make the ultimate decision about whether work will be presented to the client for approval.

But before you can even get to them, you have your own creative director to sell, as well as the account manager who is responsible for the client/agency relationship.

What do they all want?

Ideally, your creative director will be your mentor, as eager to see you succeed as you are yourself. You will have worked with him or her in real time as you developed the work you're now ready to sell, and he or she will have signed off on critical decisions at virtually every step along the way. But…now it's not just the two of you (or the three of you, the CD and your art director partner). Now the creative director's reputation, and maybe his or her job, is on the line. Don't be blind to that.

Notepad

Selling has been defined as finding a solution for someone else's problem. If you don't work in an agency, your task is a little different. You still must persuade someone that you have effectively solved the client's problem with your ad creation. But you want to do that directly with a quick benefit statement.

If you're an ad sales rep calling on a client, don't dwell on your own trivia. Instead, talk about the store owner's interests. Share how your ad will solve the retailer's problem, that you previously discovered by listening and doing your own research. Remember, to ask for the sale. It's being professional, not pushy.

What is his or her relationship with the account manager? Are they friends? Do they like each other? Tolerate each other? Hate each other? You need to know about things like this because, with the proper planning, your work could become a constructive tool, but, without it, a destructive weapon in that relationship. If their relationship is wary, you might need to position your work as a positive step forward—evidence that the creative department is supportive and can be trusted. If their relationship is friendly, then your task is easier. Your work can be another chance for them to work together to sell it (and themselves) to senior management and ultimately to the client.

How strong is their position in the agency? Are they stars, considered by senior management to be the leaders of the future? Lucky you! But if that's not the case—if they're concerned about their own survival—you have to find a way to get them to perceive your work as solid evidence of their management talent and good judgment.

Did you think good work just sold itself, that it could never be sacrificed on the altar of agency politics? Think again!

Once you have them in your corner, it's time to strategize with them about how to make sure the work survives the plans board and gets to the client intact. The client presentation is often called the *pitch*, where your persuasive verbal and visual communication skills come to the forefront.

Selling Directly to Retailers with Spec Ads

Retailers today are looking for ways to save revenue. Some of them may think that cutting back on advertising is an appropriate solution. That option is being confronted by newspaper sales representatives with speculative advertising. Spec ads—as they are called within the industry—are designed by the newspaper advertising department, and sometimes even the sales rep, and then presented to the client. Combine them with co-operative advertising dollars available to retailers and you can't lose. Unfortunately, half of all co-op dollars available from manufacturers are never claimed. Most major companies will pay retailers a set amount or a percentage of total ad costs if their product is featured in the local retailer's advertisement. Do your homework about this source of funds along with your spec ad. Unfortunately for them, many retailers are clueless about co-op opportunities.

A small market hardware store may insist advertising is irrelevant since the owner says he's the only outlet in town. A bright sales rep can remind him that hardware items are sold at drug stores, grocery stores, automotive supply retailers, and so on. Selling, as you can see, is often a follow-up requirement for copywriters and ad designers, especially for many entry-level positions filled by recent college graduates.

The enterprising sales rep will take an ad that's recently been prepared for a specific business owner who is not advertising (or not advertising enough). The goal is to sell more ads more frequently, if the employee wants to keep eating and making her car payments. That means the commissioned newspaper staffer needs to be familiar with the merchandise or service being offered by the local business. It also means establishing meaningful relationships with that customer. Keep track of birthdays and other personal data. Make non-selling calls at the retailer. Be a media consultant for the store owner. Shop there yourself.

Speculative ads could be designed in the newspaper office first thing in the morning, when it's probably too early to call on most clients. They are ready-to-run ads, subject to the business gatekeeper's approval. So doing your homework is essential. Know what services or products to promote in your spec ad. Creating a spec ad is not difficult. You already know the advertiser and the offerings. So let the prospect see an actual-size sample of the proposed ad in its finished format. Never assume the client won't be interested in your ad. Some enterprising reps will often create an ad slightly larger than they think the owner will buy. Better to slip down one notch than to cut your column inches (and your commission) in half.

A word of caution when presenting your spec ad: don't let the retailer squeeze six more items into your finished design. The advertiser may not appreciate the value of white space, for instance. You may instead attempt to line up a campaign with a series of ads, featuring the additional products. Spec ads can create long-term relationships between sales reps and local businesses, including that hardware store owner.

Exhibit 12.1

Again, you need to know what the agency's status is with the client. Strong? Precarious? Both the agency's senior management and the client will bring different eyes and a different attitude to the evaluation of your work depending on that relationship. If the relationship is a love-in, it's obviously an easier sell. However, if the client has reservations about the agency, then your work can be either a catalyst for improvement of the relationship or an excuse the client can use to beat up on the agency.

All this is about tone and purpose and positioning, and it's important for you to be aware of the selling environment. But the truth is that the heart of your sales pitch will be the same no matter what is going on among the players. Your strength is in the work you did, the research you considered, the thinking process that led you to the insight, and the talent you applied to the execution.

Never show advertising and then explain it. Explain it and *then* show it.

Walk your audience through the original assignment. Remind them of agreements along the way:

- What was the specific, measurable objective?
- Exactly whose behavior needs to be affected in order for that objective to be achieved?
- What does the prototypical person in that group think and do now?
- What do we want that person to think and do?
- What does that person want above all, relative to the product or service you're selling?
- What do we want that person to do?
- What will make him or her do that; what will his or her motivation be to take that action?

Make this person come alive. Make your audience see him or her.

Then, and only then, show the work. Walk them through how the person will experience the ad and respond to it, how the different elements work, why the visual is right, and how the headline enriches the message. Don't just read them the copy. Perform it.

Finally, explain how that process will convert into money flowing into the client's coffers. Leave no doubt that you (and your associates) believe totally in the work. Project complete confidence.

At the end of your presentation, never ask for questions. That suggests doubt. Never, ever invite comments on the creative. In your mind, it's already been approved.

When presenting to the agency senior management, move immediately to when you're scheduled to show the work to the client. Tell them who will be in the room, what everybody's role will be. Don't behave as though you're asking their permission or seeking their approval of the advertising; you're informing them. Ask them if there's anything you should know about the client; that's their area of expertise. Ask them if they have any suggestions about things you should be sure to do or say in the client presentation or if there are problems or people on the client side that you need to beware of. Get them talking about those issues and they won't feel compelled to "contribute" to the "improvement" of your work.

Similarly, when you're presenting the work to the client, immediately turn the conversation to the areas where they are expert, to their own business issues. Talk about placement, when the work will run and where.

"We're planning on the first ad appearing in the May issue of X magazine, which comes out in early April. Are we sure that the product will be on the shelves then? Will the stores have adequate inventory to supply the demand that these ads are going to create? Are there any production issues we should be aware of that might affect the timing? "

Again, don't leave any openings for them to comment on the creative. You've already made those decisions and those decisions are absolutely right. Move on to what's next.

Sell your work this way and what's next is honor and glory and gold.

Selling vs. the Competition by Content Analysis*

Advertising, of course, is about creativity. It's about the fun and the challenge of creating persuasive, memorable and clever images. But that's only part of it. Good advertising executives are not only "idea people," they're also keen observers.

In particular, advertising requires us to observe what our competitors are doing: Are they advertising as much as we are? Are they placing their ads in the same publications as us, or have they selected different periodicals? And how about their message—is it similar to ours, or does it take an entirely different approach? Maybe they're using humor, whereas we're taking a more traditional, straightforward approach that extols the qualities of our product.

*Source: *Dr. Dave Kaszuba, Susquehanna University*

Exercise

In keeping with the content analysis theme, choose a wide product category (perhaps automobiles, soft drinks or blue jeans) and examine several appropriate magazines that carry such ads. What variety did you find in the number and size of the ads? What general theme was employed in the various ads? Which brands seem to dominate? What about product-specific themes in your selected category? Create a simple chart that illustrates the comparisons you uncovered.

Only by sizing up the competition can we make informed judgments about our own tactics. Seeing what the "other guy" is doing provides a basis for comparison so that we can consider what elements of our competitors' strategy we wish to emulate, and more importantly, where and how we can work to set ourselves apart from the pack.

To formally assess how we stack up against the competition, we use a technique called **content analysis**. As the name implies, this involves analyzing media content to track the amount and types of advertising we are doing, in comparison to our competitors.

For example, we might keep track of some or all of the following:

The number of ads we run: In terms of sheer numbers, are we purchasing more or fewer ads than our competitors? If Coca-Cola notices that Pepsi has been running twice the number of magazine spots as Coke, then Coke had better consider whether it's advertising enough. In other words, is it keeping pace with its rival?

The prominence of the ads: Just because one cola company might have more ads, though, doesn't necessarily mean it has greater visibility. That's where prominence comes into play. Not all ads are created equal: Two dozen ads in a small, struggling magazine might not yield nearly the buzz as one ad in a nationally distributed, large circulation periodical. Therefore, the number of ads alone is not an effective indicator of advertising's effectiveness.

Aside from considering the number and types of readers an ad reaches, the prominence or visibility of advertising can be assessed by considering:

- The size of ads. Full-page ads are obviously more visible than half-page ads.
- The place, within a publication, that the ad appears. Does that ad appear alongside a magazine's most popular feature, where readers are likely to

turn? Is it on the back page of a magazine, where folks waiting in a doctor's office or a hair salon might see it, even if they don't open the magazine? Or does the ad appear inside the magazine, perhaps near content that is not particularly compelling?

- The place, on a page, that the ad appears. In newspapers, for example, ads that appear "above the fold" (i.e., on the top half of the page) are generally considered more prominent than those "below the fold."
- Use of color. Generally, advertisers pay more for color, reasoning that a color ad in a newspaper, for example, will be more striking and thus more prominent than a black-and-white advertisement. (Of course, in a full-color publication, one might argue that a black-and-white ad is more likely to capture interest because of its distinctiveness.)

The general themes in ads: Still another way that we can analyze content is to track the various themes that are employed in ads. Some ads focus on imparting information (e.g., "this car gets 40 miles per gallon of gas"), while others seek to conjure a mood (e.g., a person happily driving a car while listening to the stereo system and letting the wind rush through her hair), while still other ads lure readers by using humor, sex or shock value. Knowing what techniques a competitor uses might influence the approach we decide to take. In some cases, it may make sense to use the same tactic; that is, to go toe-to-toe with a rival. In other cases, we may look better by taking an entirely different approach—for example, taking the high road while your competition resorts to a message or image that smacks of bad taste.

The product-specific themes in ads: We can also track product-specific themes; in other words, what product characteristic does the ad emphasize: is it the product's dependability? Its attractive appearance? Its utility? Its association with a desired status or lifestyle? If it's a food, does the ad focus on the taste? The cost? Or on the convenience and speed associated with preparing the dish? If we sell frozen dinners by emphasizing how tasty they are—but see our competitor outdistancing our sales by running ads that instead trumpet the low-cost, no-fuss qualities of its frozen dinners—we might want to reconsider our strategy.

To perform a content analysis of ads, we might devise a chart like the following, which tracks our magazine advertising efforts compared to those of our two chief rivals.

	No. of ads	Circulation	Size	General Theme	Product Theme
Our Company	7	2–55,000 5–20,000 Avg.–30,000	2 full page	7 Information 2 full and 3 half	7 High quality, low cost
Competitor A	10	1–100,000 9–10,000 Avg.–19,000	10 half page	10 Information	5 High quality, low cost 5 Reputation/trust of brand
Competitor B	8	8–55,000 Avg.–55,000	4 full 4 half	6 Information 1 Mood (satisfaction) 1 Lifetime warranty 1 Humor	7 High quality, low cost

Having a chart like this gives us an instant snapshot of how our advertising stacks up against that of our competitors. Moreover, saving such charts allows us to look back and see how our advertising has evolved over time with respect to the strategies employed by our rivals. All in all, then, content analysis yields valuable, insightful information. It ensures that we are not devising our next ad campaign in a vacuum, without regard to what we and our competitors have done and are now doing. Content analysis reminds us that to move forward with the next winning ad, we must know where we've been, where we are, and what's around us in the form of competition. Only then can we pick the best course for our future, deciding how we want to mirror our competitors and how we want to set ourselves apart.

Recap

Ads that are finished still must be approved by internal agency supervisors and clients.

Speculative ads are ready-to-run ads shown by newspaper sales reps directly to retail managers in hopes they will buy the concept and the ad. Coupled with manufacturer-provided revenue, called co-op dollars, retailers can purchase ads and get reimbursed.

When presenting creative work to a client, first explain the targeted audience and desired action, then show the ad.

Often advertising is purchased to keep up or ahead of the competition. This is typically measured by content analysis of ads: frequency, size, placement, color, etc.

Chapter 13

Legal and Ethical Issues

> *"I saw a subliminal advertising executive, but only for a second."*
>
> Steven Wright
> Comedian

In Focus

✦ What is subliminal advertising?

✦ What are the legal implications of lottery advertising, misappropriation of personality, and model release forms?

✦ What are the prohibitions against the use of certain words or reproductions in print ads?

✦ What are the FTC's definitions of puffery and unfairness?

✦ What are the reasons for ethics codes?

✦ How widespread is sexism in print ads?

Whether you're a beginning advertising student, an entrepreneur, or a seasoned practitioner, you need to keep in mind what's ethical and what's legal on the advertising landscape. Often an issue will fit one category but not the other. Subliminal advertising—where the subconscious notices items in an ad, such as (usually female) body parts in ice cubes, that the naked eye does not see—is unethical if not illegal. No advertiser admits doing it.

Subliminal advertising is always an interesting topic of conversation, as evidenced by Steven Wright's opening joke. McDonald's even used the subliminal theme with in-store signage promoting its McSub sandwiches a few years ago. The colorful counter POPs playfully proclaimed:

THEY SAY
EVEN THE BEST
SUBLIMINAL
ADS
NEVER WORK.

Notepad

The "Sublime" 'Net

If you attempt an Internet search for subliminal advertising, prepare to have plenty of time on your hands. From movies to commercials to print ads, the charges are abundant with various examples to provide the evidence.

Academic research journals, trade publications, books, and mass media have covered the topic for decades. Try to find two or three of the most potent examples proving the existence of subliminal advertising. Is that enough to convince you about the presence of subliminal ads? Why or why not?

Vance Packard's *Hidden Persuaders* rocked the conventional world of the 1950s with exposes of how advertisers "manipulate" us into buying products or services through the use of subliminal forces. For years this hotly debated issue has been proven, disproven and back again as different interest groups attempted to make their cases. Even "Mr. Subliminal" was a popular routine on "Saturday Night Live" during the 1990s.

On one hand, every copywriter uses subliminal forces by attempting to push emotional triggers inherent in particular word choices, song titles or appeals. On the other hand, con-

NOTE: This chapter was written by Dr. Karen S. Sandell, associate dean of the graduate school and associate professor of social work at the University of North Carolina, Wilmington.

sciously manipulating subconscious forces or using techniques that make appeals invisible on the conscious level is clearly unethical.

A related trend in print advertising is the recent use of shadow ads, which are subtle gray logos submerged with text on a newspaper page. They often appear on stock market listings or sports agate pages. Blurring the line between news and editorial, shadow ads or watermark ads ignore the old maxim that disguised ads should be labeled. Most newspapers don't even have a policy about shadow ads.

Legal Concerns

Of course, it's vital to be aware of legal as well as ethical topics. Your clients, your ad agency, your publication, and your job depend on it. The Federal Trade Commission, established in 1914, targets false and deceptive advertising. It was originally designed to protect one business from another's deceptive advertising practices. Commercial-free speech is also regulated on the state and local levels. (Many states and cities ban billboards, you'll recall, from Chapter 10.) Statewide lottery advertising varies considerably, from being banned, to requiring notification of your miniscule odds of winning, to outright promotions of play and win. Internationally, China, as one example, bans all gambling ads.

Misappropriation of personality is the fancy term for illegally using someone's name, likeness, or voice without permission for commercial gain. A classic case often mentioned in textbooks involved Bette Midler, who declined to sing "Do You Wanna Dance?" for a Mercury television spot. So Ford's Mercury division and its agency went to one of her backup singers and arranged for her to perform the song in the Midler style. Needless to say, the star sued and won $400,000 for making it appear she was singing in the commercial.

On the local level, it's always wise to have signed model release forms on file before running an ad involving individuals, even if photographed in public areas. Such persons may be fair game for news photos, but not for ads intended to profit others.

Laws prohibit advertisements in which the phrases "Super Bowl," "Super Sunday," and "National Football League" appear. The NFL is quite diligent in protecting its logo and registered trademarks within any promotions or advertisements. So every winter, newspaper ad reps need to be cautious to screen retailer-provided ads for any violations of the policy. Even an Indianapolis church

Notepad

Puffery in Ads Avoids Regulation

The Federal Trade Commission considers puffery—a form of opinion statement such as "most manageable hair"—one topic that does not need to be regulated. A federal court has also applied such a legal ruling. The Better Business Bureau considers puffery to be subjective claims or personal evaluations, and not subject to tests of accuracy. Critics, however, claim the puffery defense creates a loophole for many deceptive claims. The FTC has defined puffery as claims that

1. reasonable people do not believe to be true product qualities; and
2. are incapable of being proved either true or false.

In addition to its power to regulate deceptiveness, the FTC also regulates unfair marketing practices. After more than 15 years of debate, the FTC incorporated a definition of unfairness into its own enabling act. The recent definition limits the application of the FTC's unfairness enforcement to an action or practice that

1. causes or is likely to cause substantial injury to consumers;
2. is not reasonably avoidable by consumers themselves; and
3. is not outweighed by countervailing benefits to consumers or to competition.

by Dr. Joseph Basso, J.D.,
Rowan University

was required to scale-down its 2007 Super Bowl party with a large-screen projection system after the NFL heard about its plans.

Another caution concerns the Olympic Games, rings, or other symbols in advertisements. Upset with guerilla marketing efforts to cash in on the event, the Olympic powers (and federal laws) require permission before any commercial use of such items.

The U.S. flag is one more symbol to avoid in ads, based on federal and state laws. "Although these types of statutes are rarely enforced, and raise significant constitutional issues, the PNA advises against using the flag in advertising and specifically against marking or writing on a flag in an ad," says Terri Henning, general counsel for the Pennsylvania Newspaper Association. "As an alternative, some newspapers use patriotic banners or streamers." Similarly, ads portraying U.S. presidents are prohibited.

Reproductions of U.S. dollars and Euro bills are regulated for print ads as well. Color reproduction had been prohibited, but is now allowed, if the size of the dollars is less than 75 percent or more than 150 percent of the original. As an assignment, try to look for such ads in magazines and newspapers to see if the dollars meet the legal size specifications. *USA Today* ran an illegal one for LaQuinta a few years ago, then quickly altered the $10 bill size for the next insertion when an astute reader's phone call alerted the ad staff about the requirement.

Speaking of reproductions, advertisers need to be wary of illegally using another company's trademarked item in their own ads. Even if you think Garfield would make an ideal spokescharacter for your pet store, you can't use a photo or illustration of the popular cartoon cat without written permission (and usually a hefty fee). Many local stores gamble with branded characters, hoping no one will notice or turn them in for such unlawful practice. It's often a painstakingly slow process to seek approval from the legal offices of major corporations. Our advice: forget it. Make your own cat the new mascot.

Political ads provide a quagmire of legal concerns. Many of them are based on state and local regulations, as well as individual publications' own codes. Almost all media, for example, require payment upfront, in case a losing candidate can't cover advertising expenses following the election. But other requirements concern citing who sponsored and paid for the ad, how close to the election it will accept advertising (to avoid sucker punch attack ads without time for rebuttals), and providing the same pricing structure to all candidates. An individual's state press association is a great source for updated legal advice around the political minefield.

Ethical Concerns

As mentioned at the start of Chapter 13, ads that are legal may not be ethical. That argument is not new. A 1923 advertising text, *Principles of Advertising*, by Daniel Starch, warns, "Examples of exaggeration can be found in almost any advertising medium. . . . Surely not all products of the same class can be the best or the finest."[1]

With the Web's ability to quickly share advertising mistakes with a worldwide audience, it pays to discern whether a questionable ad should run, even if it meets all legal requirements. Dr. Jef I. Richards, J.D., professor in The University of Texas Department of Advertising, summarizes the point well: "If it's not done ethically, advertising won't be trusted. If consumers don't trust it, advertising is pointless." An ethical advertising practitioner wants to help readers become discerning consumers of all ad messages.

The term *ethics* refers to principles that determine whether actions are right or wrong, proper or improper. Ethics are culturally bound so that what is viewed as good or just in one society may be viewed as heinous by another. For example, in the United States many people view the death penalty as appropriate punishment when egregious acts have been committed that violate existing laws, and perpetrators have been found guilty of such acts through due process. Other countries may view the death penalty as barbaric.

Many professions and publications ascribe to codes of ethics that guide professional behavior. These codes do not determine a single "right" course of action, but give us a way to evaluate and decide among competing options. In other words, codes of conduct offer professionals guidance on ethical conduct, that is, what is viewed as right and good. These guidelines prove helpful in determining the proper course of action when questionable ads are being submitted by clients, or being written or designed for clients.

The American Association of Advertising Agencies (AAAA) promotes a set of professional practice standards that was first adopted in 1924. Called the "Creative Code," it's based on the "belief that sound and ethical practice is good business." (You can find it and other AAAA information at www.aaaa.org/EWEB/upload/inside/standards.pdf.)

The code defines ethical conduct by stating that members cannot knowingly create claims that include:

1. False or misleading statements or exaggerations, visual or verbal.
2. Testimonials that do not reflect the real opinion of the individual(s) involved.
3. Price claims that are misleading.
4. Claims insufficiently supported or that distort the true meaning or practicable application of statements made by professional or scientific authority.
5. Statements, suggestions or pictures offensive to public decency or minority segments of the population.

AAAA recognizes that agencies operate in a competitive environment and there will be differences of interpretation and judgment in applying the code in the real world of practice. Nevertheless, the association states that its members ". . . agree not to recommend to an advertiser, and to discourage the use of, advertising that is in poor or questionable taste or that is deliberately irritating through aural or visual content or presentation." The association and other professional groups aim to help discerning consumers so that they can identify unethical and false advertising claims.

Sexism in Print Ads

It is this last statement as well as point number five above that have the most relevance to the issue of sexism in print advertisements. More specifically, how is it that an industry that has certain ethical standards is seen increasingly as creating a cultural environment that is "toxic" toward women? Sexploitation in advertising is emphasized in this chapter because its practice continues long after other advertising ills—racism, for example—have shown considerable signs of improving. Men, infrequently, are also the target of sexism in advertising. The clothing catalogs for Abercrombie and Fitch, among others, provide plenty of such examples. The focus here is primarily on females. They are the ones—whose ideal beauty and shape are unrealistically depicted in many ads—suffering from eating and psychological disorders.

Dr. Jean Kilbourne, author and lecturer, has been an ad critic for many years. She has focused particular attention on images of women in print advertising. She calls the encroachment of advertising in media, education and public spaces a "toxic cultural environment" and the focus on advertising aimed at women as "toxic" marketing. By this she means the "central message of advertising has to be that we are what we buy. And perhaps what is most insidious about this is that it takes very human, very real feelings and desires such as the need to love and be loved, the need for authentic connection, the need for meaningful work, for respect, and it yokes these feelings to products. It tells us that our ability to attain love depends upon our attractiveness."[2]

The model in Exhibit 13.1 illustrates how female bodies are often depicted in ads. That topic is the main theme in Kilbourne's video, "Slim Hopes: Advertising and the Obsession with Thinness."

The Center for Media Literacy, a nonprofit organization, offers information on the more subtle ways advertising reinforces cultural values of subservience, domination, and inequality between the sexes through tactics that include:

1. **Superiority**. This is done through size, attention, and positioning. Women may be positioned below or behind their male partners in order to appear subservient.

Exhibit 13.1 Obsession with Thin

The ultra-thin, almost boyish-looking female in Exhibit 13.1 is portrayed in a sexually provocative pose. We see her from above, a position that suggests subjugation to the male gaze. She seems to be floating on water and her legs are spread in a way that is sexually suggestive. Her hips and pubic area are highlighted. Her arms and legs are bent. Altogether the message is that this woman is waiting for something other than swimming to happen to her in her Gucci bikini.

2. **Dismemberment**. Women's bodies are often dismembered and treated as separate parts, perpetuating the concept that a woman's body is not connected to her mind and emotions. The hidden message? If a woman has great legs, who cares who she is?

3. **Clowning**. Shown alone in ads, men are often portrayed as secure, powerful, and serious. In contrast, women are pictured as playful clowns, perpetuating the attitude that women are childish and cannot be taken seriously.

4. **Canting**. People in control of their lives stand upright and ready to meet the world. The bending of body parts conveys preparedness, submissiveness, and appeasement. A picture of a woman with her upraised hand in front of her face conveys shame and embarrassment.

5. **Dominance/Violence**. Advertisements that use slogans and pictures that depict women being physically attacked glorify the violence that occurs against women every day. Furthermore, some advertisements inadvertently condone violence against children by using sexualized images of minors.

Kilbourne notes that unrealistic and unhealthy images in ads have a great power over consumers. Otherwise, she asks, why would companies spend over $200 billion a year on advertising? For example, the diet industry particularly focuses on girls, creating an obsession with thinness and sending a message to them they "need to be cut down to size, they should not be too powerful, and they should diminish themselves by being less than what they are."[3]

A study done by Brigham and Women's Hospital found "the more time a teen girl spends reading fashion magazines, the worse she feels about herself…and that's just how marketers like it. A girl feeling unattractive, overweight, and in dire need of a boyfriend is more likely to respond favorably to the countless products that promise to correct her flaws, slim her down, and prime her for romance." [4]

Ads that show girls being silenced often show images of young women with their hands over their mouths or, as in one ad, by having their mouths sewn shut. Beyond images of physical violence where women are tied up, have black eyes, or are shown as being dominated, emotional violence in advertisements sends messages that emotional intimacy is not a good thing, or that women are in competition for male attention. Kilbourne explains that "when young girls hit adolescence, at a time when they most need support from each other, they are encouraged to turn on each other in competition for men. It's tragic, because the truth is that one of the most powerful antidotes to destructive cultural messages is close and supportive female friendships." Kilbourne adds, "Ads sell a great deal more than products.

Notepad

Try This

Select ads from this Web site: www.about-face.org/ (Gallery of Offenders for sexist ads) or use ads of your choice to represent other marginalized groups, such as the elderly, different racial/ethnic groups, overweight people, people with disabilities, unattractive people, etc.:

1. What are the **attributes** of this ad? What are the **benefits**? How do they **differ**?
2. Who is the **target audience** for this ad? Discuss the particular aspects of this ad that led you to that conclusion.
3. How might this ad reinforce unrealistic cultural images, such as using young, ultra-thin, scantily clad Caucasian women to sell this product or service?
4. How might this ad play into stereotypes that portray certain groups in very limited and unflattering ways?

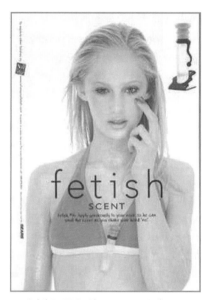

Exhibit 13.2 Glamorizing Violence

They sell values, images, and concepts or success and worth, love and sexuality, popularity and normalcy. They tell us who we are and who we should be." [5]

Ad after ad implies that girls and women don't really mean "no" when they say it, that women are only teasing when they resist men's advances. This perfume ad, running in several teen magazines, features a young woman, with eyes blackened by makeup or perhaps something else, and the copy, "Apply generously to your neck so he can smell the scent as you shake your head 'no.' " In other words, he'll understand you don't really mean it, and he can respond to the scent like any other animal. (by Jean Kilbourne)[6]

Several research studies have confirmed sexist messages are still being developed worldwide by contemporary advertising, although there has been some improvement recently. Common themes include:

1. Women are rarely seen in executive positions or making important decisions; decisions are typically simple and inexpensive ones concerning household purchases.
2. Women still portray the traditional homemaker roles of mothers and housewives.
3. Women are dependent upon men for all their needs.
4. Women are usually viewed as sex objects void of personalities.

Kilbourne reports there have been some changes in the images of women in recent years. The new woman is generally presented as a superwoman, who manages to do all the work at home and on the job (with the help of a product, of course, not of her husband or children or friends), or as the liberated woman, who owes her independence and self-esteem to the products she uses. These new images do not represent any real progress but rather create a myth of progress, an illusion that reduces complex sociopolitical problems to mundane personal ones.[7]

Certainly other offensive ads typically rile readers. Racist ads, fortunately, are much rarer than in past years, when unflattering caricatures were fairly common. Ageism is another issue still being fought in the advertising wars. Senior citizens are not universally ready for adult diapers, hearing aids, and walkers. Almost all responsible marketers now realize that a majority of older adults are still active consumers (with time, money, and AARP clout), and deserve to be treated with respect.

Why Be Ethical?

In our examination of values and ethics in advertising, we see the mandate to avoid offensive representations is increasingly in conflict with many of the depictions of women in print advertising. How does this represent a value conflict? Does this mean that some practitioners in the advertising industry rank their desires to be rich, recognized, or held in high esteem within their profession over their values of being honest, caring, and respectful toward others? And, if this is so, how can the industry move to eliminate images and representations of women that are demeaning and in conflict with professional practice standards while allowing advertisers to remain profitable?

The nonprofit Josephson Institute of Ethics (www.josephsoninstitute.org,) identifies several reasons for advertising practitioners to behave ethically, including:

1. There is inner benefit. Virtue is its own reward.
2. There is personal advantage. It is prudent to be ethical. It's good business.
3. There is approval. Being ethical leads to self-esteem, the admiration of loved ones, and the respect of peers.
4. There is religion. Good behavior can please or help serve a deity.
5. There is habit. Ethical actions can fit in with upbringing or training.

There are also obstacles to acting ethically. The ethic of self-interest is particularly salient. When our decision to act ethically is based on our own self-interest, making decisions can be reduced to estimations of risks and rewards. For example, if an ethical person is thinking about becoming a whistleblower at an ad agency, the consideration of potential negative consequences, such as losing a job or being sued, is likely to affect one's behavior. Or, if the risks from unethical behavior are low and the rewards are high, people may behave unethically based on their calculations that they have a good chance of not being caught. In such cases, moral principles can succumb to expediency. This issue is not a small one. All of us have known people who cheated on an exam or put incorrect information on a resume to make themselves look better.

Ethics is about putting our most cherished values of conduct into action. It is about being consistent between what we say and what we do. Reduced to its most basic principle, acting ethically is a matter of integrity. As current or future professionals it is important for you to assess what your core values are and how you might act when you are faced with an ethical situation. At the end of the day, the real test of our ethics is whether we are willing to do the right thing even when it is not in our self-interest.

Recap

Subliminal ads are unethical ones that supposedly contain objects that appear to the subconscious, rather than the naked eye.

Legal trouble will occur if one is not aware of federal and state laws regarding lottery ads, using one's likeness in an ad without permission (called misappropriation of personality) and model releases.

Astute copywriters need to be aware of such prohibitions as using in ads NFL or Super Bowl phrases, Olympic symbols, the U.S. flag, and U.S. paper currency and Euros. Political advertising, likewise, has regulations concerning naming its sponsor.

The Federal Trade Commission allows puffery (subjective claims by an advertiser) but protects consumers from unfair ad practices.

Despite industrywide improvement in ethics, sexist advertising is still more common than many believe.

Notes

1. Daniel Starch, *Principles of Advertising.* Chicago: A.W. Shaw Company, 1923, p. 438.
2. J. L. Pozner, "You're Soaking In It." *Salon.com.* Retrieved Dec. 8, 2007, from *www.archive.salon.com/mwt/feature/tues/2001/01/30/kilbourne/index4.html*
3. Ibid.
4 . C. Peters, "Teen girls, sexism, and marketeering." *ZNetDailyCommentaries.* Retrieved Aug. 8, 2007, from *www.zmag.org/ZSustainers/ZDaily/1999-03/mar_16peters.htm.*
5. J. L. Pozner, "You're Soaking In It." *Salon.com.*
6. Clea Simon, "Hooked on Advertising." *Ms.com.* Retrieved Dec. 8, 2007, from *www.msmagazine.com/jan01/hooked_jan01.html.*
7 . Center for Media Literacy. "Sexist advertisements: How to See Through the Soft Sell." Retrieved Dec. 8, 2007, from www.medialit.org/reading_room/article41.html.

For Further Reading

Anthony J. Cortese, *Provocateur: Images of Women and Minorities in Advertising.* Lanham, MD: Rowman & Littlefield, 2004.

Marilyn Kern-Foxworth, *Aunt Jemima, Uncle Ben, and Rastus: Blacks in Advertising, Yesterday, Today and Tomorrow.* Westport, CT: Greenwood Press, 1994.

Don Pember and Clay Calvert, *Mass Media Law: 2007-2008.* New York: Mc-Graw-Hill, 2007.

Robert Trager, Joseph Russomanno and Susan Dente Ross, *The Law of Journalism and Mass Communication.* New York: McGraw-Hill, 2007.

About the Authors

RANDY HINES is a professor in the Communications Department at Susquehanna University. He has received three professor of the year awards during his 25-year teaching career. His doctorate is from Texas A&M in public relations, a profession in which he has obtained universal accreditation (APR). He has a B.A. and an M.A. in journalism from Kent State University. He also earned an M.Div. at Bethel Theological Seminary.

Prior to joining Susquehanna in 2002, he taught in the University of North Carolina system, where he served as chair of the Mass Communications Department at UNC-Pembroke.

He has also taught at East Tennessee State University and Kent State University. He has been active in the American Advertising Federation, starting a chapter at ETSU where he also served in the local AAF professional chapter, holding several positions, including first vice-president.

His consulting work has included such clients as: American Water Heater Company,

Creative Energy, Doe River Gorge Conference Center, Duke University, Eastman Chemical, Georgia Press Association, Hotel Günther, Johnson City Medical Center, Mid-Atlantic Newspaper Advertising Marketing Executives, New England Newspaper Association, Nuclear Fuel Services, Siemens, Sire Advertising, Tennessee Press Association and Wyoming Press Association.

He publishes articles in various consumer, professional and academic publications. Since 1993 he has written monthly columns for 20 state press associations. He is also a regular columnist for the Southern Newspaper Press Association.

He is lead co-author of *The Writer's Toolbox: A Comprehensive Guide for PR and Business Communication* (Kendall/Hunt, 2005). He also co-authored *Feeling at Home in God's Family* in 2006 with Dr. Stewart Brown

Locally, he provides pro bono services for regional nonprofits and serves as copy editor of *Susquehanna Life Magazine*.

ROBERT LAUTERBORN is the James L. Knight Professor of Advertising in the UNC-Chapel Hill School of Journalism and Mass Communication, a distinguished chair made possible by a million-dollar grant from the Knight Foundation "to improve the teaching of advertising."

Bob is a co-author of the best-selling book *Integrated Marketing Communication: Pulling It Together and Making It Work* (NTC, 1993), now translated into 13 languages.

Prior to joining academia, Lauterborn was Director of Marketing Communication & Corporate Advertising for International Paper worldwide. He also spent 16 years with General Electric, principally in creative functions. As creative director of GE's 400-person house agency, he developed the FOCUS approach to improve creative performance and consistency across the group's 15 U.S. and overseas offices.

In 2004, he was named "Advertising Educator of the Year" by Advertising Club of the Triangle, which set up two scholarships in his name, and in 2005 he received the Silver Medal Award, the American Advertising Federation's highest honor.

Always active in the industry, he has been vice chairman of the Association of National Advertisers, chairman of the Business Marketing Association International and the Business Advertising Research Council, and a board member of several organizations, including the Advertising Research Foundation.

In 1999, he was presented with the G.D. Crain, Jr. Award (named after the founder of Advertising Age) for "lifetime contributions to the development and improvement of business marketing," and inducted into the Business Marketing Hall of Fame.

Over the past dozen years, he has consulted or conducted seminars and workshops for more than 50 organizations in 21 countries on five continents, including IBM, General Motors, ExxonMobil, Hewlett Packard, Monsanto, AT&T, Bank of America, BASF, Kellogg's, Eli Lilly and Philips.

American Advertising Federation (AAF)

Advertising Ethics and Principles*

Truth
Advertising shall tell the truth, and shall reveal significant facts, the omission of which would mislead the public.

Substantiation
Advertising claims shall be substantiated by evidence in possession of the advertiser and advertising agency, prior to making such claims.

Comparisons
Advertising shall refrain from making false, misleading, or unsubstantiated statements or claims about a competitor or his/her products or services.

Bait Advertising
Advertising shall not offer products or services for sale unless such offer constitutes a bona fide effort to sell the advertised products or services and is not a device to switch consumers to other goods or services, usually higher priced.

Guarantees and Warranties
Advertising of guarantees and warranties shall be explicit, with sufficient information to apprise consumers of their principal terms and limitations or, when space or time restrictions preclude such disclosures, the advertisement should clearly reveal where the full text of the guarantee or warranty can be examined before purchase.

Price Claims
Advertising shall avoid price claims that are false or misleading, or saving claims that do not offer provable savings.

Testimonials
Advertising containing testimonials shall be limited to those of competent witnesses who are reflecting a real and honest opinion or experience.

Taste And Decency
Advertising shall be free of statements, illustrations, or implications which are offensive to good taste or public decency.

*Most recent version, adopted by the American Advertising Federation Board of Directors, March 2, 1984, San Antonio, Texas.
http://www.aaaa.org/EWEB/upload/inside/standards.pdf

The Power of the Printed Word

An Award-Winning Advertising Campaign
Prepared by Ogilvy & Mather
for its client, International Paper Company

The Power of the Printed Word

Publishers, to be successful, need an audience—people who *read*.

Unfortunately, young Americans are losing their ability to read and write well.

Our strategy for our International Paper client was: to try to build a strong future audience for publishers of books, magazines and newspapers by helping young people—high school and college students and recent graduates—read and write better; to help them feel comfortable with and make more and better use of *the printed word*.

This way, International Paper would demonstrate its commitment to its publishing customers, and at the same time help, if even in a small way, to turn around the major literacy problem facing our nation.

The campaign has hit a responsive chord. For the three years it has been running, International Paper has averaged a thousand letters a day commenting on the advertising or requesting reprints. To date, more than eleven million have been sent out.

It was this overwhelming reaction to the series that encouraged us to put reprints of the articles together in this booklet.

We hope you will enjoy reading the twelve articles which have been produced so far. You might also know some young person who could use this booklet to advantage. Let us know if you would like extra copies.

At Ogilvy *&* Mather, we too believe in the power of the printed word.

How to write a business letter

Some thoughts from Malcolm Forbes

President and Editor-in-Chief of Forbes Magazine

International Paper asked Malcolm Forbes to share some things he's learned about writing a good business letter. One rule, "Be crystal clear."

A good business letter can get you a job interview.

Get you off the hook.

Or get you money.

It's totally asinine to blow your chances of getting *whatever* you want—with a business letter that turns people off instead of turning them on.

The best place to learn to write is in school. If you're still there, pick your teachers' brains.

If not, big deal. I learned to ride a motorcycle at 50 and fly balloons at 52. It's never too late to learn.

Over 10,000 business letters come across my desk every year. They seem to fall into three categories: stultifying if not stupid, mundane (most of them), and first rate (rare). Here's the approach

I've found that separates the winners from the losers (most of it's just good common sense)—it starts *before* you write your letter:

Know what you want

If you don't, write it down—in one sentence. "I want to get an interview within the next two weeks." That simple.

List the major points you want to get across—it'll keep you on course.

If you're *answering* a letter, check the points that need answering and keep the letter in front of you while you write. This way you won't forget anything—*that* would cause another round of letters.

And for goodness' sake, answer promptly if you're going to answer at all. Don't sit on a letter—*that* invites the person on the other end to sit on whatever you want from *him*.

Plunge right in

Call him by name—not "Dear Sir, Madam, or Ms." "Dear Mr. Chrisanthopoulos"—and be sure to spell it right. That'll get him (thus, you) off to a good start.

(Usually, you can get his name just by phoning his company—or from a business directory in your nearest library.)

Tell what your letter is about in the first paragraph. One or two sentences. Don't keep your reader guessing or he might file your letter away—even before he finishes it.

In the round file.

If you're answering a letter, refer to the date

it was written. So the reader won't waste time hunting for it.

People who read business letters are as human as thee and me. Reading a letter shouldn't be a chore—*reward* the reader for the time he gives you.

Write so he'll enjoy it

Write the entire letter from his point of view—what's in it for *him*? Beat him to the draw—surprise him by answering the questions and objections he might have.

Be positive—he'll be more receptive to what you have to say.

Be nice. Contrary to the cliché, genuinely nice guys most often finish first or very near it. I admit it's not easy when you've got a gripe. To be agreeable while disagreeing—that's an art.

Be natural—write the way you talk. Imagine him sitting in front of you—what would you *say* to him?

Business jargon too often is cold, stiff, unnatural.

Suppose I came up to you and said, "I acknowledge receipt of your letter and I beg to thank you." You'd think, "Huh? You're putting me on."

The acid test—read your letter *out loud* when you're done. You

"Be natural. Imagine him sitting in front of you—what would you say to him?"

might get a shock—but you'll know for sure if it sounds natural.

Don't be cute or flippant. The reader won't take you seriously. This doesn't mean you've got to be dull. You prefer your letter to knock 'em dead rather than bore 'em to death.

Three points to remember:

Have a sense of humor. That's refreshing *anywhere*—a nice surprise in a business letter.

Be specific. If I tell you there's a new fuel that could save gasoline, you might not believe me. But suppose I tell you this:

"Gasohol"—10% alcohol, 90% gasoline—works as well as straight gasoline. Since you can make alcohol from grain or corn stalks, wood or wood waste, coal— even garbage, it's worth some real follow-through.

Now you've got something to sink your teeth into.

Lean heavier on nouns and verbs, lighter on adjectives. Use the active voice instead of the passive. Your writing will have more guts.

Which of these is stronger? Active voice: "I kicked out my money manager." Or, passive voice: "My money manager was kicked out by me." (By the way, neither is true. My son, Malcolm Jr., manages most Forbes money—he's a brilliant moneyman.)

"I learned to ride a motorcycle at 50 and fly balloons at 52. It's never too late to learn anything."

Give it the best you've got

When you don't want something enough to make *the* effort, making *an* effort is a waste.

Make your letter look appetizing —or you'll strike out before you even get to bat. Type it—on good-quality 8½" x 11" stationery. Keep it neat. And use paragraphing that makes it easier to read.

Keep your letter short—to one page, if possible. Keep your paragraphs short. After all, who's going to benefit if your letter is quick and easy to read?

You.

For emphasis, underline impor-

tant words. And sometimes indent sentences as well as paragraphs.

Like this. See how well it works? (But save it for something special.)

Make it perfect. No typos, no misspellings, no factual errors. If you're sloppy and let mistakes slip by, the person reading your letter will think you don't know better or don't care. Do you?

Be crystal clear. You won't get what you're after if your reader doesn't get the message.

Use good English. If you're still in school, take all the English and writing courses you can. The way you write and speak can really help —or *hurt*.

If you're not in school (even if you are), get the little 71-page gem by Strunk & White, *Elements of Style*. It's in paperback. It's fun to read and loaded with tips on good English and good writing.

Don't put on airs. Pretense invariably impresses only the pretender.

Don't exaggerate. Even once. Your reader will suspect everything else you write.

Distinguish opinions from facts. Your opinions may be the best in the world. But they're not gospel. You owe it to your reader to let him know which is which. He'll appreciate it and he'll admire you. The dumbest people I know are those who Know It All.

Be honest. It'll get you further in the long run. If you're not, you won't rest easy until you're

found out. (The latter, not speaking from experience.)

Edit ruthlessly. Somebody ~~has~~ said that words are ~~a lot~~ like inflated money—the more ~~of them that~~ you use, the less each one ~~of them~~ is worth. ~~Right on.~~ Go through your entire letter ~~just~~ as many times as it takes. ~~Search out and~~ **A**nnihilate all unnecessary words, ~~and~~ sentences—even ~~entire~~ *paragraphs*.

"Don't exaggerate. Even once. Your reader will suspect everything else you write."

Sum it up and get out

The last paragraph should tell the reader exactly what you want *him* to do—or what *you're* going to do. Short and sweet. "May I have an appointment? Next Monday, the 16th, I'll call your secretary to see when it'll be most convenient for you."

Close with something simple like, "Sincerely." And for heaven's sake sign legibly. The biggest ego trip I know is a completely illegible signature.

Good luck.

I hope you get what you're after.

Sincerely,

Malcolm S. Forbes

How to improve your vocabulary

By Tony Randall

International Paper asked Tony Randall—who is on The American Heritage Dictionary Usage Panel, and loves words almost as much as acting—to tell how he has acquired his enormous vocabulary.

Words can make us laugh, cry, go to war, fall in love.

Rudyard Kipling called words the most powerful drug of mankind. If they are, I'm a hopeless addict—and I hope to get you hooked, too!

Whether you're still in school or you head up a corporation, the better command you have of words, the better chance you have of saying exactly what you mean, of understanding what others mean—and of getting what you want in the world.

English is the richest language —with the largest vocabulary on earth. Over 1,000,000 words!

You can express shades of meaning that aren't even *possible* in other languages. (For example, you can differentiate between "sky" and "heaven." The French, Italians and Spanish cannot.)

Yet, the average adult has a vocabulary of only 30,000 to 60,000 words. Imagine what we're missing!

Here are five pointers that help me learn—and remember— whole *families* of words at a time.

They may not *look* easy—and

won't be at first. But if you stick with them you'll find they *work!*

What's the first thing to do when you see a word you don't know?

1. Try to guess the meaning of the word from the way it's used

You can often get at least *part* of a word's meaning—just from how it's used in a sentence.

That's why it's so important to read as much as you can— different *kinds* of things: magazines, books, newspapers you don't normally read. The more you *expose* yourself to new words, the more words you'll pick up *just by seeing how they're used.*

For instance, say you run across the word "manacle":

> "The manacles had been on John's wrists for 30 years. Only one person had a key— his wife."

You have a good *idea* of what "manacles" are—just from the context of the sentence.

But let's find out *exactly* what the word means and where it comes from. The only way to do this, and to build an extensive vocabulary *fast*, is to go to the dictionary. (How lucky, you *can*— Shakespeare *couldn't*. There *wasn't* an English dictionary in his day!)

So you go to the dictionary. (NOTE: Don't let dictionary abbreviations put you off. The front tells you what they mean, and even has a guide to pronunciation.)

2. Look it up

Here's the definition for "manacle" in *The American Heritage*

Dictionary of the English Language.

man-a-cle (mǎn'ə-kəl) *n.* Usually plural. **1.** A device for confining the hands, usually consisting of two metal rings that are fastened about the wrists and joined by a metal chain; a handcuff. **2.** Anything that confines or restrains.—*tr. v.* **manacled, -cling, -cles. 1.** To restrain with manacles. **2.** To confine or restrain as if with manacles; shackle; fetter. [Middle English *manicle*, from Old French, from Latin *manicula*, little hand, handle, diminutive of *manus*, hand. See **man-²** in Appendix.*]

The first definition fits here: A device for confining the hands, usually consisting of two metal rings that are fastened about the wrists and joined by a metal chain.

Well, that's what you *thought* it meant. But what's the idea *behind* the word? What are its *roots?* To really understand a word, you need to know.

Here's where the detective work—and the *fun*—begins.

3. Dig the meaning out by the roots

The root is the basic part of the word—its heritage, its origin. (Most of our roots come from

"Your main clue to remembering a word is its root—its origin."

"'Emancipate' has a Latin root. Learn it and you'll know other words at a glance."

Latin and Greek words at least 2,000 years old—which come from even earlier Indo-European tongues!)

Learning the roots: 1) Helps us *remember* words. 2) Gives us a deeper understanding of the words we *already* know. And 3) allows us to pick up whole families of *new* words at a time. That's why learning the root is the *most important part of going to the dictionary.*

Notice the root of "manacle" is *manus* (Latin) meaning "hand."

Well, that makes sense. Now, other words with this root, <u>man</u>, start to make sense, too.

Take <u>manual</u>—something done "by hand" (<u>man</u>ual labor) or a "handbook." And <u>man</u>age—to "handle" something (as a <u>man</u>ager). When you e<u>man</u>cipate someone, you're taking him "from the hands of" someone else.

When you <u>man</u>ufacture something, you "make it by hand" (in its original meaning).

And when you finish your first novel, your publisher will see your—originally "handwritten"—<u>man</u>uscript.

Imagine! A whole new world of words opens up—just from one simple root!

The root gives the *basic* clue to the meaning of a word. But there's another important clue that runs a close second—the *prefix.*

4. Get the powerful prefixes under your belt

A prefix is the part that's sometimes attached to the front of a word. Like—well, *prefix!* There aren't many—less than 100 major prefixes—and you'll learn them in no time at all just by becoming more aware of the meanings of words you already know. Here are a few. (Some of the "How-to" vocabulary-building

books will give you the others.)

PREFIX		MEANING	EXAMPLES	
(Lat.)	(Gk.)			(Literal sense)
com, con, co, col, cor	sym, syn, syl	with, very, together	conform	(form with)
			sympathy	(feeling with)
in, im, il, ir	a, an	not, without	innocent	(not wicked)
			amorphous	(without form)
contra, counter	anti, ant	against, opposite	contravene	(come against)
			antidote	(give against)

Now, see how the *prefix* (along with the context) helps you get the meaning of the italicized words:

• "If you're going to be my witness, your story must <u>corr</u>oborate my story." (The literal meaning of *corroborate* is "strength together.")

• "You told me one thing—now you tell me another. Don't <u>contra</u>dict yourself." (The literal meaning of *contradict* is "say against".)

• "Oh, that snake's not poisonous. It's a completely <u>in</u>nocuous little garden snake." (The literal meaning of *innocuous* is "not harmful".)

Now, you've got some new words. What are you going to do with them?

5. Put your new words to work at once

Use them several times the first day you learn them. Say them out loud! Write them in sentences.

Should you "use" them on *friends?* Careful—you don't want them to think you're a stuffed shirt. (It depends on the situation. You *know* when a word sounds natural—and when it sounds stuffy.)

How about your *enemies?* You have my blessing. Ask one of them

if he's read that article on pneumonoultramicroscopicsilicovolcanoconiosis. (You really can find it in the dictionary.) Now, you're one up on him.

So what do you do to improve your vocabulary?

Remember: 1) Try to guess the meaning of the word from the way it's used. 2) Look it up. 3) Dig the meaning out by the roots. 4) Get the powerful prefixes under your belt. 5) Put your new words to work at once.

That's all there is to it—you're off on your treasure hunt.

Now, do you see why I love words so much?

Aristophanes said, "By words, the mind is excited and the spirit elated." It's as true today as it was

"The more words you know, the more you can use. What does 'corroborate' really mean? See the text."

when he said it in Athens—2,400 years ago!

I hope you're now like me—hooked on words forever.

Tony Randall

How to read faster

By Bill Cosby

International Paper asked Bill Cosby—who earned his doctorate in education and has been involved in projects which help people learn to read faster—to share what he's learned about reading more in less time.

When I was a kid in Philadelphia, I must have read every comic book ever published. (There were fewer of them then than there are now.)

I zipped through all of them in a couple of days, then reread the good ones until the next issues arrived.

Yes indeed, when I was a kid, the reading game was a snap.

But as I got older, my eyeballs must have slowed down or something! I mean, comic books started to pile up faster than my brother Russell and I could read them!

It wasn't until much later, when I was getting my doctorate, I realized it wasn't my eyeballs that were to blame. Thank goodness. They're still moving as well as ever.

The problem is, there's too much to read these days, and too little time to read every word of it.

Now, mind you, I still read comic books. In addition to contracts, novels, and newspapers. Screenplays, tax returns and correspondence. Even textbooks about how people read. And which techniques help people read more in less time.

I'll let you in on a little secret. There are hundreds of techniques you could learn to help you read

faster. But I know of 3 that are especially good.

And if I can learn them, so can you—and you can put them to use *immediately*.

They are commonsense, practical ways to get the meaning from printed words quickly and efficiently. So you'll have time to enjoy your comic books, have a good laugh with Mark Twain or a good cry with *War and Peace*. Ready?

Okay. The first two ways can help you get through tons of reading material—fast—*without reading every word*.

They'll give you the *overall meaning* of what you're reading. And let you cut out an awful lot of *unnecessary* reading.

1. Preview—if it's long and hard

Previewing is especially useful for getting a general idea of heavy reading like long magazine or newspaper articles, business reports, and nonfiction books.

It can give you as much as half the comprehension in as little as one tenth the time. For example, you should be able to preview eight or ten 100-page reports in an hour. After previewing, you'll be able to decide which reports (or which *parts* of which reports) are worth a closer look.

<u>Here's how to preview:</u> Read the entire first two paragraphs of whatever you've chosen. Next read only the *first sentence of* each successive paragraph.

"Learn to read faster and you'll have time for a good laugh with Mark Twain—and a good cry with War and Peace."

Then read the entire last two paragraphs.

Previewing doesn't give you all the details. But it does keep you from spending time on things you don't really want—or need—to read.

Notice that previewing gives you a quick, overall view of *long, unfamiliar* material. For short, light reading, there's a better technique.

2. Skim—if it's short and simple

Skimming is a good way to get a general idea of light reading—like popular magazines or the sports and entertainment sections of the paper.

You should be able to skim a weekly popular magazine or the second section of your daily paper in less than *half* the time it takes you to read it now.

Skimming is also a great way to review material you've read before.

<u>Here's how to skim:</u> Think of your eyes as magnets. Force them to move fast. Sweep them across each and every line of type. Pick up *only a few key words in each line*.

Everybody skims differently.

You and I may not pick up exactly the same words when we skim the same piece, but we'll both get a pretty similar idea of what it's all about.

To show you how it works, I circled the words I picked out when I skimmed the following story. Try it. It shouldn't take you more than 10 seconds.

My brother Russell thinks monsters live in our bedroom closet at night. But I told him he is crazy. "Go and check then," he said. I didn't want to. Russell said I was chicken.

"Am not," I said.

"Are so," he said.

So I told him the monsters were going to eat him at midnight. He started to cry. My Dad came in and told the monsters to beat it. Then he told us to go to sleep.

"If I hear any more about monsters," he said, "I'll spank you." We went to sleep fast. And you know something? They never did come back.

Skimming can give you a very good idea of this story in about half

'Read with a good light—and with as few friends as possible to help you out. No TV, no music. It'll help you concentrate better—and read faster.''

the words—and in *less* than half the time it'd take to read every word.

So far, you've seen that previewing and skimming can give you a *general idea* about content—fast. But neither technique can promise more than 50 percent comprehension, because you aren't reading all the words. (Nobody gets something for nothing in the reading game.)

To *read faster and understand most*—if not all—of what you read, you need to know a third technique.

3. Cluster—to increase speed and comprehension

Most of us learned to read by looking at each word in a sentence—*one at a time.*

Like this:

My—brother—Russell—thinks—monsters...

You probably still read this way sometimes, especially when the words are difficult. Or when the words have an extra-special meaning—as in a poem, a Shakespearean

play, or a contract. And that's O.K.

But word-by-word reading is a rotten way to read faster. It actually *cuts down* on your speed.

Clustering trains you to look at *groups* of words instead of one at a time—to increase your speed enormously. For most of us, clustering is a *totally different way of seeing what we read.*

Here's how to cluster: Train your eyes to see *all* the words in clusters of up to 3 or 4 words at a glance.

Here's how I'd cluster the story we just skimmed:

My brother Russell thinks monsters live in our bedroom closet at night. But I told him he is crazy.

"Go and check then," he said. I didn't want to. Russell said I was chicken.

"Am not," I said.

"Are so," he said.

So I told him the monsters were going to eat him at midnight. He started to cry. My Dad came in and told the monsters to beat it. Then he told us to go to sleep.

"If I hear any more about monsters," he said, "I'll spank you."

We went to sleep fast. And you know something? They never did come back.

Learning to read clusters is not something your eyes do naturally. It takes constant practice.

Here's how to go about it: Pick something light to read. Read it as fast as you can. Concentrate on seeing 3 to 4 words at once rather than one word at a time. Then reread

"Preview, skim, and cluster to read faster—except the things you want to read word for word."

the piece at your normal speed to see what you missed the first time. Try a second piece. First cluster, then reread to see what you missed in this one.

When you can read in clusters without missing much the first time, your speed has increased. Practice 15 minutes every day and you might pick up the technique in a week or so. (But don't be disappointed if it takes longer. Clustering *everything* takes time and practice.)

So now you have 3 ways to help you read faster. Preview to cut down on unnecessary heavy reading. Skim to get a quick, general idea of light reading. And cluster to increase your speed *and* comprehension.

With enough practice, you'll be able to handle *more* reading at school or work—and at home—*in less time.* You should even have enough time to read your favorite comic books—*and War and Peace!*

Today, the printed word is more vital than ever. Now there is more need than ever for all of us to *read* better, *write* better, and *communicate* better.

International Paper offers this series in the hope that, even in a small way, we can help.

If you'd like to share this article with others—students, friends, employees, family—we'll gladly send you reprints. So far we've sent out over 8,000,000 in response to requests from people everywhere.

Please write: "Power of the Printed Word," International Paper Company, Dept. HW, P.O. Box 954, Madison Square Station, New York, NY 10010. ©1982, INTERNATIONAL PAPER COMPANY

INTERNATIONAL PAPER COMPANY
We believe in the power of the printed word.

How to write clearly

By Edward T. Thompson

Editor-in-Chief, Reader's Digest

International Paper asked Edward T. Thompson to share some of what he has learned in nineteen years with Reader's Digest, a magazine famous for making complicated subjects understandable to millions of readers.

If you are afraid to write, don't be.

If you think you've got to string together big fancy words and high-flying phrases, forget it.

To write well, unless you aspire to be a professional poet or novelist, you only need to get your ideas across simply and clearly.

It's not easy. But it *is* easier than you might imagine.

There are only three basic requirements:

First, you must *want* to write clearly. And I believe you really do, if you've stayed this far with me.

Second, you must be willing to *work hard*. Thinking means work—and that's what it takes to do anything well.

Third, you must know and follow some *basic guidelines*.

If, while you're writing for clarity, some lovely, dramatic or inspired phrases or sentences come to you, fine. Put them in.

But then with cold, objective eyes and mind ask yourself: "Do they detract from clarity?" If they do, grit your teeth and cut the frills.

Follow some basic guidelines

I can't give you a complete list of "dos and don'ts" for every writing problem you'll ever face.

But I can give you some fundamental guidelines that cover the most common problems.

1. Outline what you want to say.

I know that sounds grade-schoolish. But you can't write clearly until, *before you start*, you know where you will stop.

Ironically, that's even a problem in writing an outline (i.e., knowing the ending before you begin).

So try this method:

• On 3"x 5" cards, write—one point to a card—all the points you need to make.

• Divide the cards into piles—one pile for each group of points *closely related* to each other. (If you were describing an automobile, you'd put all the points about mileage in one pile, all the points about safety in another, and so on.)

• Arrange your piles of points in a sequence. Which are most important and should be given first or saved for last? Which must you present before others in order to make the others understandable?

• Now, *within* each pile, do the same thing—arrange the *points* in logical, understandable order.

There you have your outline, needing only an introduction and conclusion.

This is a practical way to outline. It's also flexible. You can add, delete or change the location of points easily.

2. Start where your readers are.

How much do they know about the subject? Don't write to a level higher than your readers' knowledge of it.

CAUTION: Forget that old—and wrong—advice about writing to a 12-year-old mentality. That's insulting. But do remember that your prime purpose is to *explain* something, not prove that you're smarter than your readers.

3. Avoid jargon.

Don't use words, expressions, phrases known only to people with specific knowledge or interests.

Example: A scientist, using scientific jargon, wrote, "The biota exhibited a one hundred percent mortality response." He could have written: "All the fish died."

4. Use familiar combinations of words.

A speech writer for President Franklin D. Roosevelt wrote, "We are endeavoring to construct a more inclusive society." F.D.R. changed it to, "We're going to make a country in which no one is left out."

CAUTION: By familiar combinations of words, I do *not* mean incorrect grammar. *That* can be *un*clear. Example: John's father says he can't go out Friday. (Who can't go out? John or his father?)

5. Use "first-degree" words.

These words immediately bring an image to your mind. Other words must be "translated" through the first-degree word before you see

"Outline for clarity. Write your points on 3"x 5" cards—one point to a card. Then you can easily add to, or change the order of points—even delete some."

"Grit your teeth and cut the frills. That's one of the suggestions I offer here to help you write clearly. They cover the most common problems. And they're all easy to follow."

the image. Those are second/third-degree words.

First-degree words	Second/third-degree words
face	visage, countenance
stay	abide, remain, reside
book	volume, tome, publication

First-degree words are usually the most precise words, too.

6. Stick to the point.

Your outline—which was more work in the beginning—now saves you work. Because now you can ask about any sentence you write: "Does it relate to a point in the outline? If it doesn't, should I add it to the outline? If not, I'm getting off the track." Then, full steam ahead—on the main line.

7. Be as brief as possible.

Whatever you write, shortening—*condensing*—almost always makes it tighter, straighter, easier to read and understand.

Condensing, as *Reader's Digest* does it, is in large part artistry. But it involves techniques that anyone can learn and use.

• *Present your points in logical ABC order:* Here again, your outline should save you work because, if you did it right, your points already stand in logical ABC order—A makes B understandable, B makes C understandable and so on. To write in a straight line is to say something clearly in the fewest possible words.

• *Don't waste words telling people what they already know:* Notice how we edited this: "Have you ever

wondered how banks rate you as a credit risk? ~~You know, of course, that it's some combination of facts about your income, your job, and so on. But actually,~~ Many banks have a scoring system...."

• *Cut out excess evidence and unnecessary anecdotes:* Usually, one fact or example (at most, two) will support a point. More just belabor it. And while writing about some-

Writing clearly means avoiding jargon. Why didn't he just say: "All the fish died!"

thing may remind you of a good story, ask yourself: "Does it *really help* to tell the story, or does it slow me down?"

(Many people think *Reader's Digest* articles are filled with anecdotes. Actually, we use them sparingly and usually for one of two reasons: either the subject is so dry it needs some "humanity" to give it life; or the subject is so hard to grasp, it needs anecdotes to help readers understand. If the subject is both lively and easy to grasp, we move right along.)

• *Look for the most common word wasters:* windy phrases.

Windy phrases	Cut to...
at the present time	now
in the event of	if
in the majority of instances	usually

• *Look for passive verbs you can make active:* Invariably, this produces a shorter sentence. "The cherry tree *was* chopped down by George Washington." (Passive verb and nine words.) "George Washington *chopped* down the cherry tree." (Active verb and seven words.)

• *Look for positive/negative sections from which you can cut the negative:* See how we did it here:"The answer ~~does not rest with carelessness or incompetence. It lies largely in~~ having enough people to do the job."

• Finally, to write more clearly by saying it in fewer words: when you've finished, stop.

Edward T. Thompson

How to write with style

By Kurt Vonnegut

International Paper asked Kurt Vonnegut, author of such novels as "Slaughterhouse-Five," "Jailbird" and "Cat's Cradle," to tell you how to put your style and personality into everything you write.

Newspaper reporters and technical writers are trained to reveal almost nothing about themselves in their writings. This makes them freaks in the world of writers, since almost all of the other ink-stained wretches in that world reveal a lot about themselves to readers. We call these revelations, accidental and intentional, elements of style.

These revelations tell us as readers what sort of person it is with whom we are spending time. Does the writer sound ignorant or informed, stupid or bright, crooked or honest, humorless or playful – ? And on and on.

Why should you examine your writing style with the idea of improving it? Do so as a mark of respect for your readers, whatever you're writing. If you scribble your thoughts any which way, your readers will surely feel that you care nothing about them. They will mark you down as an egomaniac or a chowderhead – or, worse, they will stop reading you.

The most damning revelation you can make about yourself is that you do not know what is interesting and what is not. Don't you yourself like or dislike writers mainly for what they choose to show you or make you think about? Did you ever admire an empty-headed writer for his or her mastery of the language? No.

So your own winning style must begin with ideas in your head.

1. Find a subject you care about

Find a subject you care about and which you in your heart feel others should care about. It is this genuine caring, and not your games with language, which will be the most compelling and seductive element in your style.

I am not urging you to write a novel, by the way – although I would not be sorry if you wrote one, provided you genuinely cared about something. A petition to the mayor about a pothole in front of your house or a love letter to the girl next door will do.

2. Do not ramble, though

I won't ramble on about that.

3. Keep it simple

As for your use of language: Remember that two great masters of language, William Shakespeare and James Joyce, wrote sentences which were almost childlike when their subjects were most profound. "To be or not to be?" asks Shakespeare's Hamlet. The longest word is three letters long. Joyce, when he was frisky, could put together a sentence as intricate and as glittering as a necklace for Cleopatra, but my favorite sentence in his short story "Eveline" is this one: "She was tired." At that point in the story, no other words could break the heart of a reader as those three words do.

Simplicity of language is not only reputable, but perhaps even sacred. The *Bible* opens with a sentence well within the writing skills of a lively fourteen-year-old: "In the beginning God created the heaven and the earth."

4. Have the guts to cut

It may be that you, too, are capable of making necklaces for Cleopatra, so to speak. But your eloquence should be the servant of the ideas in your head. Your rule might be this: If a sentence, no matter how excellent, does not illuminate your subject in some new and useful way, scratch it out.

5. Sound like yourself

The writing style which is most natural for you is bound to echo the speech you heard when a child. English was the novelist Joseph Conrad's third language, and much that seems piquant in his use of English was no doubt colored by his first language, which was Polish. And lucky indeed is the writer who has grown up in Ireland, for the English spoken there is so amusing and musical. I myself grew up in Indianapolis, where common speech sounds like a band saw cutting galvanized tin,

"Keep it simple. Shakespeare did, with Hamlet's famous soliloquy."

'Be merciless on yourself. If a sentence does not illuminate your subject in some new and useful way, scratch it out.'

and employs a vocabulary as unornamental as a monkey wrench.

In some of the more remote hollows of Appalachia, children still grow up hearing songs and locutions of Elizabethan times. Yes, and many Americans grow up hearing a language other than English, or an English dialect a majority of Americans cannot understand.

All these varieties of speech are beautiful, just as the varieties of butterflies are beautiful. No matter what your first language, you should treasure it all your life. If it happens not to be standard English, and if it shows itself when you write standard English, the result is usually delightful, like a very pretty girl with one eye that is green and one that is blue.

I myself find that I trust my own writing most, and others seem to trust it most, too, when I sound most like a person from Indianapolis, which is what I am. What alternatives do I have? The one most vehemently recommended by teachers has no doubt been pressed on you, as well: to write like cultivated Englishmen of a century or more ago.

6. Say what you mean to say

I used to be exasperated by such teachers, but am no more. I understand now that all those antique essays and stories with which I was to compare my own work were not magnificent for their datedness or foreignness, but for saying precisely what their authors

meant them to say. My teachers wished me to write accurately, always selecting the most effective words, and relating the words to one another unambiguously, rigidly, like parts of a machine. The teachers did not want to turn me into an Englishman after all. They hoped that I would become understandable – and therefore understood. And there went my dream of doing with words what Pablo Picasso did with paint or what any number of jazz idols did with music. If I broke all the rules of punctuation, had words mean whatever I wanted them to mean, and strung them together higgledy-piggledy, I would simply not be understood. So you, too, had better avoid Picasso-style or jazz-style writing, if you have something worth saying and wish to be understood.

Readers want our pages to look very much like pages they have seen before. Why? This is because they themselves have a tough job to do, and they need all the help they can get from us.

7. Pity the readers

They have to identify thousands of little marks on paper, and make sense of them immediately. They have to *read*, an art so difficult that most people don't really master it even after having studied it all through grade school and high school – twelve long years.

"Pick a subject you care so deeply about that you'd speak on a soapbox about it."

So this discussion must finally acknowledge that our stylistic options as writers are neither numerous nor glamorous, since our readers are bound to be such imperfect artists. Our audience requires us to be sympathetic and patient teachers, ever willing to simplify and clarify – whereas we would rather soar high above the crowd, singing like nightingales.

That is the bad news. The good news is that we Americans are governed under a unique Constitution, which allows us to write whatever we please without fear of punishment. So the most meaningful aspect of our styles, which is what we choose to write about, is utterly unlimited.

8. For really detailed advice

For a discussion of literary style in a narrower sense, in a more technical sense, I commend to your attention *The Elements of Style*, by William Strunk, Jr., and E.B. White (Macmillan, 1979).

E.B. White is, of course, one of the most admirable literary stylists this country has so far produced.

You should realize, too, that no one would care how well or badly Mr. White expressed himself, if he did not have perfectly enchanting things to say.

Today, the printed word is more vital than ever. Now there is more need than ever for all of us to *read* better, *write* better, and *communicate* better.

International Paper offers this series in the hope that, even in a small way, we can help.

If you'd like to share this article with others—students, friends, employees, family—we'll gladly send you reprints. So far we've sent out over 8,000,000 in response to requests from people everywhere.

Please write: "Power of the Printed Word," International Paper Company, Dept. 5 X, P.O. Box 954, Madison Square Station, New York, NY 10010. ©1982 INTERNATIONAL PAPER COMPANY

Ⓐ INTERNATIONAL PAPER COMPANY
We believe in the power of the printed word.

How to use a library

By James A. Michener

International Paper asked Pulitzer Prize-winning novelist James A. Michener, author of "Tales of the South Pacific," "Hawaii," "Centennial" and "Chesapeake," to tell how you can benefit from the most helpful service in your community.

You're driving your car home from work or school. And something goes wrong. The engine stalls out at lights, holds back as you go to pass.

It needs a tune-up—and soon. Where do you go? The library.

You can take out an auto repair manual that tells step-by-step how to tune up your make and model.

Or your tennis game has fallen off. You've lost your touch at the net. Where do you go?

The library—for a few books on improving your tennis form.

"The library!" you say. "That's where my teacher sends me to do –ugh–homework."

Unfortunately, I've found that's exactly the way many people feel. If you're among them, you're denying yourself the easiest way to improve yourself, enjoy yourself and even cope with life.

It's hard for me to imagine what I would be doing today if I had not fallen in love, at the ripe old age of seven, with the Melinda Cox Library in my hometown of Doylestown, Pennsylvania. At our house, we just could not afford books. The books in that free library would change my life dramatically.

Who knows what your library can open up for you?

My first suggestion for making the most of your library is to do what I did: read and read and read. For pleasure—and for understanding.

How to kick the TV habit

If it's TV that keeps you from cultivating this delicious habit, I can offer a sure remedy. Take home from the library a stack of books that might look interesting.

Pile them on the TV set. Next time you are tempted to turn on a program you really don't want to see, reach for a book instead.

Over the years, some people collect a mental list of books they mean to read. If you don't have such a list, here is a suggestion. Take from the library some of the books you might have enjoyed dramatized on TV, like Remarque's "All Quiet on the Western Front," Clavell's "Shōgun," Tolkien's "The Hobbit," or Victor Hugo's "Les Misérables."

If you like what you read, you can follow up with other satisfying books by the same authors.

Some people in their reading limit themselves to current talked-about best sellers. Oh, what they miss! The library is

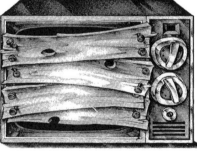

"You don't have to go this far to cut back on the TV habit and enjoy reading more. See my suggestions here."

full of yesterday's best sellers; and they still make compelling reading today. Some that I've enjoyed: A.B. Guthrie's "The Big Sky," Carl Van Doren's "Benjamin Franklin," Mari Sandoz's "Old Jules," and Norman Mailer's "The Naked and the Dead."

How do you find these or any other books you're looking for? It's easy—with the card catalog.

Learn to use the card catalog

Every time I go to the library—and I go more than once a week—I invariably make a beeline to the card catalog before anything else. It's the nucleus of any public library.

The card catalog lists every book in the library by:

1. author; 2. title; 3. subject.

Let's pick an interesting subject to look up. I have always been fascinated by astronomy.

You'll be surprised at the wealth of material you will find under "astronomy" to draw upon. And the absorbing books you didn't know existed on it.

CAUTION: Always have a pencil and paper when you use the card catalog. Once you jot down the numbers of the books you are interested in, you are ready to find them on the shelves.

Learn to use the stacks

Libraries call the shelves "the stacks." In many smaller libraries which you'll be using, the stacks will be open for you to browse.

To me there is a special thrill in tracking down the books I want in the stacks! For invariably, I find books about which I knew nothing, and these often turn out to be the very ones I need. You will find the same thing happening to you when you start to browse in the stacks. "A learned mind is the end product of browsing."

'Every time I go to the library, I make a beeline to the card catalog. Learn to use it. It's easy."

CAUTION: If you take a book from the stacks to your work desk, do not try to return it to its proper place. That's work for the experts. If you replace it incorrectly, the next seeker won't be able to find it.

Learn to know the reference librarian

Some of the brightest and best informed men and women in America are the librarians who specialize in providing reference help.

Introduce yourself. State your problem. And be amazed at how much help you will receive.

CAUTION: Don't waste the time of this expert by asking silly questions you ought to solve yourself. Save the reference librarian for the really big ones.

Learn to use *The Reader's Guide to Periodical Literature*

This green-bound index is one of the most useful items in any library. It indexes all the articles in the major magazines, including newspaper magazine supplements.

Thus it provides a guide to the very latest expert information on any subject that interests you.

So if you want to do a really first-class job, find out which magazines your library subscribes to, then consult *The Reader's Guide* and track down recent articles on your subject. When you use this wonderful tool effectively, you show the mark of a real scholar.

Four personal hints

Since you can take most books home, but not magazines, take full notes when using the latter.

Many libraries today provide a reprographic machine that can quickly copy pages you need from magazines and books. Ask about it.

If you are working on a project of some size which will require repeated library visits, keep a small notebook in which you record the identification numbers of the books you will be using frequently. This will save you valuable time, because you won't have to consult the card catalog or search aimlessly through the stacks each time you visit for material you seek.

Some of the very best books in any library are the reference books, which may not be taken home. Learn what topics they cover and how best to use them, for these books are wonderful repositories of human knowledge.

Your business and legal advisor

Your library can give you help on *any* subject. It can even be your business and legal advisor.

How many times have you scratched your head over how to get a tax rebate on your summer job? You'll find answers in tax guides at the library. Thinking of buying or renting a house? You'll find guides to that. Want to defend yourself in traffic court? Find out how in legal books at the library.

Library projects can be fun — and rewarding

Here are a few ideas:

1. *What are your roots?* Trace your ancestors. Many libraries specialize in genealogy.

2. *Did George Washington sleep nearby?* Or Billy the Kid? Your library's collection of local history books can put you on the trail.

3. *Cook a Polynesian feast.* Or an ancient Roman banquet. Read how in the library's cookbooks.

4. *Take up photography.* Check the library for consumer reviews of cameras before you buy. Take out books on lighting, composition, or darkroom techniques.

Or — you name it!

If you haven't detected by now my enthusiasm for libraries, let me offer two personal notes.

I'm particularly pleased that in recent years two beautiful libraries have been named after me: a small community library in Quakertown,

"I discover all kinds of interesting books just by browsing in the stacks. I encourage you to browse."

Pennsylvania, and the huge research library located at the University of Northern Colorado in Greeley. And I like libraries so much that I married a librarian.

James A. Michener

How to enjoy the classics

By Steve Allen

International Paper asked Steve Allen, television comedian, composer, writer of the television series "Meeting of Minds," author of 22 books and lover of the classics, to tell how you can appreciate man's greatest written works.

Why is it? In school we learn one of the most amazing and difficult feats man has ever accomplished – *how to read* – and at the same time we learn to hate to read the things worth reading most!

It's happened to us all – with assignment reading! It happened to me. The teacher assigned *Moby Dick.* I didn't want to read it. So I fought it. I disliked it. I thought I won.

But I lost. My struggle to keep at arm's length from *Moby Dick* cost me all the good things that can come from learning to come to terms with those special few books we call the "classics."

I've come back to *Moby Dick* on my own since. I *like* it. And I've discovered a new level of pleasure from it with each reading.

What is a classic? A classic is a book that gives you that exhilarating feeling, if only for a moment, that you've finally uncovered part of the meaning of life.

A classic is a book that's stood the test of time, a book that men and women all over the world keep reaching for throughout the ages for its special enlightenment.

Not many books can survive such a test. Considering all the volumes that have been produced since man first put chisel to stone,

classics account for an infinitesimal share of the total – less than .001 percent. That's just a few thousand books. Of those, under 100 make up the solid core.

Why should you tackle the classics? Why try to enjoy them?

I suggest three good reasons:
1. Classics open up your mind.
2. Classics help you grow.
3. Classics help you understand your life, your world, yourself.

That last one is the big one. A classic can give you insights into yourself that you will get nowhere else. Sure, you can get pleasure out of almost any book. But a classic, once you penetrate it, lifts you up high! Aeschylus's *Oresteia* was written nearly 2,500 years ago – and it still knocks me out!

But I can hear you saying, "I've *tried* reading classics. They are hard to understand. I can't get into them."

Let me offer some suggestions that will help you open up this wondrous world. Pick up a classic you've always promised to try. Then take Dr. Allen's advice.

Know what you're reading

Is it a novel, drama, biography, history? To find out, check the table of contents, read the book cover, the preface, or look up the title or author in *The Reader's Encyclopedia.*

Don't read in bed

Classics can be tough going; I'll admit it. You need to be alert, with your senses sharp. When you read in bed you're courting sleep – and you'll blame it on the book when you start nodding off.

Don't let a lot of characters throw you

Dostoevsky tosses fifty major characters at you in *The Brothers*

Karamazov. In the very first chapter of *War and Peace,* Tolstoy bombards you with twenty-two names – long, complicated ones like Anna Pavlovna Scherer, Anatole and Prince Bolkonski. Don't scurry for cover. Stick with it. The characters will gradually sort themselves out and you'll feel as comfortable with them as you do with your own dear friends who were strangers, too, when you met them.

Give the author a chance

Don't say "I don't get it!" too soon. Keep reading right to the end.

Sometimes, though, you may not be ready for the book you're trying to get into. I tackled Plato's *Republic* three times before it finally opened up to me. And man, was it worth it! So if you really can't make a go of the book in your lap, put it aside for another day, or year, and take on another one.

Read in big bites

Don't read in short nibbles. How can you expect to get your head into anything that way? The longer you stay with it, the more you get into the rhythm and mood – and the more pleasure you get from it.

When you read *Zorba the Greek* try putting bouzouki music on the record player; Proust, a little Debussy; Shakespeare, Elizabethan theater music.

Read what the author read

To better understand where the author is

"'Moby Dick' escaped me when it was assigned reading. I've landed it since and loved it. Don't let assigned reading spoil the classics for you."

coming from, as we say, read the books he once read and that impressed him. Shakespeare, for example, dipped into North's translation of Plutarch's *Lives* for the plots of *Julius Caesar, Antony and Cleopatra* and *A Midsummer Night's Dream*. It's fun to know you're reading what *he* read.

Read about the author's time

You are the product of your time. Any author is the product of *his* time. Knowing the history of that time, the problems that he and others faced, their attitudes–will help you understand the author's point of view. *Important point:* You may not agree with the author. No problem. At least he's made you think!

Read about the author's life

The more you know about an author's own experiences, the more you'll understand why he wrote what he wrote. You'll begin to see the autobiographical odds and ends that are hidden in his work.

A writer can't help but reveal himself. Most of our surmises about Shakespeare's life come from clues found in his plays.

Read the book again

All classics bear rereading. If after you finish the book you're intrigued but still confused, reread it then and there. It'll open up some more to you.

If you did read a classic a few years back and loved it, read it again. The book will have so many new things to say to you, you'll hardly believe it's the same one.

A few classics to enjoy

You can find excellent lists of the basic classics compiled by helpful experts, like Clifton Fadiman's *Lifetime Reading Plan,* the *Harvard Classics* and Mortimer J. Adler's *Great Books.* Look into them.

But before you do, I'd like to suggest a few classics that can light up your life. Even though some might have been spoiled for you by the required reading stigma, try them. Try them. And *try* them.

1. Homer: *Iliad* and *Odyssey*. The Adam and Eve of Western literature. Read a good recent translation. My favorite is by Robert Fitzgerald.

2. Rabelais: *Gargantua and Pantagruel*. A Gargantuan romp. I recommend the Samuel Putnam translation.

"Some of my best friends come out of the pages of the classics I suggest to you here. They'll be your best friends, too, for they'll help you better understand your life, your world and yourself."

3. Geoffrey Chaucer: *Canterbury Tales*. Thirty folks on a four-day pilgrimage swapping whoppers. Don't be surprised if the people you meet here are like people you know in *your* life.

4. Cervantes: *Don Quixote.* The first modern novel, about the lovable old Don with his "impossible dream." How could you go through life without reading it *once?*

5. Shakespeare: *Plays.* Shake-speare turned out 37 plays. Some are flops, some make him the greatest writer ever. All offer gold. His best: "Hamlet," "Macbeth" and "Romeo and Juliet." (See them on the stage, too.)

6. Charles Dickens: *Pickwick Papers.* No one can breathe life into characters the way Dickens can. Especially the inimitable Samuel Pickwick, Esq.

7. Mark Twain: *Huckleberry Finn.* Maybe you had to read this in school. Well, climb back on that raft with Huck and Jim. You'll find new meaning this time.

Of course, these few suggestions hardly scratch the surface.

Don't just dip your toe into the deep waters of the classics. Plunge in! Like generations of bright human beings before you, you'll find yourself invigorated to the marrow by thoughts and observations of the most gifted writers in history.

You still enjoy looking at classic paintings. You enjoy hearing musical classics. Good books will hold you, too.

Someone has said the classics are the diary of man. Open up the diary. Read about yourself– and *understand* yourself.

How to read an annual report

International Paper asked Jane Bryant Quinn, business commentator for the CBS-TV Morning News, columnist for Newsweek, and author of Everyone's Money Book, to tell how anyone can understand and profit from a company's annual report.

To some business people I know, curling up with a good annual report is almost more exciting than getting lost in John le Carré's latest spy thriller.

But to you it might be another story. "Who needs that?" I can hear you ask. You do—if you're going to gamble any of your future working for a company, investing in it, or selling to it.

Why should you bother?
Say you've got a job interview at Galactic Industries. Well, what does the company do? Does its future look good? Or will the next recession leave your part of the business on the beach?

Or say you're thinking of investing your own hard-earned money in its stock. Sales are up. But are its profits getting better or worse?

Or say you're going to supply it with a lot of parts. Should you extend Galactic plenty of credit or keep it on a short leash?

How to get one
You'll find answers in its annual report. Where do you find that? Your library should have the annual reports of nearby companies plus leading national ones. It also has listings of companies' financial

officers and their addresses so you can write for annual reports.

So now Galactic Industries' latest annual report is sitting in front of you ready to be cracked. How do you crack it?

Where do we start? Not at the front. At the back! We don't want to be surprised at the end of this story.

Start at the back
First, turn back to the report of the certified public accountant. This third-party auditor will tell you right off the bat if Galactic's report conforms with "generally accepted accounting principles."

Watch out for the words "subject to." They mean the financial report is clean only if you take the company's word about a particular piece of business, and the accountant isn't sure you should. Doubts like this are usually settled behind closed doors. When a "subject to" makes it into the annual report, it could mean trouble.

What else should you know before you check the numbers?

Stay in the back of the book and go to

the footnotes. Yep! The whole profits story is sometimes in the footnotes.

Are earnings down? If it's only because of a change in accounting, maybe that's good! The company owes less tax and has more money

in its pocket. Are earnings up? Maybe that's bad. They may be up because of a special windfall that won't happen again next year. The footnotes know.

For what happened and why
Now turn to the letter from the chairman. Usually addressed "to our stockholders," it's up front, and should be in more ways than one. The chairman's tone reflects the personality, the well-being of his company.

In his letter he should tell you how his company fared this year. But more important, he should tell you why. Keep an eye out for sentences that start with "Except for..." and "Despite the..." They're clues to problems.

Insights into the future
On the positive side, a chairman's letter should give you insights into the company's future and its stance on economic or political trends that may affect it.

While you're up front, look for what's new in each line of business. Is management getting the company in good shape to weather the tough and competitive 1980's?

"Reading an annual report can be (almost) as exciting as a spy thriller—if you know how to find the clues. I'll show you how to find the most important ones here."

Now—and no sooner—should you dig into the numbers!

One source is the balance sheet. It is a snapshot of how the company stands at a single point in time. On the left are assets – everything the company owns. Things that can quickly be turned into cash are *current assets.* On the right are *liabilities*—everything the company owes. *Current liabilities* are the debts due in one year, which are paid out of current assets.

The difference between current assets and current liabilities is *net working capital,* a key figure to watch from one annual (and quarterly) report to another. If working capital shrinks, it could mean trouble. One possibility: the company may not be able to keep dividends growing rapidly.

Look for growth here

Stockholders' equity is the difference between total assets and liabilities. It is the presumed dollar value of what stockholders own. You want it to grow.

Another important number to watch is *long-term debt.* High and rising debt, relative to equity, may be no problem for a growing business. But it shows weakness in a company that's leveling out. (More on that later.)

The second basic source of numbers is the *income statement.* It shows how much money Galactic made or lost over the year.

Most people look at one figure first. It's in the income statement at the bottom: *net earnings per share.* Watch out. It can fool you. Galactic's management could boost earnings by selling off a plant. Or by cutting the budget for research and advertising. (See the footnotes!) So don't be smug about net earnings until you've found out how they happened—and how they might happen next year.

Check net sales first

The number you *should* look at first in the income statement is *net sales.* Ask yourself: Are sales going *up at a faster rate* than the last time around? When sales increases start to slow, the company may be in trouble. Also ask: Have sales gone up faster than inflation? If not, the company's *real* sales may be behind. And ask yourself once more: Have sales gone down because the company is selling off a losing business?

If so, profits may be soaring.

(I never promised you that figuring out an annual report was going to be easy!)

Get out your calculator

Another important thing to study today is the company's debt. Get out your pocket calculator, and turn to the balance sheet. Divide long-term liabilities by stockholders' equity. That's the *debt-to-equity ratio.*

A high ratio means that the company borrows a lot of money to spark its growth. That's okay—*if* sales grow, too, and *if* there's enough cash on hand to meet the payments. A company doing well

TOP BRASS ONLY

"For inside information, an annual report is second only to meeting with the brass behind closed doors. Come on in!"

on borrowed money can earn big profits for its stockholders. But if sales fall, watch out. The whole enterprise may slowly sink. Some companies can handle high ratios, others can't.

You have to compare

That brings up the most important thing of all: *One* annual report, *one* chairman's letter, *one* ratio won't tell you much. You have to compare. Is the company's debt-to-equity ratio better or worse than it

used to be? Better or worse than the industry norms? Better or worse, after this recession, than it was after the last recession? In company-watching, *comparisons are all.* They tell you if management is staying on top of things.

Financial analysts work out many other ratios to tell them how the company is doing. You can learn more about them from books on the subject. Ask your librarian.

But one thing you will *never* learn from an annual report is how much to pay for a company's stock. Galactic may be running well. But if investors expected it to run better, the stock might fall. Or, Galactic could be slumping badly. But if investors see a better day tomorrow, the stock could rise.

Two important suggestions

Those are some basics for weighing a company's health from its annual report. But if you want to know *all* you can about a company, you need to do a little more homework. First, see what the business press has been saying about it over recent years. Again, ask your librarian.

Finally, you should keep up with what's going on in business, economics and politics here and around the world. All can—and will—affect you and the companies you're interested in.

Each year, companies give you more and more information in their annual reports. Profiting from that information is up to you. I hope you profit from *mine.*

Jane Bryant Quinn

How to make a speech

By George Plimpton

International Paper asked George Plimpton, who writes books about facing the sports pros (like "Paper Lion" and "Shadow Box"), and who's in demand to speak about it, to tell you how to face the fear of making a speech.

One of life's terrors for the uninitiated is to be asked to make a speech.

"Why me?" will probably be your first reaction. "I don't have anything to say." It should be reassuring (though it rarely is) that since you were asked, somebody must think you do. The fact is that each one of us has a store of material which should be of interest to others. There is no reason why it should not be adapted to a speech.

Why know how to speak?

Scary as it is, it's important for anyone to be able to speak in front of others, whether twenty around a conference table or a hall filled with a thousand faces.

Being able to speak can mean better grades in any class. It can mean talking the town council out of increasing your property taxes. It can mean talking top management into buying your plan.

How to pick a topic

You were probably asked to speak in the first place in the hope that you would be able to articulate a topic that you know something about. Still, it helps to find out about your audience first. Who are they? Why are they there? What are they interested in? How much do they already know about your subject? One kind of talk would be appropriate for the Women's Club of Columbus, Ohio, and quite another for the guests at the Vince Lombardi dinner.

How to plan what to say

Here is where you must do your homework.

The more you sweat in advance, the less you'll have to sweat once you appear on stage. Research your topic thoroughly. Check the library for facts, quotes, books and timely magazine and newspaper articles on your subject. Get in touch with experts. Write to them, make phone calls, get interviews to help round out your material.

In short, gather—and learn—far more than you'll ever use. You can't imagine how much confidence that knowledge will inspire.

Now start organizing and writing. Most authorities suggest that a good speech breaks down into three basic parts—an introduction, the body of the speech, and the summation.

Introduction: An audience makes up its mind very quickly. Once the mood of an audience is set, it is difficult to change it, which is why introductions are important. If the speech is to be lighthearted in tone, the speaker can start off by telling a good-natured story about the subject or himself.

But be careful of jokes, especially the shaggy-dog

"What am I doing wrong? Taking refuge behind the lectern, looking scared to death, shuffling pages, and reading my speech. Relax. Come out in the open, gesture, talk to your audience!"

variety. For some reason, the joke that convulses guests in a living room tends to suffer as it emerges through the amplifying system into a public gathering place.

Main body: There are four main intents in the body of the well-made speech. These are 1) to entertain, which is probably the hardest; 2) to instruct, which is the easiest if the speaker has done the research and knows the subject; 3) to persuade, which one does at a sales presentation, a political rally, or a town meeting; and finally, 4) to inspire, which is what the speaker emphasizes at a sales meeting, in a sermon, or at a pep rally. (Hurry-Up Yost, the onetime Michigan football coach, gave such an inspiration-filled half-time talk that he got carried away and at the final exhortation led his team on the run through the wrong locker-room door into the swimming pool.)

Summation: This is where you should "ask for the order." An ending should probably incorporate a sentence or two which sounds like an ending—a short summary of the main points of the speech, perhaps, or the repeat of a phrase that most embodies what the speaker has hoped to convey. It is valuable to think of the last sentence or two as something which might produce applause. Phrases which are perfectly appropriate to signal this are: "In closing…" or "I have one last thing to say…"

Once done—fully written, or the main

points set down on 3″ x 5″ index cards—the next problem is the actual presentation of the speech. Ideally, a speech should not be read. At least it should never appear or sound as if you are reading it. An audience is dismayed to see a speaker peering down at a thick sheaf of papers on the lectern, wetting his thumb to turn to the next page.

How to sound spontaneous

The best speakers are those who make their words sound spontaneous even if memorized. I've found it's best to learn a speech point by point, not word for word. Careful preparation and a great deal of practicing are required to make it come together smoothly and easily. Mark Twain once said, "It takes three weeks to prepare a good ad-lib speech."

Don't be fooled when you rehearse. It takes longer to deliver a speech than to read it. Most speakers peg along at about 100 words a minute.

Brevity is an asset

A sensible plan, if you have been asked to speak to an exact limit, is to talk your speech into a mirror and stop at your allotted time; then cut the speech accordingly. The more familiar you become with your speech, the more confidently you can deliver it.

As anyone who listens to speeches knows, brevity is an asset. Twenty minutes are ideal. An hour is the limit an audience can listen comfortably.

In mentioning brevity, it is worth mentioning that the shortest inaugural address was George Washington's—just 135 words. The longest was William Henry Harrison's in 1841. He delivered a two-hour 9,000-word speech into the teeth of a freezing northeast wind. He came down with a cold the

following day, and a month later he died of pneumonia.

Check your grammar

Consult a dictionary for proper meanings and pronunciations. Your audience won't know if you're a bad speller, but they will know if you use or pronounce a word improperly. In my first remarks on the dais, I used to thank people for their "fulsome introduction," until I discovered to my dismay that "fulsome" means *offensive* and *insincere*.

"*Why should you make a speech?* There are four big reasons (left to right): to inspire, to persuade, to entertain, to instruct. I'll tell you how to organize what you say."

On the podium

It helps one's nerves to pick out three or four people in the audience—preferably in different sectors so that the speaker is apparently giving his attention to the entire room—on whom to focus. Pick out people who seem to be having a good time.

How questions help

A question period at the end of a speech is a good notion. One would not ask questions following a tribute to the company treasurer on his re-

tirement, say, but a technical talk or an informative speech can be enlivened with a question period.

The crowd

The larger the crowd, the easier it is to speak, because the response is multiplied and increased. Most people do not believe this. They peek out from behind the curtain and if the auditorium is filled to the rafters they begin to moan softly in the back of their throats.

What about stage fright?

Very few speakers escape the so-called "butterflies." There does not seem to be any cure for them, except to realize that they are beneficial rather than harmful, and never fatal. The tension usually means that the speaker, being keyed up, will do a better job. Edward R. Murrow called stage fright "the sweat of perfection." Mark Twain once comforted a fright-frozen friend about to speak: "Just remember they don't expect much." My own feeling is that with thought, preparation and faith in your ideas, you can go out there and expect a pleasant surprise.

And what a sensation it is—to hear applause. Invariably after it dies away, the speaker searches out the program chairman—just to make it known that he's available for next month's meeting.

George Plimpton

How to write a resume

by Jerrold G. Simon, Ed.D.
Harvard Business School

International Paper asked Jerrold G. Simon, Ed.D., psychologist and career development specialist at Harvard Business School, who has counseled over a thousand people in their search for jobs, to tell you how to go after the job you really want.

If you are about to launch a search for a job, the suggestions I offer here can help you whether or not you have a high school or college diploma, whether you are just starting out or changing your job or career in midstream.

"What do I want to do?"

Before you try to find a job opening, you have to answer the hardest question of your working life: "What do I want to do?" Here's a good way.

Sit down with a piece of paper and don't get up till you've listed all the things you're proud to have accomplished. Your list might include being head of a fund-raising campaign, or acting a juicy role in the senior play.

Study the list. You'll see a pattern emerge of the things you do best and like to do best. You might discover that you're happiest working with people, or maybe with numbers, or words, or well, you'll see it.

Once you've decided what job area to go after, read

more about it in the reference section of your library. "Talk shop" with any people you know in that field. Then start to get your resume together.

There are many good books that offer sample resumes and describe widely used formats. The one that is still most popular, the *reverse chronological*, emphasizes where you worked and when, and the jobs and titles you held.

How to organize it

Your name and address go at the top. Also phone number.

What job do you want? That's what a prospective employer looks for first. If you know exactly, list that next under *Job Objective*. Otherwise, save it for your cover letter (I describe that later), when you're writing for a specific job to a specific person. In any case, make sure your resume focuses on the kind of work you can do and want to do.

Now comes *Work Experience*. Here's where you list your qualifications. Lead with your most important credentials. If you've had a distinguished work history in an area related to the job you're seeking, lead

off with that. If your education will impress the prospective employer more, start with that.

Begin with your most recent experience first and work backwards. Include your titles or positions held. And list the years.

Figures don't brag

The most qualified people don't always get the job. It goes to the person who presents himself most persuasively in person and on paper.

So don't just list where you were and what you did. This is your chance to tell *how well you did*. Were you the best salesman? Did you cut operating costs? Give numbers, statistics, percentages, increases in sales or profits.

No job experience?

In that case, list your summer jobs, extracurricular school activities, honors, awards. Choose the activities that will enhance your qualifications for the job.

Next list your *Education*—unless you chose to start with that. This should also be in reverse chronological order. List your high school only if you didn't go on to college. Include college degree, postgraduate degrees, dates conferred, major and minor courses you took that help qualify you for the job you want.

"'Who am I? What do I want to do?' Writing your resume forces you to think about yourself."

Also, did you pay your own way? Earn scholarships or fellowships? Those are impressive accomplishments.

No diplomas or degrees?

Then tell about your education: special training programs or courses that can qualify you. Describe outside activities that reveal your talents and abilities. Did you sell the most tickets to the annual charity musical? Did you take your motorcycle engine apart and put it back together so it works? These can help you.

Next, list any *Military Service*. This could lead off your resume if it is your only work experience. Stress skills learned, promotions earned, leadership shown.

Now comes *Personal Data*. This is your chance to let the reader get a glimpse of the personal you, and to further the image you've worked to project in the preceding sections. For example, if you're after a job in computer programming, and you enjoy playing chess, mention it.

"Talk about a hobby if it'll help get the job. Want to be an automotive engineer? Tell how you built your own hot rod."

Chess playing requires the ability to think through a problem.

Include foreign languages spoken, extensive travel, particular interests or professional memberships, *if* they advance your cause.

Keep your writing style simple. Be brief. Start sentences with impressive action verbs: "Created," "Designed," "Achieved," "Caused."

No typos, please

Make sure your grammar and spelling are correct. And no typos!

Use 8½" x 11" bond paper—white or off-white for easy reading. Don't cram things together.

Make sure your original is clean and readable. Then have it professionally duplicated. No carbons.

Get it into the right hands

Now that your resume is ready, start to track down job openings. How? Look up business friends, personal friends, neighbors, your minister, your college alumni association, professional services. Keep up with trade publications, and read help-wanted ads.

And start your own "direct mail" campaign. First, find out about the companies you are interested in—their size, location, what they make, their competition, their advertising, their prospects. Get their annual report—and read it.

No "Dear Sir" letters

Send your resume, along with a cover letter, to a specific person in the company, not to "Gentlemen" or "Dear Sir." The person should be the top person in the area where you want to work. Spell his name properly! The cover letter should appeal to your reader's own needs. What's in it for him?

Quickly explain why you are approaching *his* company (their product line, their superior training program) and what you can bring to the party. Back up your claims with facts. Then refer him to your enclosed resume and ask for an interview.

Oh, boy! An interview!

And now you've got an interview! Be sure to call the day before to confirm it. Meantime, *prepare yourself*. Research the company and the job by reading books and business journals in the library.

On the big day, arrive 15 minutes early. Act calm, even though, if you're normal, you're trembling inside at 6.5 on the Richter scale. At every chance, let your interviewer see that your personal skills and qualifications relate to the job at hand. If it's a sales position, for example, go all out to show how articulate and persuasive you are.

Afterwards, follow through with a brief thank-you note. This is a fine opportunity to restate your qualifications and add any important points you didn't get a chance to bring up during the interview.

Keep good records

Keep a list of prospects. List the dates you contacted them, when they replied, what was said.

And remember, someone out there is looking for someone *just like you*. It takes hard work and sometimes luck to find that person. Keep at it and you'll succeed.

Jerrold Simon

Today, the printed word is more vital than ever. Now there is more need than ever for all of us to *read* better, *write* better, and *communicate* better.

International Paper offers this series in the hope that, even in a small way, we can help.

If you'd like to share this article with others—students, friends, employees, family—we'll gladly send you reprints. So far we've sent out over 8,000,000 in response to requests from people everywhere.

Please write: "Power of the Printed Word," International Paper Company, Dept. 10X, P.O. Box 954, Madison Square Station, New York, NY 10010. © 1982 INTERNATIONAL PAPER COMPANY

(A) INTERNATIONAL PAPER COMPANY
We believe in the power of the printed word.

How to enjoy poetry

by James Dickey

International Paper asked James Dickey, poet-in-residence at the University of South Carolina, winner of the National Book Award for his collection of poems, "Buck-dancer's Choice," and author of the novel, "Deliverance," to tell you how to approach poetry so it can bring special pleasure and understanding to your life.

What is poetry? And why has it been around so long? Many have suspected that it was invented as a school subject, because you have to take exams on it. But that is not what poetry is or why it is still around. That's not what it feels like, either. When you really feel it, a new part of you happens, or an old part is renewed, with surprise and delight at being what it is.

Where poetry is coming from

From the beginning, men have known that words and things, words and actions, words and feelings, go together, and that they can go together in thousands of different ways, according to who is using them. Some ways go shallow, and some go deep.

Your connection with other imaginations

The first thing to understand about poetry is that it comes to you from outside you, in books or in words, but that for it to live, something from within you must come to it and meet it and complete it. Your response with your own mind and body and memory and emotions gives the poem its ability to work its magic; if you give to it, it will give to you, and give plenty.

When you read, don't let the poet write down to you; read up to him. Reach for him from your gut out, and the heart and muscles will come into it, too.

Which sun? Whose stars?

The sun is new every day, the ancient philosopher Heraclitus said. The sun of poetry is new every day, too, because it is seen in different

"The things around us—like water, trees, clouds, the sun—belong to us all. How you see them can enhance my way of seeing them. And just the other way around."

ways by different people who have lived under it, lived with it, responded to it. Their lives are different from yours, but by means of the special spell that poetry brings to the fact of the sun—everybody's sun; yours, too—

you can come into possession of many suns: as many as men and women have ever been able to imagine. Poetry makes possible the deepest kind of personal possession of the world.

The most beautiful constellation in the winter sky is Orion, which ancient poets thought looked like a hunter, up there, moving across heaven with his dog Sirius. What is this hunter made out of stars hunting for? What does he mean? Who owns him, if anybody? The poet Aldous Huxley felt that he did, and so, in Aldous Huxley's universe of personal emotion, he did.

> Up from among the emblems of the
>   wind into its heart of power,
> The Huntsman climbs, and all his
>   living stars
> Are bright, and all are mine.

Where to start

The beginning of your true encounter with poetry should be simple. It should bypass all classrooms, all textbooks, courses, examinations, and libraries and go straight to the things that make your own existence exist: to your body and nerves and blood and muscles. Find your own way–a secret way that just maybe you don't know yet–to open yourself as wide as you can and as deep as you can to the moment, the *now* of your own existence and the endless mystery of it, and perhaps at the same time to one other thing that is not you, but is out there: a handful of gravel is a good place to start. So is an ice cube–what more mysterious and beautiful *interior* of something has there ever been?

As for me, I like the sun, the source of all living things, and on certain days very good-feeling, too. "Start with the sun," D.H. Lawrence said, "and everything will slowly, slowly happen." Good advice. And a lot *will* happen.

What is more fascinating than a rock, if you really feel it and *look* at it, or more interesting than a leaf?

> Horses, I mean; butterflies, whales;
> Mosses, and stars; and gravelly
> Rivers, and fruit.
>
> Oceans, I mean; black valleys; corn;
> Brambles, and cliffs; rock, dirt, dust, ice…

Go back and read this list–it is quite a list, Mark Van Doren's list!– item by item. Slowly. Let each of these things call up an image out of your own life.

Think and feel. What moss do you see? Which horse? What field of corn? What brambles are *your* brambles? Which river is most yours?

The poem's way of going

Part of the spell of poetry is in the rhythm of language, used by poets who understand how powerful a factor rhythm can be, how compelling and unforgettable. Almost anything put into rhythm and rhyme is more memorable than the same thing said in prose. Why this is, no one knows completely, though the answer is surely rooted far down in the biology by means of which we exist; in the circulation of the blood that goes forth from the heart and comes back, and in the repetition of breathing. Croesus was a rich Greek king, back in the sixth century before Christ, but this tombstone was not his:

> No Croesus lies in the grave you see;
> I was a poor laborer, and this suits me.

That is plain-spoken and definitive. You believe it, and the rhyme helps you believe it and keep it.

Some things you'll find out

Writing poetry is a lot like a contest with yourself, and if you like sports and games and competitions of all kinds, you might like to try writing some. Why not?

The possibilities of rhyme are great. Some of the best fun is in making up your own limericks. There's no reason you can't invent limericks about anything that comes to your mind. No reason. Try it.

The problem is to find three words that rhyme and fit into a meaning. "There was a young man from…" *Where* was he from? What

situation was he in? How can these things fit into the limerick form–a form everybody knows–so that the rhymes "pay off," and give that sense of completion and inevitability that is so deliciously memorable that nothing else is like it?

How it goes with you

The more your encounter with poetry deepens, the more your experience of your own life will deepen, and you will begin to see things by means of words, and words by means of things.

You will come to understand the world as it interacts with words, as it can be re-created by words, by rhythms and by images.

You'll understand that this condition is one charged with vital possibilities. You will pick up meaning more quickly–and you will *create* meaning, too, for yourself and for others.

Connections between things will exist for you in ways that they never did before. They will shine with unexpectedness, wide-openness, and you will go toward them, on your own path. "Then…" as Dante says, "…Then will your feet be filled with good desire." You will know this is happening the first time you say, of something you never would have noticed before, "Well, would you look at *that!* Who'd 'a thunk it?" (Pause, full of new light)

"*I* thunk it!"

How to spell

By John Irving

International Paper asked John Irving, author of "The World According to Garp," "The Hotel New Hampshire," and "Setting Free the Bears," among other novels— and once a hopelessly bad speller himself— to teach you how to improve your spelling.

Let's begin with the bad news.

If you're a bad speller, you probably think you always will be. There are exceptions to every spelling rule, and the rules themselves are easy to forget. George Bernard Shaw demonstrated how ridiculous some spelling rules are. By following the rules, he said, we could spell <u>fish</u> this way: <u>ghoti</u>. The "f" as it sounds in enou<u>gh</u>, the "i" as it sounds in w<u>o</u>men, and the "sh" as it sounds in fi<u>ti</u>on.

With such rules to follow, no one should feel stupid for being a bad speller. But there are ways to improve. Start by acknowledging the mess that English spelling is in—but have sympathy: English spelling changed with foreign influences. Chaucer wrote "gesse," but "guess," imported earlier by the Norman invaders, finally replaced it. Most early printers in England came from Holland; they brought "ghost" and "gherkin" with them.

If you'd like to intimidate yourself—and remain a bad speller forever—just try to remember the 13 different ways the sound "sh" can be written:

<u>sh</u>oe	suspi<u>ci</u>on
<u>s</u>ugar	nau<u>se</u>ous
o<u>ce</u>an	con<u>sci</u>ous
i<u>ss</u>ue	<u>ch</u>aperone
na<u>ti</u>on	man<u>si</u>on
<u>sch</u>ist	fu<u>ch</u>sia
p<u>sh</u>aw	

Now the good news

The good news is that 90 percent of all writing consists of 1,000 basic words. There is, also, a method to most English spelling and a great number of how-to-spell books. Remarkably, all these books propose learning the same rules! Not surprisingly, most of these books are humorless.

Just keep this in mind: If you're familiar with the words you use, you'll probably spell them correctly—and you shouldn't be writing words you're unfamiliar with anyway. USE a word—out loud, and more than once—before you try writing it, and make sure (with a new word) that you know what it means before you use it. This means you'll have to look it up in a dictionary, where you'll not only learn what it means, but you'll see how it's spelled. Choose a dictionary you enjoy browsing in, and guard it as you would a diary. You wouldn't lend a diary, would you?

A tip on looking it up

Beside every word I look up in my dictionary, I make a mark.

"Love your dictionary."

Beside every word I look up more than once, I write a note to myself —about WHY I looked it up. I have looked up "strictly" 14 times since 1964. I prefer to spell it with a <u>k</u>— as in "stri<u>k</u>tly." I have looked up "ubiquitous" a dozen times. I can't remember what it means.

Another good way to use your dictionary: When you have to look up a word, for any reason, learn— and learn to *spell*—a *new* word at the same time. It can be any useful word on the same page as the word you looked up. Put the date beside this new word and see how quickly, or in what way, you forget it. Eventually, you'll learn it.

Almost as important as knowing what a word means (in order to spell it) is knowing how it's pronounced. It's go<u>ve</u>rnment, not go<u>ve</u>rment. It's Feb<u>r</u>uary, not Feb<u>u</u>ary. And if you know that <u>anti</u>- means against, you should know how to spell <u>anti</u>dote and <u>anti</u>biotic and <u>anti</u>freeze. If you know that <u>ante</u>- means before, you shouldn't have trouble spelling <u>ante</u>chamber or <u>ante</u>cedent.

Some rules, exceptions, and two tricks

I don't have room to touch on <u>all</u> the rules here. It would take a book to do that. But I can share a few that help me most:

What about -<u>ary</u> or -<u>ery</u>? When a word has a primary accent on the first syllable and a secondary accent on the next-to-last syllable (sec're- tar'y), it usually ends in -<u>ary</u>. Only six important words like this end in -<u>ery</u>:

cemetery monastery
millinery confectionery
distillery stationery
  (as in pap<u>e</u>r)

Here's another easy rule. Only four words end in -<u>efy</u>. Most people misspell them—with -<u>ify</u>, which is usually correct. Just memorize these, too, and use -<u>ify</u> for all the rest.

stupefy putrefy
liquefy rarefy

As a former bad speller, I have learned a few valuable tricks. Any good how-to-spell book will teach you more than these two, but these two are my favorites. Of the 800,000 words in the English language, the most frequently misspelled is <u>alright</u>; just remember that <u>alright</u> is <u>all wrong</u>. You wouldn't write <u>alwrong</u>, would you? That's how you know you should write <u>all</u> right.

The other trick is for the truly *worst* spellers. I mean those of you who spell so badly that you can't get close enough to the right way to spell a word in order to even FIND it in the dictionary. The word you're looking for is there, of course, but you won't find it the way you're trying to spell it. What to do is look up a synonym—another word that means the same thing. Chances are good that you'll find the word you're looking for under the definition of the synonym.

Demon words and bugbears

Everyone has a few demon words—they never look right, even when they're spelled correctly. Three of my demons are <u>medieval</u>, <u>ecstasy</u>, and <u>rhythm</u>. I have learned to hate these words, but I have not learned to spell them; I have to look them up every time.

And everyone has a spelling rule that's a bugbear—it's either too difficult to learn or it's impossible to remember. My personal bugbear among the rules is the one governing whether you add -<u>able</u> or -<u>ible</u>. I can teach it to you, but I can't

remember it myself.
You add -<u>able</u> to a full word: adapt, adaptable; work, workable. You add -<u>able</u> to words that end in <u>e</u>—just remember to drop the final <u>e</u>: love, lovable. But if the word ends in two <u>e</u>'s, like agree, you keep them both: agreeable.
You add -<u>ible</u> if the base is not a full word that can stand on its own: credible, tangible, horrible, terrible. You add -<u>ible</u> if the root word ends in -<u>ns</u>: responsible. You add -<u>ible</u> if the root word ends in -miss: permissible. You add -<u>ible</u> if the root word ends in a soft <u>c</u>

"This is one of the longest English words in common use. But don't let the length of a word frighten you. There's a rule for how to spell this one, and you can learn it."

(but remember to drop the final <u>e</u>!): force, forcible.
Got that? I don't have it, and I was introduced to that rule in prep school; with that rule, I still learn one word at a time.

Poor President Jackson

You must remember that it is permiss<u>ible</u> for spelling to drive you crazy. Spelling had this effect on Andrew Jackson, who once blew his stack while trying to write a Presidential paper. "It's a damn poor mind that can think of only one way to spell a word!" the President cried.
When you have trouble, think of poor Andrew Jackson and know that you're not alone.

What's really important

And remember what's really important about good writing is not good spelling. If you spell badly but write well, you should hold your head up. As the poet T.S. Eliot recommended, "Write for as large and miscellaneous an audience as possible"—and don't be overly concerned if you can't spell "miscellaneous."
Also remember that you can spell correctly and write well and still be misunderstood. Hold your head up about that, too.
As good old G.C. Lichtenberg said, "A book is a mirror: if an ass peers into it, you can't expect an apostle to look out"—whether you spell "apostle" correctly or not.

John Irving

Ogilvy & Mather
Advertising

2 East 48th Street, New York, N.Y. 10017

Glossary

AAAA American Association of Advertising Agencies, a national trade association founded in 1917; its members place approximately 80 percent of all U.S. agency advertising; also called 4A's.

ABC Audit Bureau of Circulation, an independent organization that audits and verifies circulation sizes of publications.

account executive an individual liaison in an ad agency who calls on and services clients; often called a "suit" because the person represents the agency to the client and vice versa.

account planner an individual within an ad agency who functions as a representative for consumer interests in the research and creative process.

ad banking a common practice of many magazines to have multiple pages of advertisements in the front of their book, cluttered before and after the table of contents.

Ad Council formerly the War Advertising Council, this nonprofit organization provides public service campaigns to the media for social issues and nonprofit causes.

agate a measurement of type that is typically the smallest used for print publications; traditionally it was 5.5 points, although 6 points is often used today as agate size.

ascender that part of the lowercase letter that rises above the midline (or x-height) of that particular font; such letters include f, l and t. *(see also descender)*

balance a design principle regarding placement of items within an advertisement so they complement one another.

billboards the traditional form of outdoor advertising; standard billboard is a 30-sheet poster panel (or 12 by 25 feet), but a variety of sizes is available.

bleed an ad that has an element (graphic, background color, etc.) that extends to the extreme edge of the page; full bleed means elements expand to all four edges.

boldface a thicker, heavier style font, usually used for emphasis.

border the outside boundary of an ad, often with lines of varying thicknesses or small graphics, such as flowers or stars.

brand a name, symbol, design or combination that identifies a company, its products or services; used to distinguish it from competitors.

bullets graphic devices used to highlight a line or list of items, usually dots or squares, although individualized bullets can be used.

campaign a planned advertising strategy that encompasses several similar ads, often through various media, over an extended period of time.

caption title or description found under or beside illustrations and photos; also called cutline or legend.

center spread *(see double truck)*

classified display ad an ad in the classified section of the newspaper that stands out because of a combination of larger type, borders, photos, white space or color.

collateral various sales materials (such as article reprints or data sheets) inserted in a direct mailing that complement the letter itself.

column inch measurement of newspaper advertising in which space is one column wide and one inch deep; magazine space is typically sold by pages or fractions of pages.

cooperative advertising system to share costs of ads between the manufacturer and the retailer; percentage paid by the manufacturer for such ads varies greatly; called co-op.

copy testing research technique to assess the effectiveness of an ad or parts of an ad (such as text, creative message, photo, graphic) before final production.

copyright legal protection for the originator of artistic effort or intellectual property, such as a book.

copywriter individual who is responsible for the message and actual text of an ad; often suggests visuals for ad.

CPM cost per thousand (Roman numeral M = 1,000), a measurement device used to compare cost effectiveness of ad placements; direct mailers often use CPR, for cost per response from a mailing.

corporate advertising *see institutional advertising*

creative brief a guiding statement that determines issues that need to be included in an ad and describes its target audience.

creative director individual in an agency who supervises the writers and graphic artists in the final execution of the ad.

crosshead small, boldfaced headline found within the copy of an ad, used to create contrast and help guide readers through long copy blocks; also called a subhead.

cume the unduplicated readership of a medium that accumulates over a given number of issues or time frame.

deckhead *(see also drophead)*

demographics descriptive and quantifiable characteristics (age, income, education, etc.) that help advertisers target consumers. *(see also psychographics)*

descender that part of the lowercase letter that extends below the line of that particular font; such letters include g, j and y. *(see also ascender)*

dimensional mail a form of direct mail that stands out because the envelope is not a plain, flat one; also called bulky mail to reflect the contents of the package.

display advertising ads that run throughout a publication, often next to editorial material; they often use eye-catching devices such as color, photos, large headlines and white space.

drophead a headline that drops below the main headline, usually in a smaller size; also called a readout, especially when the main thought continues into the lower headline.

double truck the two facing pages in the middle of a newspaper section or magazine; because the two pages are printed on one piece of paper, ads can run from one page to the other across the gutter; also called center spread. *(see center spread)*

fair use concept that a portion of a copyrighted work can be used without permission; mostly used by educators and researchers, not for commercial publications.

flip technique to turn over a photograph's negative so a person will be looking the opposite direction when printed (often toward a product rather than away).

font the complete set of type characters (letters, numbers, punctuation marks, etc.) within a particular typeface and size.

four color printing process combining blue (cyan), red (magenta), yellow and black to create full-color or four-color artwork and photos.

frequency the number of times an ad can potentially be seen within a specified time period.

gatefold magazine cover or page that folds open for additional ad pages; usually used to create a three-page ad, but some are longer.

hairline extremely thin line useful for borders or within ads.

hammer a main headline of only one or two words, with a longer but smaller headline beneath or beside it; also called a reverse kicker.

headline larger type used to attract attention to an ad, often used in conjunction with a photo or illustration.

IMC integrated marketing communications; a process in which all elements of an organization (advertising, sales, public relations, marketing) complement one another in creating a unified message to targeted audiences.

initial cap a large and usually bold uppercase letter used to begin the first line of a text block.

inside card interior transit ad signs that appeal to riders; the most common size is 14 inches by 28 inches.

institutional advertising paid promotional efforts to enhance an organization's image, rather than to sell its products or services; also called corporate advertising.

island a lone newspaper display advertisement that is totally surrounded by stock market listings, or, in magazines, by editorial matter.

island half similar format for magazine in which an ad appears in the middle portion of a two-page spread, with editorial matter on both sides and either the top or bottom.

italics a thin, sloping-to-the-right, type style option; *italics.*

Johnson box a small rectangular box at the top of a direct mail letter that summarizes the major points in the mailing.

justify equal-length line of type that is aligned evenly on both the left and right margins.

kerning process of moving type elements closer or farther apart than normal; often used to eliminate extra spacing between headline letters.

leading process of adjusting horizontal spacing between lines of text; 72 points equals one inch.

list broker individual who coordinates renting contact information of potential consumers to direct-mail advertisers.

logo also called logotype, the visual symbol of a brand name.

lumpy term describing direct mail that is not flat; often containing samples or promotional products.

make-good an ad that is run for free to compensate for an error that appeared in the original version; publications usually have guidelines on informing them quickly in case of errors to qualify for a make-good.

merge-purge a process to eliminate duplicate names when two or more mailing lists are combined.

model release a legal form signed by the subject of a photograph allowing its use and specifying any payment for such use; minors must have a parental signature.

OAAA Outdoor Advertising Association of America, founded in 1891, represents and promotes out-of-home media operators and suppliers.

orphan the last line of a paragraph that is continued to the top of the next column of text; try to avoid at all costs. *(see also widow)*

out-of-home all-encompassing term for billboards, transit, shelter and other forms of out-of-home advertising.

outdoor *(see out-of-home)*

PASS *(see SAU)*

pica in printing, a standard unit for horizontal type measurement; 6 picas equal one inch.

point in printing, a standard unit of measure for text height and display type; 12 points equal one pica, 72 points equal one inch.

P-O-P point-of-purchase signs and other displays provided by a manufacturer for use inside a retail store; also called point-of-sale or POS.

positioning how a consumer evaluates and ranks a product or service vs. its competition.

psychographics quantifiable characteristics related to personality and lifestyle traits (hobbies, attitudes, etc.) that help advertisers target consumers. *(see also demographics)*

puffery a legally allowed subjective statement made by an advertiser needing no verification or testing; "Easy to apply" or "Best-looking hair" are such examples.

pullout a selection from the text of the ad—either a direct quote or a key phrase—that's set in larger or bolder type for emphasis; may be set apart from text with rules; also called a sandwich or a pull quote.

ragged left or right a reference to a line of text that is not evenly justified at one end of the line.

rate card a publication's brochure for the advertising sales department to share with potential advertisers, listing prices for various-sized ads, deadlines, quantity discounts and other information.

reach percentage of a demographic group having the opportunity to be reached by a publication during a specific time frame.

retouching the manipulation of a photograph with airbrushes, inks, etc., to change details or to remove defects in the original exposure.

reverse white (or light colored) letters printed within a black or dark background; it should be used with caution because of reduced legibility.

reverse kicker *(see hammer)*

ROP a term that means "run of press;" typically it's the most economical means of print advertising since the publication determines the ad's placement.

rule a line of various thickness useful for borders or within ads.

SAU Standard Advertising Unit, a system of uniform column widths; the switch by newspapers to several narrower page sizes has made SAU not as universal. PASS (Preferred Ad Submission Size) is a system developed following the decline of SAU.

sans serif type letters without finishing strokes at the ends.

serif type letters containing finishing strokes at the ends; usually considered slightly more readable for text than sans serif type.

shadow ad somewhat controversial practice of printing a grayscale logo or brand name within editorial matter (such as stock market listings); also called watermark ad.

shelter advertising poster-type ads found outside and inside mass transit shelters where passengers wait for rides.

showing a term indicating how much exposure a billboard campaign generates; a 100 showing indicates that the daily exposure equaled the market's total population.

signature a collective term that includes the advertiser's name and contact information found within an ad.

small caps letters that are capitalized, but not much larger than lowercase letters; for example, SMALL CAPS.

spec ad a print ad that has not been requested by a client; its design is merely on speculation that the client may decide to run it.

spectaculars large billboards with special features: flashing graphics, movement, 3D effects, etc.

spot color the addition of one additional color to parts of an ad.

statement stuffer a piece of paper advertising a service or product that is included in a customer's regular billing envelope from, for example, a utility or department store.

subhead a small boldfaced headline that helps to break up long copy; also called break head or crosshead.

subliminal ads controversial advertising practice in which the advertiser has inserted a symbol or word that registers with the subconscious, rather than the naked eye of the consumer.

total circulation the number of copies of a publication, including subscriptions, single-copy sales and complimentary issues.

trademark a word, symbol or name used by manufacturers and legally registered to distinguish their products from competitors.

traffic manager the person in an ad agency who coordinates the tracking of various projects from client, to account manager, to creative, to printing, etc.

transit advertising ads located on or inside mass transit vehicles.

type weight type thickness, ranging from light to extra bold letters.

uppercase type using capital letters, as opposed to lowercase.

widow the last word or word fragment of a paragraph that sits alone on the last line of a paragraph. *(see also orphan)*

x-height literally, it refers to the height of the letter x in any font.

Illustration Credits

Exhibit 2.1   Jill Lauterborn
Exhibit 2.2   Randy Hines
Exhibit 4.2   © United Negro College Fund
Exhibit 4.3   © Red Square Marketing/Public Relations
Exhibit 4.4   http://pzrservices.typepad.com/.shared/image.html?/photos/
uncategorized/stock_image_a.jpeg
Exhibit 5.1   © Radio Advertising Bureau
Exhibit 5.3   © Volkswagen, North America
Exhibit 7.6   © Jaguar
Exhibit 8.1   © Crest
Exhibit 10.1   Zheng Shen
Exhibit 10.2   Stephanie L. Hines
Exhibit 10.3   Robert J. Rapp III
Exhibit 10.4   Robert J. Rapp III
Exhibit 10.6   Randy Hines
Exhibit 10.8   © Corbis
Exhibit 11.1A   © Red Square Marketing/Public Relations
Exhibit 11.1B   © Red Square Marketing/Public Relations
Exhibit 13.1   © Gucci

Index

Volvo 64
Vonnegut, Kurt 68

W

The Wall Street Journal 98, 120, 121
West, Mae 44
White space, in ad design 93–94, 95
Whitman, David 104
Williams, Robin 75, 84, 89
Winterberry Group 107
Women, as shown in print advertising
    169–73
  gender inequality 169–70
  superwoman myth 172
  thinness obsession 169, 170, 171

violence 171
Women, role in purchasing decisions 46
Wood, Evelyn 2–3
Wood, Tiger 145
Word count, headlines and 54
Word–of–mouth advertising 30
WPP Group 124
Wright, Steven   163

Y

Yahoo 120

Z

Z pattern 91